Acclaim for JOSEPH EPSTEIN
and *Narcissus Leaves the Pool*

"The modern essay has regained a good deal of its literary status in our time, much to the credit of Joseph Epstein." —KARL SHAPIRO

"One of America's best living essayists . . . Joseph Epstein is a man on whom nothing is lost." —*Hudson Review*

"Wry and engaging." —*Boston Globe*

"Epstein's essays have some of the qualities one associates with a conversation with a good friend: directness, ease, sincerity, and affability . . . Deftly blending gravity with a saving touch of levity, his essays exude a civilized urbanity."—*Christian Science Monitor*

"Erudite and charming."—*Economist*

"To read a Joseph Epstein essay is to witness a natural talent at work in his element . . . He is a splendid essayist, a graceful and dexterous writer who makes it look easy." —*Raleigh News and Observer*

"Must reading [from] one of the country's premier men of letters."
—*Weekly Standard*

"If Epstein's ultimate ancestor is Montaigne, his more immediate master is Mencken. Like Mencken, he has fashioned a style that successfully combines elegance and even bookishness with a street-smart colloquial directness. And there is nothing remote or aloof about him."—JOHN GROSS, *Chicago Tribune*

"Epstein's work is well in the Addisonian line of succession that Cyril Connolly saw petering out in *Punch* and the professional humorists . . . Epstein is a great deal more sophisticated than they were, and a great deal more readable."—PHILIP LARKIN

Narcissus Leaves the Pool

ESSAYS

▼

Joseph Epstein

A MARINER BOOK

HOUGHTON MIFFLIN COMPANY

BOSTON ✦ NEW YORK

First Mariner Books edition 2007

Copyright © 1999 by Joseph Epstein

ALL RIGHTS RESERVED

For information about permission to reproduce selections
from this book, write to Permissions, Houghton Mifflin Company,
215 Park Avenue South, New York, New York 10003.

Visit our Web site: www.houghtonmifflinbooks.com.

The Library of Congress has cataloged the
hardcover edition as follows:

Epstein, Joseph, date.
Narcissus leaves the pool : familiar essays / Joseph Epstein.
p. cm.
Essays originally published in *The American Scholar,*
The New Yorker, and *The Hudson Review.*
ISBN 0-395-94403-1
I. Title.

PS3555.P6527N37 1999
814'.54 — dc21   98-43791 CIP
ISBN-13: 978-0-618-87216-9 (pbk.)
ISBN-10: 0-618-87216-7 (pbk.)

Printed in the United States of America

Book design by Robert Overholtzer

QUM 10 9 8 7 6 5 4 3 2 1

Grateful acknowledgment is given to *The American Scholar,*
The New Yorker, and *The Hudson Review,* for which these
essays were originally written. The excerpt from "Prologue
at Sixty (for Friedrich Heer)" is from *Collected Poems*
by W. H. Auden, edited by Edward Mendelson. Copyright
© 1967 by W. H. Auden. Reprinted by permission of
Random House, Inc. The excerpt from *Black Boy* by Richard
Wright copyright 1937, 1942, 1944, 1945 by Richard Wright.
Copyright renewed 1973 by Ellen Wright.

FOR
Paul R. McHugh

Contents

Author's Note

AMONG THE various kind and generous things said and written about my five previous books of familiar essays — the book in your hand is my sixth such book — the one that makes me most edgy is to have myself compared to Michel de Montaigne, the father of the essay form and a central figure in not only French but world literature. Sucker for praise though I am, even I, rendered all trembly gullible by egotism, find it difficult to believe that one. Montaigne is broader, deeper, more acute than I; he had a better character, a subtler mind, a more complex and ripe philosophy. He also happens to have lived a more active and richer life. Otherwise there is scarcely any difference between us.

The one quality I do have over Montaigne, however, is garrulity, loquacity, sheer prolixity. His *Essays,* in the M. A. Screech translation, number a mere 1,269 pages. Mine, with this book, number more than 1,700 (a case, as the poet Philip Larkin once suggested in a review of one of my books, "of supply rather than demand"). I begin to see, too, that like Montaigne, my familiar essays, taken cumulatively, constitute an autobiography of sorts. The notion of progression implicit in autobiography is also implicit in some of the titles of my earlier collections of familiar essays: *The Middle of My Tether, Once More Around the Block, With My Trousers Rolled.*

Narcissus Leaves the Pool suggests further progression. It suggests — it is meant to suggest — the time has come for an end to preening, to thinking oneself still youthful, to regarding the future as endlessly expandable. It also suggests, I suppose, that it is time to enter upon a new stage in life, time — my God! — to get serious. I believe I can achieve all things implicit in my title but this last. I find it difficult to get serious, or at least wholly serious, or to remain so for long. Time passes, the day darkens, the grave yawns — and yet I still cannot resist a joke, a witty formulation, a piece of well-made frivolity. Narcissus may have left the pool, but as he departs, stage left, I hope you can still discern the echo of his laughter.

Narcissus
Leaves the Pool

Narcissus Leaves the Pool

E MERGING from the shower, I stand naked in front of my bathroom mirror. This, let the truth be told, is not an altogether enrapturing sight. (Had he grown well into middle age, Narcissus himself would surely have spent a lot less time gazing into the pool.) Contemplating myself, I feel a brief wave of pity for my wife who, night after night, has to sleep next to this body; I, more fortunate soul, have only to sleep *in* it. The bathroom has good light and a mirror extending nearly its full length; there is a soft rug, muted wallpaper, and ample blocks and slabs of cool, cream-colored marble. To paraphrase Bishop Heber on Ceylon, this bathroom is a place where every prospect pleases and only I am vile.

I note that my body seems slightly out of proportion to my head, which is a size $7\frac{3}{8}$. My shoulders are not wide — they are, more precisely, sloped — and my posture, a good deal less than perfect, has caused a slight humpiness where my neck runs into my back. Only the muscles in my calves and forearms could pass for youthful. My stomach is flat just now, but any weight I gain usually goes, like the blows of the late, punishing welterweight Carmen Basilio, straight to the midsection. The skin at my throat has begun to sag. I have old-guy elbows whose skin is dry, wrinkled, and reddish. If I lift my arms out to the side, the skin here, too, is loose, anticipating old age. My buttocks, I do believe, have begun to droop — not an inspiriting sight, drooping buttocks. The hair has long since disappeared from my shins, transferred perhaps to the backs of my shoulders, where I have only recently begun to notice it. My ankles, owing to what must be hundreds of broken capillaries, are purplish and descend into small, rather duckishly wide feet.

In the mirror before me, then, is an assemblage of hair, veins, and flesh that bears little more than what might be called a species resemblance to either Michelangelo's or Donatello's David. About Praxiteles' Hermes I wish not even to speak. And this, you understand, is the result of fairly clean living. What if I had lived with the throttle full-out, drinking heavily, smoking steadily, keeping late hours, eating with the happy gluttony of which I am capable? I have to conclude that, as protection against the ravages of age, a quiet life, a careful diet, plenty of fresh air, and regular flossing may not be all they are cracked up to be.

My favorite physical feature is my hands, and over the years I have spent a fair amount of time staring at them. My fingers are longish and shapely; the backs of my hands and my knuckles are still covered by dark hair; turquoise veins stand out in high relief; the knuckles at mid-finger are large; the nails are strong and cut straight across — the whole presenting (to me at least) a pleasing complication. A woman once told me that I had sexy wrists, an odd compliment that, unfortunately, came too late to be useful. Had I known earlier, when I was a bachelor and still engaged in the sex wars, I might have gone with this strength and taken to wearing gaudy watches, gold identification bracelets, and extravagant cuff links.

My most notable physical attribute is my ears, which are large and stand well out from my head. Caricaturists quickly pick this up. They haven't yet picked up on the hair that is beginning to grow ever so lightly on the rims of these ears. The hair on my head is now more gray than brown, and I note that my eyebrows have begun to turn white. Below my eyes rest substantial bags, two-suiters distinctly not by Louis Vuitton. My skin color is high, somewhat tan in all seasons, and this, combined with the darkness of my whiskers and the manifold wrinkles and creases of my skin, works well to camouflage my face's various blemishes and mottlings. When I go out in the evening, I frequently have to shave a second time because my five o'clock shadow, owing to my being an early riser, sets in around three in the afternoon.

Henry James, in an essay with the very Jamesian title "The Question of the Possibilities," refers to the American businessman of his day as "seamed all over with the scars of the marketplace." I think often about how lucky I am to have been spared all such scars, both metaphorical and real, of the marketplace and of the medical office. I suppose the chief scar of our day is that left by heart surgery, from simple to quintuple bypass. Lifesaving though this operation has proved to be, I am pleased to have avoided it and want ardently to depart the planet without its particular rococo medical tattoo.* Hence my blasted careful diet.

How little, really, has been exacted from this body over nearly six decades traipsing the earth! Apart from some rudimentary athletic training as a boy, and a few long marches and moderately strenuous calisthenics in the army, my body has never been truly tested. As for how easy my physical life has been, let me count the ways: I have never been tortured; I have never been shot or stabbed; I have never, after the age of ten, been in a

---

* Not quite. See p. 254

serious fight; I have never fallen from a horse; I have never been hungry or thirsty for more than a few hours. Perhaps only an American in the twentieth century can make such a happy claim, but in the physical realm I have known almost nothing of pain, deprivation, or humiliation.

In the sixteenth century, certainly, no one would have been so privileged. The great Montaigne is full of talk of the body: of impotence, flatulence, smells, rheums, fluxions of gout, coronary palpitations, migraines, and gallstones (which "monstrously unlecher me"). He informs readers of the foods he likes ("I am not over-fond of salads nor of any fruit except melons"), of the rhythm of his defecations, of the kind of bed he prefers to sleep in (hard, with rather too many covers, and he likes to sleep alone). He tells of the time he was thrown from his horse, when he lost consciousness and had his first premonition of death.

Death, the closing down of the body, and old age, the beginning of that process, are perpetually on Montaigne's mind: "God shows mercy to those from whom he takes away life a little at a time: this is the sole advantage of growing old; the last death which you die will be all the less total and painful: it will only be killing off half a man, or a quarter." Montaigne thought long about defeating the fear of death, which he seems to have achieved. His own taste ran to a death among strangers, so that he wouldn't have to expend his last breaths consoling others about his dying. Owing to his gallstones, a condition that also killed his father, Montaigne, from his forty-fifth year on, lived with great, sometimes unbearable, pain. This pain, which never let him for long forget his body, helped make him a thinker more thoroughly grounded in reality, even though he seemed to deny it. "What does it matter," he asks, "if our arms flay about as long as our thoughts do not?"

While I feel fortunate to have lived in a century in which pain has in many quarters been muted, if not defeated, I feel, at the same time, ever so mildly deprived that my body has not been placed in danger. Like every male, I wonder how I would have acted in battle with bullets whizzing by, bombs dropping around me, in hand-to-hand combat. Would I have kept my courage and won through? Every boy bred on World War II movies has wondered how much torture he could have stood without giving up military secrets that would have betrayed his comrades and his country. As a man now much too old for military service, I still wonder, when reading about the Nazi death camps or the Soviet slave-labor camps, how much, under pressure that was at bottom physical, I could have taken in the way of such punishment.

A boy lives in his body with an intensity and completeness that perhaps only professional athletes know as adults. His physical qualities count for nearly everything. Imperfections — plumpness, a big nose, poor skin, unruly hair — can bring him endless cruel teasing. How fast he can run, how far throw, how high jump, how artfully dodge, how willing to accept dares — these are the only questions that seem to matter in boyhood, or at least they did in mine. I grew up with many otherwise quite witless boys who were held in the highest regard because they could unfailingly field a grounder, throw a football fifty yards, or smash a tennis ball with a nicely controlled fury.

As a boy, I accepted without scruple the sovereignty of the physical — which meant the supremacy of athletic ability — as a guide to human quality. I was a respectable athlete myself, at any rate through grade school. Because I was small, my hope was to be a stylish athlete, an athlete with finesse, one who could make the quick, the smooth, the elegant move: to be the punch hitter, the agile dribbler with the deadly long shot, the smooth stroker. My talent was for pastiche; like many another boy, I was able to put together a fairly convincing hodge-podge imitation of the older boys and the professional athletes I had seen.

All this I brought off fairly well, at least for a while, but I lacked proper aggression. By proper aggression I really mean physical courage. Physical courage is probably an unteachable quality, and while I greatly admired it, I didn't have it in great abundance. In a clutch situation, I don't recall ever chickening out, but I was not ready on a regular basis to sacrifice my body, except when not to do so meant clear public disgrace.

A boy I grew up with who was always ready to sacrifice his body was Marty Summerfield. Not much bigger than I, Marty would run into a wall to catch a ball; stand unflinching at home plate to tag out a base runner thirty or forty pounds heavier than he who was about to steamroll him; catapult his body, kamikaze-like, into a defensive line to score a touchdown from two yards out. Marty lived on different terms with his body than did I or most of the other kids with whom we played. I considered the proposition of pain and quickly concluded that, on balance and where possible, it was best avoided; Marty never, as we should say nowadays, "factored in" pain. He just blazed ahead. Most of us were not cowards, but Marty was absolutely fearless. He had had a number of concussions and other interesting injuries. He had a generously chipped front tooth that I envied. That chipped tooth seemed the boyhood equivalent of a dueling scar, a bit of shrapnel in the hip, a Purple Heart.

The one gift bestowed upon my boyish body was excellent coordination. I don't recall ever feeling awkward. My body could do almost anything I wanted it to do: turn, twist, leap, calculate perfectly the arrival of a football in my hands, a baseball in my glove, and a tennis ball on my racket. What I couldn't do with my body was get it to grow taller.

The comic books that I read passionately as a kid regularly ran two ads on their back covers that were aimed at boys like me. These ads held out the promise of building up our bodies. In one, a man whose muscles were oiled and tensed offered to make us Commando Tough!, exclamation mark and all. In an even more popular ad, the famous bodybuilder Charles Atlas promised to convey the secrets of a muscle-building program he called "Dynamic Tension." Atlas's ad asked if one was tired of being a ninety-eight-pound weakling and showed cartoon drawings of such a weakling on the beach getting sand kicked in his face and losing his girlfriend to a bully.

At age nine, I was a good deal less than ninety-eight pounds when I sent away for the free sepia-colored pamphlet that Atlas pledged would change my life. Among the photographs it contained was one of a man stopping a railroad train in its progress with his bare arms: just the lightest touch of photo-hyperbole, perhaps. The deal was that I should send away, at no insubstantial cost, for a continuing series of pamphlets that would teach me how to build up my various muscle groups. To acquire the entire set, a couple of hundred bucks was required — no small sum for a boy of nine. When I asked my father for financial help, he replied, while turning the pages of the *Chicago Daily News* and not bothering to look up, "Whaddaya, kiddin' me?"

I had never been more serious. Yet "Dynamic Tension" would not have done the job, for it entailed a regular round of exercises, and it was the boring regularity of exercise of which I was incapable. Besides, I really didn't want to have the bulky, thickly veined muscles of the weight lifter. I wanted instead to have the smooth, long muscles of the graceful athlete. (Weight lifting was then thought to destroy athletic coordination. To-day every collegiate athletic program has its weight room, and weight training is suggested even for baseball and tennis players.)

In the realm of the physical, the first rule is to feel discontent with what one has. I note that no woman, no matter how beautiful, is ever quite satisfied with her looks; and the better looking she is, the more troubling are her minor flaws. "She was pretty," says a flapper in F. Scott Fitzgerald's *The Beautiful and Damned*, "except that she had big ankles." And in the realm of the physical, too, nothing is ever quite satisfactorily repairable — at least not exactly in the way one had hoped. Cosmetic surgeons, I am told, ask to be paid their entire fee in advance for the sensible reason that almost no one is ever entirely satisfied with their work.

In adolescence, my body controlled me. Along with every other boy of my age I knew, I became, in spirit if not (alas) in actuality, a complete, if also completely unfulfilled, sex fiend. I must have thought about other things during this time but none with the same pure concentration as I thought about sex. Adolescent boys, to speak plainly, are beasts. I don't care how well they do on the SATs, how nicely they conduct themselves around the house, or how great their pretensions to be interested in science, sports, music, their computers, or good causes — they are never to be trusted and are probably better assigned to a road gang until the age of twenty-five.

One of the many divisions of humankind is that between those who live in their bodies and those who live outside them. Here social class often enters in. In *My Ántonia*, Willa Cather has her young hero, Jim Burden, compare the immigrant country girls to the richer town girls. He says that outdoor work had given the former "a vigour which, when they got over their first shyness on coming to town, developed into a positive carriage and freedom of movement," whereas the town girls, though jolly and pretty, had "bodies [that] never moved inside their clothes" and "muscles [that] seemed to ask but one thing — not to be disturbed."

I thought of this passage the other day when I saw a famous professor from the university where I teach carrying hand weights as he walked home. He was doing it in such a herky-jerky fashion that I could read into his every step a boy who had never known physical grace. At chamber music concerts, too, most of the people in the audience look as if they have not used their bodies very much. Someone I knew who grew up in the working class, when asked in later life about the differ-ence between the working and the middle classes, remarked that almost everyone in the latter seemed to have retained ten fingers. This made me recall noticing, when I worked in a discount store in downtown Chicago, how many farmers and factory workers had lost fingers in accidents with farm machin-ery or on the assembly line. With some exceptions (F. Scott Fitzgerald's first description of the wealthy Tom Buchanan in *The Great Gatsby:* his "was a body capable of enormous leverage — a cruel body"), to be of the working class is to live in greater dependence on one's body.

My own adolescent body was efficient enough, but, it almost goes without saying, it was far from everything I wanted it to be. I wished, among other things, for larger arms, especially at the biceps. To help bring this about, I once bought two ten-pound dumbbells and began doing the weight-lifting exercise known as curls, which, out of boredom, I soon gave up. For bodybuilding, I should have much preferred a summer con-struction job of the kind much admired in my high school days. In such a job you labored at heavy work in the blazing sun for relatively high wages, ate an Italian sausage sandwich and washed it down with a quart of beer for lunch, leered at passing girls, belched grandly, swore profusely among fellow workers, and got a great tan. Or so I idealized such work, which I was never able to get. The closest I came to doing physical labor was unloading trucks in the receiving room of a phonograph needle factory; not enough trucks came in, though, to give me the kind of exercise that would have built me up.

I wished also for the growth of facial hair that would allow me to shave regularly, but it didn't come until I was eighteen or nineteen. I associated the end of boyhood with the beginning of regular shaving. Although I was already taller than my father, I hoped to cheat genetics and to grow a good deal taller still. People in those days talked about boys "shooting up," and it seemed that the time for shooting up was summer. At fourteen, fifteen, sixteen, seventeen, or even eighteen, boys could suddenly achieve another four or five inches in height. I waited, hopefully, for mine. They never arrived.

It is not all that easy for people with small bodies to imagine living in large bodies, or for large people to imagine living in small bodies. When T. S. Eliot first met Igor Stravinsky, he told him that he expected a taller man: Stravinsky was 5 feet 3 inches and weighed 120 pounds. Stravinsky, in return, had expected that Eliot would have "less imposing proportions; his big, somewhat stolid and cumbrous frame seemed an unnecessarily large refuge even for such over-endowed shyness and modesty as his." I don't know exactly how large Eliot was, but for a man so large he was very adroit at deploying semicolons. Edmund Wilson reports in his journals that Stephen Spender, an immense man, claimed that "he lacked energy on account of being so tall." Aldous Huxley, another tall man, apparently once told Spender that neither of them qualified as geniuses "because when you are tall, your head is too far from your solar plexus." A friend of mine thinks that it is a mistake of a fundamental kind to be over six feet tall and not a good basketball player — "wasted height," he calls it. Dragging my own rather abbreviated carcass around on certain logy days, I feel grateful that I am not a foot taller and a hundred pounds heavier.

At some point in life, not long after adolescence, one has to become reconciled to one's body, to play the cards one was dealt, to say, in effect, this is it, this is the skin I was intended to travel in, and so I shall. And thus, historically, people have done. But not quite any longer. The current belief, widely held, is that we can do a lot to change things: lose weight, tone things up, somehow or other cheat the dealer. We can, I suppose, for a while. I have tried to cheat him myself — I am still at it, puffing away on my NordicTrack WalkFit four or five mornings a week, trudging off, I must somehow believe, into life everlasting.

But finally, as they say in Vegas, you can't hope to beat the House. The House will trip you up in ways you don't expect. For an illness, I once took a drug whose side effect caused something called avascular necrosis, which meant for me a loss of tissue in my hip. So stiffened up was my right leg that I needed, for a few months, to use a cane. Though I was never in great pain, this provided a small lesson in how any minor physical malfunction can upset one's life. One of the wretched things about carrying a cane is that you lose the use of the hand in which you hold the damn thing. I found myself standing at my front door, cane in one hand, two plastic bags of groceries in the other, and no hand free to take the keys from my pants pocket. Or when I needed to use the bathroom in the middle of the night, I first had to locate my cane. A hundred other little inconveniences resulted from the medically caused jiggeroo that prevented my right hipbone from fitting smoothly into its socket.

But this was bush-league stuff. Imagine how desolating it would be to walk around nauseated all the time or to be unable to use your hands or to hear. Imagine being hostage to some devastating debilitating disease such as lupus or multiple sclerosis. Even temporarily unpleasant physical conditions are not all that easily imagined: great thirst, for example, or a horrendous sensation of itching. Dan Jacobson, writing about going down into a Zambian copper mine in his South African travel book, *The Electronic Elephant,* notes that the experience "left me with a thoroughgoing scepticism about the power of the written word ever to convey the inward nature of any extreme physical experience: of war, say, or polar exploration, or even severe illness." Not even the effects of a cold are easily described. Which is partly why *The Magic Mountain,* with its concentrated and sustained description of the effects, physical and mental, of tuberculosis, and *Cancer Ward,* in which Solzhenitsyn does the same thing for cancer, are such impressive works.

In literature the great connoisseurs of the body seem to be the French. The tradition began even before Montaigne with Rabelais, who viewed the body as a magnificent fleshly vessel for containing vast quantities of wine and food (and oh so useful for energetic fornication). Rabelais, with his tales of comic defecation, vomiting, uncontrollable micturation, and other temporary maladies and permanent human indignities, is always reminding us how body-bound we are. "Without health life is not life," wrote Rabelais, "life is not livable. . . . Without health life is nothing but languor; life is but the simulacrum of death."

But, then, Rabelais was a physician, and, as the narrator of

Marguerite Yourcenar's great novel *Memoirs of Hadrian* reminds us, "it is difficult to remain an emperor in the presence of a physician, and difficult even to keep one's essential quality as a man." I have always thought the problem might be quite as difficult the other way around — that it is difficult to keep one's essential quality as a man when one is a physician. A part of me much admires physicians, but as great a part is repelled by their work of picking and probing in the big muddy that is the human body. I speak, though, as someone who is quite squeamish. I don't, for example, like to contemplate much of what goes on in my body beneath the skin. I don't even like to think that I possess kidneys, a liver, a spleen, a pancreas, and the rest of it. An old joke has it that a psychoanalyst is a Jewish boy who can't stand the sight of blood. A writer, at least this writer, may be a Jewish boy who not only can't stand the sight of blood but doesn't wish to spend all that much time listening to other people's problems.

While respecting what they do and realizing the need for them, I have tried, to the best of my ability, to steer clear of physicians. I find that, given a chance, they discover things I would rather not know about. But as I get older, I find myself calling upon them more often. I have finally reached the age when I call my physicians by their first names, for I am now older than the various doctors and dentists on, so to speak, my staff. This should be a good thing. Being younger, they are likely to survive me — to be there, as the English say, to see me out.

My internist is, I think, a penetrating diagnostician and a very nice guy: sensible, good-natured, likable in every way. Yet I cannot say I enjoy his searches upon my body for lumps, bumps, protuberances, dangerous distensions, little bubbles on major veins and arteries. One day, of course, he will find that for which he has been looking. He will call me into his office and tell me

— nothing positive of course, nothing for me to worry about *yet* — that he would like to run further tests. I shall respond stoically, with good humor on my face and terror in my heart, joking with him yet knowing that this is it, *ball game*. My body has had enough. Bored with its occupant or repaying old if minor abuses, it has determined to devour itself — and me with it — in disease.

I often envision that day. I am no hypochondriac; only your normal thanatophobe. With death at the door — the Ruffian on the Stair, the poet W. E. Henley called it — I hope to have a little time to cut loose. From my physician's office, I shall betake myself to an ice cream shop for a banana split, after which I shall stop off for a large packet of a candy I have always been partial to known as Spearmint Leaves. I may pick up a pack of cigarettes. A restaurant known as Chicago Joe's, a steak joint with a specialty in cheesecake and key lime pie, will, in the time remaining, get to see a lot of me. I shall cease flossing.

My guess is that I am not alone in thinking such thoughts, playing out the scenario of being told by a physician that there is little time left; for we all live in anticipation of that moment nowadays. I don't think I go too far when I say that many of us organize our diets and our daily lives so that we can put off that moment for as long as possible. Despite lots of cheating, I try to eat foods that will help me escape colon cancer or a heart attack. Worse to report: when I have eaten carefully through the day, I feel as though I am one up on the Ruffian on the Stair. I assume that he's going to be discouraged and depart because I have had a fruit salad for lunch and salmon and two vegetables for dinner. Foolish of me. He has plenty of patience, the Ruffian.

A few years ago I purchased an exercise bicycle on which, for twenty-five or so minutes every morning, I would ride off into imaginary sunsets listening to Louis Prima and reading magazines. I have now graduated, as I mentioned earlier, to a Nordic-Track WalkFit treadmill. Both of these modern torture racks exist chiefly to help the user lose weight and stay slim — which will in turn, presumably, help the user avoid a heart attack. The true meaning behind all this careful eating and joyless exercise is that I, and countless others like me, have begun to live, at least on the physical level, defensively. The Ruffian on the Stair must smile at our hopeless contrivances to outwit him, knowing that, even if our plan works for a while, his old pal Senile Dementia awaits.

Working out is, as T. S. Eliot described poetry, a mug's game. It is so because one cannot finally win at it. All muscles, after all, eventually break down. The *New York Times* not long ago ran an article on the need for the very old to work out. "Even among the very old, it is never too late to benefit from getting in shape," the article happily begins. It then goes on to cite the results of a study about to be published in that good news/bad news journal of our day, the *New England Journal of Medicine*. Half the people in the study, the article reports, were demented. Even when you are out of your mind, exercise is apparently good for you. How the Ruffian must be giggling!

My own relationship with my body has changed gradually over the years. I used to think it an agreeable companion that yielded me great pleasure on many fronts. Today I look at it somewhat paranoically, chiefly for signs of betrayal, for ways it might let me down. The least change or irregularity is worrisome, indicating some (probably) fatal disease. ("Anyone who is afraid of suffering," writes Montaigne, "suffers already of being afraid.") The obituary pages are filled with the deaths of people younger than I. Serious breakdown, while not necessarily imminent, now has to be considered a distinct possibility.

Until four or five years ago, I was a gamesman — I played

games to give my body a workout. My last game was racquet-ball. Racket and paddle games have always been my favorite sports because they don't call for great size but they do put my good coordination to felicitous use. Ping-Pong, badminton, tennis — I was a more than respectable player in all these games. But I think I may have been best of all at racquetball, a four-wall court game that enjoyed a great flurry of popularity in the 1970s and has all but fizzled out today.

I don't want to overrate my ability — when Joe DiMaggio and Marilyn Monroe divorced, Oscar Levant said that he supposed no man could excel at two national pastimes — but I think I was fairly good at racquetball. The game held an aesthetic excitement for me that seems to have been inseparable from every pleasure I have known in games through a long and mediocre athletic career: the clean pickup of a grounder, the sweet swish of the basketball net, the clear *pock* of an overhead smash.

Racquetball gave me the most intense physical pleasure of all. I loved racing back to take a shot off the back wall and send the ball careening off the front wall for a winner. I loved crushing a return of the other player's service down the backhand side. The game had various "kill shots," of which my own favorite involved standing near the service line, waiting until the very last moment before the ball hit the floor for the second time, and whacking the ball — *whap!* — into the right-hand corner for an unreturnable shot. Sometimes, just before falling asleep at night, I would rehearse that shot — *whap! whap! whap!* — and it gave me delight even to think about it. While playing racquetball my body was on automatic pilot; the horse, so to speak, knew the way. My hip injury put an end to all that.

The other day, a bright Wednesday afternoon, a generous friend took me out to hit some tennis balls, something I had not done for more than a decade. With my hip now healed, I harbored a new fantasy, and I wished to try it out. The fantasy was that I would play a businesslike, middle-aged game of tennis, without any of the old competitiveness of youth, any of the anger directed at myself for errors of judgment and prowess. I thought I might hire a young pro to rally with me, to smooth over those things in my game that had become too rough. Maturity, late to arrive though it may have been, would at last be in the saddle. Mild-mannered, middle-aged tennis would be the ass on which into Jerusalem I would ride, in white shorts, shirt, and shoes, graphite racket in hand, the very picture of cool and natural elegance, playing this happily controlled tennis game.

It didn't work out as I had planned. Not only did I fail to hit many balls well — my forehand was particularly atrocious; my backhand, a more grooved stroke, was still intact — but even those balls I did hit well gave me, as René Lacoste might have put it, *non frisson*. Or, as the telephone answering machine of Will "the Thrill" Clark, the first baseman of the Texas Rangers, is reported to announce, the thrill is gone. The magic wasn't there; the fantasy refused to take wing. Ken Rosewall and Rod Laver needn't worry; neither is likely to be knocked out of the early rounds of a seniors tournament by an amiable, unseeded, altogether unknown midwesterner with red elbows, purple ankles, and slightly drooping buttocks.

I have decided to put off my comeback as a tennis player because, without the physical pleasure, it all seems pointless. Hitting a service ace, a crisp volley, a crosscourt winner — the prospect of these acts no longer lights my fire. A new and distinctly different set of fantasies is required. So, too, is a new relationship with that now old companion, my body, or, as the kids say, me bod. My mother lived to the age of eighty-one; my father is still alive at ninety-one. With luck and enough boringly safe meals, I might be walking the planet for another twenty-five or so years.

Little as I wish to own up to it, I have begun thinking about my body less and less as a receiving room for pleasure and a hall for physical delights. It won't do any longer to think myself Fred Astaire or Jim Thorpe, let alone Casanova. Shocking to confess, I am a man who stares furtively (I hope) at beautiful women. But I remind myself that my interest in such matters is now not even theoretical but entirely museological. Similarly, when I lose my temper over poor service or a breach of etiquette, I have to understand, more poignantly than ever before, that the notion of a physical threat behind my loss of temper is quite pathetic. ("What else could I do?" I imagine the service manager at my car dealership patiently explain over beers with a friend about his stormy dealings with me. "I had no choice. I punched the old guy out.") The time has come when I really have to take seriously the dictum to act my age.

I have been reading Sherwin B. Nuland's best-selling book *How We Die.* A book not excessively loaded with jokes, Dr. Nuland's. I don't think I shall be giving away the plot when I report that the answer to the question posed in his title is that we die too quickly or all too slowly, drearily, painfully, sloppily, undignifiedly, horrendously, but — and here is the genuinely bad news — inevitably. "We rarely go gently into that good night," he writes. He reports that "our own bodies are simultaneously and subtly undergoing the same inexorable process that will lead eventually to senescence and death." Dr. Nuland has enough grim material well in hand not to have to bring up the little unpractical jokes the body likes to play, such as giving an abscessed tooth to a man who is fighting leukemia. He is especially strong on what the brain loses in functioning power after the age of fifty. I would pass some of this information along to you, but, being sixty-one myself, I don't remember most of what he wrote.

Sometimes I see my reflection in a store window or in a restaurant mirror, and I am a little shocked. Who is this grayish, rather sour-faced fellow? It takes me a second to remember and then another few moments to remind myself to get used to him. He and I have to come to terms. So many people I know in their eighties have told me that, in their minds, they feel forty or fifty years younger. In my own early sixties, I still think of myself as in my thirties. It won't do. My body daily gives testimony that it won't.

The body is the reality in which each of us is grounded. The world surely looks different to a man of 350 pounds than it does to a man of 130 pounds. Not only do we obtain much of our information about the world through our senses — which is to say, through our bodies — but, as all philosophers of good standing can convincingly argue, our senses enjoy almost nothing so much as deceiving us. The limitations of knowledge are best exhibited in the lack of control we have over our physique. Mind will go only so far over matter. Did their logic, asks Montaigne, console Varro and Aristotle for their gout? Does having read Proust twice all the way through make having stomach flu any easier? It's a serious mistake to forget for a moment that we are held hostage by these fleshly prison cells, our bodies.

All things considered, the one assigned to me hasn't been a lemon. Despite its compactness, ·it is sufficiently commodious. It has chugged along pretty well and required relatively little servicing. Since by now it is long out of warranty, I hesitate to take sharp corners with it or to put it to endurance tests of any impressive kind. With so much mileage on it, breakdowns oughtn't come as a surprise. Replacement parts, they say, are possible to obtain, but about this I remain a bit dubious. A new body, clearly, is called for, but what dealer would take mine as a trade-in?

Thrift and prudence may, with luck, make one wealthy. Thoughtfulness and learning may, with even more luck, make one wise. But there stands the body to mock both wealth and wisdom and every other kind of accumulation. The body exists to demonstrate, if demonstration is needed, that progress has its limitations. "Every day in every way I get better and better" is a notion that the body refutes. Beyond a certain point one ceases to grow stronger, more beautiful, more desirable. Neither all the king's personal trainers nor all the king's cosmetic surgeons can put any of us together again. The body reminds us that we are in the swim only for a short, however glorious, while. Then, no matter what one's station in life, or what one's natural endowments, the whistle blows and it's everybody but everybody out of the pool, and that includes you — which is to say me — Narcissus, baby.

An Extremely
Well Informed SOB

McKisco was "well-informed" on a range of
subjects wider than Goethe's — it was interesting
to listen to the innumerable facile combinations
that he referred to as his opinions.

— F. SCOTT FITZGERALD, *Tender Is the Night*

T HE OTHER MORNING, over coffee, I had one of those
Eureka moments. I was indulging in some splendidly
useless reading, in this instance the *Selected Letters of
Raymond Chandler.* I have never read a Raymond Chandler novel,
but, from an earlier dip in his letters, I have come to have a
genuine regard for Chandler. He was not an academic or an
intellectual, but he was more than a bit of an artist, though not
in the least a pretentious one. Above all, he was a smart guy. He
was too easily irascible to be wise, perhaps too leery of being
conned to be disinterestedly penetrating, but he was smart in
the sense of having a good interior radar for the kind of lies and
nonsense that most of us get caught up in. He had a strong
notion of what counted and what didn't in a life of limited
years. He held a low, not easily refuted, and probably salubrious
view of human nature: "The best way to find out if you have

any friends," he wrote to his agent Carl Brandt, "is to go broke. The ones that hang on longest are your friends. I don't mean the ones that hang on forever. There aren't any of these."

Drinking coffee, I read a letter that Chandler wrote in 1950 to a friend which said that he was about to cancel his subscription to the *Saturday Review of Literature.* He had decided that it wasn't good enough to warrant bringing into a house already overloaded with magazines, despite the magazine's claim to improve its readers' minds. "But I must be one of the few living Americans who do not crave to have their minds improved," Chandler wrote. "I know too much already. I would be happier knowing less."

There it was: Eureka! Pow! Zowie! not to say &, *, #, and @! We read certain writers for those moments when they tell us what in our hearts we already know but, for one reason or another, haven't managed to formulate for ourselves. This was such a moment for me.

On the table where I was drinking my coffee and reading Raymond Chandler's letters were the following magazines: the *New York Review of Books,* the *Chronicle of Higher Education,* two copies of *Publishers Weekly,* three issues of the London *Times Literary Supplement,* a *Harper's,* a *New Yorker,* the *Atlantic,* the *New Republic, Poetry,* the *New York Times Book Review,* and the *New York Times Magazine.*

On the same table were the following books: *The AIA Guide to the Architecture of Washington, D.C.; Memories & Commentaries* by Igor Stravinsky and Robert Craft; *Mrs. Thatcher's Minister: The Private Diaries of Alan Clark; The Mezzanine* by Nicholson Baker; *Barbarian Asia and the Greek Experience* by Pericles Georges; *Dr. Johnson and Mr. Savage* by Richard Holmes; *The Ruin of Kasch* by Roberto Calasso; *Mosaic* by Lincoln Kirstein; *The Primary Colors* by Alexander Theroux; *Clear and Simple as the Truth: Writing*

Classic Prose by Francis-Noël Thomas and Mark Turner; *The Journals of James Boswell*, selected and edited by John Wain; *Ukulele Music — Perduta Gente*, poems by Peter Reading; and, finally, *Characters* by La Bruyère. None of these books, be it noted, has any direct connection with anything I am working on at the moment.

Elsewhere in this apartment there are bookmarks in books I have begun reading by V. S. Naipaul, Mario Vargas Llosa, Kingsley Amis, Julius Meier-Graefe, Paul Auster, Ryszard Kapuscinski, Maurice Ravel, Dan Jacobson, Stendhal, E. J. Dent, Carl Zuckmayer, E. R. Curtius, Nicholas Mosley, Ned Rorem, and, in the bathroom, sits an extraordinary novel about Wittgenstein and Bertrand Russell titled *The World As I Found It*, written by a man named Bruce Duffy. None of these books, either, has to do with anything I am working on or plan to be working on.

I read the daily national edition of the *New York Times*. (I probably should but don't read the *Chicago Tribune*, the largest paper in the city in which I live.) Along with the magazines mentioned above, I read *Commentary*, the *New Criterion*, the *Hudson Review*, the *Sewanee Review*, the *Virginia Quarterly Review*, and the *Kenyon Review*. I do not so much read as breeze through *Vanity Fair*, *Esquire*, and *Gentlemen's Quarterly*, to all of which I subscribe. I read though do not subscribe to *Tikkun*, the *American Spectator*, the *Nation*, and the *National Review*. I read Hilton Kramer on the visual arts in the weekly *New York Observer* and glimpse the rest of that peach-colored rag for gossip about men and women in magazine and book publishing. Add the things that I read for my work — writing, teaching, editing — and, taken all in all, a fair amount of print finds its way into this apartment and into my brain.

Given all this reading — maybe it adds up to near half my waking hours — you might think me an extremely well informed SOB. Funny, but I don't in the least feel well informed. If anything, I feel less and less informed as the years go by. Once upon a time, and not so long ago as all that, one could posit what an educated man or woman ought to know: what languages, what historical narratives, what works of philosophy, literature, music, and art. Since the job description for the educated person seems to have changed a good bit of late — I'm not sure that knowledge of ancient Greek and Latin are still required — what might the well-informed, as distinct from the well-educated, man or woman of our day know? Would he or she be able to name the nine political parties in Mexico (I can name one), recall who Kristen McMenamy, Ron Jeremy, and Tony Little are (I can't), explain a nickel defense, a twelve-tone scale, a neutron (beats me)?

What, really, is the point of being well informed? Perhaps the first answer to that question is that it relieves one of the embarrassment of seeming ignorant. Having information, knowing the score, the true gen (as Hemingway called it), the real lowdown, brings a thrill of its own special kind. Not only does it separate one from the ignoranti — cognoscenti 48, ignoranti 0 — but it gives one the feeling that one is living the life of one's time. As an editor and writer, I have felt an extra inducement for keeping myself informed about the trends, issues, questions, and problems of the day, so that I can write or induce other people to write about them.

Of late, however, I have been feeling the strain of information overload. My storage and retrieval system doesn't seem to function as smoothly as it once did. Some might say that this is the effect of putting on too many winters, but I suspect that the problem is with the amount of information that just keeps piling up until there isn't enough room left in the file cabinets of my mind to sort it out. (I am old enough, after all, to know about SEATO and NATO and the Green Hornet's man whose name was Cato.) Over lunch someone explains to me, in intricate detail, what the import of the salary cap is in the then baseball strike. Pretending to listen intently, hoping that my eyes do not show the thick glaze of a franchise doughnut, I ask myself how can I most efficiently forget all this information, every scrap?

I suppose one of the reasons for being well informed on everything is so that one can have an opinion on everything. The culture seems very opinionated just now. ("Ron Perelman and Richard Perle," Cathleen Schine writes of her heroine in her novel *Rameau's Niece;* "she knew she disapproved of them both, but which one for which reason?") No one is more opinionated than an intellectual. I am an intellectual. (Finish the syllogism on your own.) One of the delights of being an intellectual is that one is expected to have opinions on everything while incurring responsibility for nothing. But for the formation of these opinions at least a smattering of information is required.

Alas, on an increasingly wide range of subjects, I find I am perfectly pleased to be without any opinion at all. On so many political questions, social scandals, academic disputes, I find my antipathies nicely riven down the center, which makes forming an opinion favoring one side or the other a bit difficult. Besides, opinion generally — and my own in particular — has come to seem less and less interesting to me. A human being, after all, is not an op-ed page; the least impressive of thoughts are formulated in the personal equivalent of editorials. In his novel *Guerrillas,* V. S. Naipaul remarks about a character he clearly despises that she had a great many opinions but, taken together, these did not add up to a point of view.

Opinions are most impressive, of course, when backed up with vast quantities of information. Yet, when one does accrue a fair amount of information, someone is almost certain to come along with even more. The hotter the subject, the more intense the controversy, the greater the amount of information available. Take the four great American political controversies of the twentieth century: the Sacco-Vanzetti case, the Rosenberg spy trial, the Hiss-Chambers case, and the Kennedy assassination. To have all the information available on these controversies, so that one can arrive at the most reasoned opinion, would take just a little longer than a longish lifetime. To study any of them in anything like full detail is to step into the swamp with Ferragamo loafers — just not a sensible move. The truth, it is said, will set you free, but, pursued with the ardor some matters require, it can cause you to miss dinner and many a pleasant evening afterward. Most people, I suspect, must do what I do: hold, on most matters of genuine controversy, an opinion based less on solid information than on hunch, temperament, and one's general politics and point of view.

At the precise time that our age is going bonkers for more and more information, with people talking confidently of "the information society" and "the knowledge economy of the twenty-first century," with all the chatter about fiber-optic cables, direct broadcast satellites, digital technology, video E-mail, and the rest, I find myself longing for rather less information. Why do I have to know the politics of Michael Lerner — or even who Michael Lerner is? Why do I have to know that the golfer Greg Norman's sobriquet is "the White Shark"? I am pleased not to know what quantity is contained in the unit of a "ball" of cocaine. I am pleased — proud even — never to have heard Howard Stern or Don Imus on the radio, but I'm a little sad to have to admit that I know who they are. I'd rather be as ignorant of them as I am of Beavis and Butt-head. I am, again, pleased not to know what "lap dancing" is — and I shall make a concerted effort not to find out. I feel no sorrow at my ignorance of whole subcultures. Plenty of time to learn them, I figure, in the next life.

Instant information and instant communication — these are among the goals of the current age. I not long ago had a letter from a man who, on his letterhead, listed, along with his address, three phone numbers (home, office, and car), two fax numbers, and his E-mail code. When I saw that great jumble of numbers, I said to myself, "The hell with it. This guy's altogether too easy to get in touch with. I'm not going to answer his letter." I eventually did answer it, though, and not long after, I met him. Sorry to report, he turned out to be an amiable fellow. How much less complicated life would be if you could judge a man by his letterhead!

The states or conditions or degrees of informedness, I have concluded, are four: being well informed, being knowledgeable, being hip, and being cultivated. An example of someone well informed might be a television newsman in the upper reaches — a Sam Donaldson, say, or a Cookie Roberts — someone who chats away about the news for a living and for whom knowing who voted how on health care or on defense spending is more important than knowing the names of the books of the Bible or when Proust died or who Poulenc was. Being well informed suggests, at least to me, people mired in the news whose outlook and limits are bounded physically by the Washington Beltway and chronologically by the last ten years. They may have bits of historical knowledge, but they are really defined by the up-to-the-moment. *Au courant* and all current, the well informed live almost wholly in the Now.

The knowledgeable are more wide-ranging in their information. Although often in possession of information about the Now, they know a vast deal about the Then. They are not usually specialized in what they know. If 1950s quiz shows hadn't all been fixed, one could cite their contestants as perfect examples of the knowledgeable. A knowledgeable person could, I suppose, tell you who led the final sacking of Constantinople in 1453, who won the Preakness in 1926, and whence tarragon derives.

I recently had a student of remarkable knowledgeability, a refreshment in an age when professors are wont to claim that the young have no historical knowledge. This young man has a wonderfully absorbent mind and an attractive manner of mastering the factual substance of any subject that interests him. He knows baseball, the Arab world, an impressive amount about serious music, much history, and so many other things that when he didn't know a discrete fact I felt slightly amazed, as if I had found a flaw in an almanac or encyclopedia of good repute. I was not surprised to learn that he had been a member of his quite good high school's — St. Albans's, in Washington, D.C. — quiz bowl team.

Knowledgeability, however, has its limits. It is chiefly, though not wholly, about facts, and the world's facts are simply too many for even the most absorbent brain to retain. During the investigation of cheating on quiz shows, one of the producers of a fifties quiz show called *Dotto* told an attorney from the New York district attorney's office that, given the range of factual knowledge, nobody could be expected to answer more than two of any ten randomly asked questions. "You cannot ask random questions of people and have a show," he declared. "You simply have failure, failure, failure, and that does not make for entertainment." That is perhaps the best explanation, though no justification, for the fixing of those quiz shows, and contained within it is a description of the natural limits of knowledgeability.

If to be informed is to know about the Now, and to be knowledgeable is to know about the Then, to be hip is to know about what's going on in those lively waters outside the boring mainstream, where life is reputedly lived with the intensity it merits. The truly hip would find much that interests the informed and the knowledgeable more than a little beside the point. The hip think of themselves as blasting through the façade of quotidian life to discover what is going on in the inner rooms. The hip man or woman is an avant-gardist of information: he or she knows what's happening — and feels that what's happening is the only thing genuinely worth knowing.

I have known people — all have been men — who prided themselves on their hipness, but one friend in particular went, I think it fair to say, hip full-time. I first met Al in New York. He had written a Ph.D. dissertation about plagiarism in Thomas De Quincey, and he taught in the School of General Studies at Columbia, which he always referred to, in good, amusing hip fashion, as "working the lounge at Columbia." He was the first person I knew who, having had the talent to be either, preferred being hip to being learned.

Like many who pride themselves on their hipness, Al knew an extraordinary amount about jazz — with a special interest in its more out-on-the-edge aspects: the barbaric appetites of Charlie Parker, the elegant viciousness of Miles Davis — and he wrote about it in rather febrile prose. He had been in psychoanalysis — in those days itself still something of an advance-guard activity — which was one source of his humor. This humor featured many jokes about repression, or, more precisely, about cutting loose from repression. "Could you lower the lights, bring me a paper cup and a towel, and turn on Peggy Lee singing 'Fever'?" he once asked me when he sat down to read his own galley proofs at a magazine where I worked.

Al's great moment came when he discovered the comedian Lenny Bruce. He eventually wrote a substantial tome, a work of 565 pages, about him. Like Charlie Parker and Miles Davis, Lenny Bruce was another of Al's heroic anti-repressors. Bruce's specialty, as Al argued in an early article he wrote about him, was to serve as a shaman of sorts by breaking taboos — of decorous speech, of false sentiment — that the rest of us were apparently too timid to confront. In this, Lenny Bruce was the hippest of the hip, telling the truths that we all knew — about sex, religion, drugs — but were too uptight (a word not yet current), too frozen with fright, to admit. Al became something of a Bruce hanger-on, and my guess is that, as a frustrated comedian himself whose only stage was "the lounge" at Columbia, he would have traded places with Lenny Bruce without hesitation, except for the squalor of the comedian's drug-laden life.

Al later wrote thick books about Elvis and John Lennon — books underwritten, it was said, by million-dollar advances. The John Lennon book was an international bestseller whose revelations angered a great many people. (I once heard, on television, the rock singer Elton John, in reaction to the John Lennon book, call Al "human vermin," which is certainly a long way from the kind of response his work on plagiarism in De Quincey had received.) Al died of a heart attack in his middle sixties, but had he lived longer, I don't doubt he would have written a book about Michael Jackson; for what interested him most seemed to be the investigation of the world of popular-culture figures, behind which he found, as the very hip are inclined to do, drugs, strange sexual practices, disorder, and early sorrow.

I'm afraid I make an old friend sound rather a creep. Al wasn't. He had, in fact, beneath all his relentless hipness, a kind of natural refinement and charm. With his receding hairline, his mustache (later shaved off), his small wire-rimmed glasses, his scholar's stoop, his good if sometimes excessively modish clothes, he resembled S. J. Perelman, but a sexier, hipper, much flippier S. J. Perelman. We didn't keep in regular touch, and, after I moved from New York, years would go by without our meeting. But whenever I saw him, I found myself pleased to be in his company.

Al was never boring, and he had a lovely, snorting adenoidal laugh, which, when I could, I enjoyed invoking. I never read his Elvis or John Lennon books — friendship, after all, has its limits. I used to think his condition inherently a little sad: being hip, molding an entire personality out of one's hipness, appeared to me more than a touch unseemly for a man of a certain age. The only people I know who can bring off hipness past the age of fifty are the older black jazz musicians; it's almost always a mistake for white guys to attempt it.

When Al was working on his Lenny Bruce book, he asked me, as a favor, to do a bit of "research" for him — remember when that was a real word, something scientists did in laboratories? Could I find a few hours to interview a druggist in Chicago who was known to have supplied Lenny Bruce with lots of drugs when he played The Gate of Horn and other Chicago nightclubs? I agreed and met the druggist, who was absolutely forthcoming not only about Lenny Bruce but about other comedians, musicians, and singers whom he supplied with an impressive range of drugs. They used to take these drugs at his house near Rush Street, then Chicago's chief nightclub center. "In those days, we used to call the house," he said with a prideful smile, "the shooting gallery." For three hours or so, this man rattled on and on, and here I was, for the first and only time in my life, in possession of inside, altogether hippish information about all these show-business characters. The thrill, I have to report, just wasn't there.

One could, I suppose, be informed, knowledgeable, and hip all at once — though clogging one's mind with much useless information would be a terrible strain — but no one could be all three things and cultivated into the bargain. To be cultivated is, of the four possibilities, the most desirable. I have had a few friends who have achieved this elevated status. The cultivated not only know a great deal but, more important, they know what is significant — they know, not to put too fine a point on it, what is really worth knowing.

Part of being a cultivated person is knowing what to forget. Gertrude Stein recorded the happy moment when she realized she couldn't read all the books in the world. The truly cultivated person realizes that he probably hasn't a chance to read even all the good books in the world. He knows the mind is best not used as a sponge, ready to soak up everything that falls on the counter. The names David Koresh, Kimba Wood, and Webster Hubbell, he would know instinctively, are not for storage and retrieval. The cultivated person is good at the art of extrapolation: at imagining the unknown on the evidence of the known. He has a strong historical sense, so that he tends to be less impressed by the crisis of the week that agitates the news media, which they in turn use to agitate the rest of us. From his historical sense, he knows that this caravan has passed before, and that another, not very different one will pass through next week and another the week after that. The cultivated person is interested in information that either has been around for a while or will probably be around in the future. He is also likely to possess knowledge that goes a step or two deeper down than that which ordinary, decently educated people have.

My late friend Arnaldo was not merely cultivated, he was immensely erudite — the most learned man I expect ever to know — but his impressive cultivation made the erudition all the more striking. As someone who had been forced by the Fascists to depart his native Italy, as someone who had lost family in Hitler's death camps, Arnaldo knew politics was serious business. Yet I rarely heard him talk "politics" in the mundane sense of elections, or personalities, or changing governments. He seemed to know the darker side of politics — its tendency to get under people's skin to affect their fairness, decency, and honor.

Although there was not a hint of one-upmanship about him, Arnaldo made one feel the poverty of one's own knowledge. It had taken me many years to become just shallowly conversant about such names as Lampedusa, Fokine, and Simmel, yet Arnaldo, a great scholar of the ancient world, not only knew more about these figures than I, but had an intellectual archaeology that went much deeper in every regard. Where I was still digging away at Troy III, he was already at Troy VIII. In conversation, he might make casual mention of, say, the founder of Romanian folklore. He knew an immense amount about Edward and Constance Garnett. Once, at the University of Chicago, I was having breakfast with Leon Edel, who was then setting out to write a book about Bloomsbury. Arnaldo joined us and spoke with such astonishing penetration about the importance to the Bloomsbury group of Duncan Grant that a stranger, freshly arrived at our table, might have thought that Arnaldo had just completed a book about Bloomsbury. If there had been a parlor game called Serious Pursuit, Arnaldo would have been its champion.

I sometimes think God not a very good economist in allowing people such as Arnaldo to die, because with his death all that information not set out in his books simply — poof! — disappears. No one will need to make the same charge against God at my demise. The information stored in my mind is neither so interesting nor so carefully stored as Arnaldo's. Often I will recall what seems to me an interesting point, insight, or observation, but I won't be able to recall where I read it, even though I am confident I read it only a day or so before. This comes, I suspect, from too much desultory reading.

Elizabeth Bishop, the poet, herself a steady reader, felt likewise. In a letter written from her redoubt in Brazil to her friend Pearl Kazin, she wrote: "And — oh well, we read and read and read, all the time, and the books pile up, and I remember a little here and there, and the magazines are snowing us under . . . and what good it all does drifting around in this aging brain I don't know." Miss Bishop was ten years younger than I when she wrote that. But concern about what the mind retains, what the endless acquisition of information all comes down to, had long been much on her mind. As early as 1937, when she was only twenty-six, she wrote a strange little story, "The Sea & Its Shore," about a man hired to pick up scraps from a beach who finds himself reading everything he picks up. He divides his reading, or studies as he calls it, into three categories: things that related to himself, things about people who had caught his fancy, and things he couldn't understand at all that interested him nonetheless. The story also contains the following amusing passage: "This was the type of warning that worried him: 'the habit of perusing periodical works may properly be added to Averrhoe's catalogue of ANTI-MNEMONICS, or weakeners of the memory.'"

Am I suffering an information overload by reading too many magazines? Mightn't I simplify somewhat my intellectual life by dropping my subscriptions to *Esquire, Vanity Fair,* and *Gentle-*

men's Quarterly? Why do I read them in the first place? Do I really need to know more — or anything at all, really — about Strobe Talbott or Liam Neeson? You are reading the words of a man who actually took an hour out of his life to read an interview by Norman Mailer of Madonna. If any lingering respect you might have had for me has vanished and you wish to stop reading me here, I shall of course quite understand.

I read these magazines in the first place — there is no second place — in the hope that in doing so I shall keep up with some of the things that preoccupy the culture in its wider, sometimes more youthful, often wildly excessive aspects. I tell myself I do so because it is the duty of a writer to try to grasp the unique quality of his time and make sense of it. I see movies — never at full price, but on videotapes — whose politics present no surprises, in the hope of understanding why so many contemporary intellectuals continue to be so pleased by the predictable. Somehow, I cannot take the awfulness of these things on faith; I must look into them on my own.

For largely the same reasons, I continue to read a modest number of new novelists. The novel, as the old cliché has it, brings the news, or at least it used to. I take pleasure in reading well-made stories, but I also read new novels in anticipation of learning about shifts in sensibility. I know I am likely to get news of this sort of thing late, but I don't want to miss out on it altogether. I read the last two novels of Louis Begley, for example, to bring myself up to date on current snobberies. These novels brought me lots of information on clothes, food, real estate, fancy fornication (I seem to have forgotten their larger themes or messages). The only question is, what am I supposed to do with this information?

The other day I was talking with a friend, a former *New Yorker* writer, who told me that his contract at that magazine had not been renewed under its new editor. "Your problem," I found myself saying in reaction to his not entirely surprising news, "is that your writing for that magazine was merely interesting." The "merely interesting" seems, for the moment, to have had it, not only at *The New Yorker* but elsewhere in the culture.

Be brief, be blunt, and be gone — the rules that used to apply to Catholic confession — are increasingly the rules of journalism. Keep the information moving — and move it does. With so much loose information flying around, information must now come tidily packaged and is most sought after when labeled "inside." The appetite for inside information, stoked beyond all previous imagining by technological invention, continues to grow. I was recently at a meeting where an after-dinner speaker said that he was going to reveal the results of a Times Mirror poll on American public opinion that wouldn't be officially released until 4:00 the following afternoon. I looked at my watch. It was 8:30 P.M. I and my fellow diners had a seventeen-and-a-half-hour scoop. One could feel the small *frisson* afforded by our little advantage go shivering through the room. So elated was I at being one of the recipients of this scoop that I nearly forgot that I didn't care about the poll and that I enjoy few journalistic moments better than when pollsters are proved dead wrong.

Still, I am as vulnerable to being in on inside information as the next chump. I cannot resist checking the *National Enquirer* and the rest of the grocery press — America's very own gutter press — as I go through the checkout line at supermarkets. The *National Enquirer* seems to be particularly good at informing its readers about who has cancer or AIDS, which gives one a macabre little jump on the obituary page; the paper must have informants in hospitals who supply them with this information. Such allure as the novels of John Gregory Dunne have seems to me built on the prospect of his supplying insider information about politicians, priests, and the culture of Hollywood. In a recent novel, Dunne remarks that screenwriters are contemptuous of writers of books. Is this true? Assuming that it is, what does it profit me to know this? Nothing, except perhaps it gives me possession of yet another tidbit of insider information. Information, I am certain, isn't wisdom, but is it even, in most cases, knowledge? My reaction to the Sunday *New York Times*, all three or four pounds of it, is sheer depression. The only thing about it that cheers me up is that I don't have to help produce all this bumf. When young, I would have loved to have been a newspaper reporter, which I thought excellent training for a writer, as the careers of Stephen Crane, Dreiser, Hemingway, and Willa Cather all attest. But nowadays working on a newspaper, each day weighting down the information stone for poor, hopeless Sisyphus, seems to me simply hell. It's bad enough to have to wade through all this information, deciding which of it to ignore; to be actually responsible for supplying some of it seems even worse.

Yet, when one hears all the talk about the information superhighway and the rest of it, one gathers that large numbers of people long for not less but even more information and want it coming in quicker than ever before. I, for my part, would rather it were all slowed down. Of course, I am someone who is still being dragged into the twentieth century and am far from ready for the twenty-first. Car phones, VCRs, personal computers — I fought them all and I now own and use them all. I am still fighting getting a fax, though I have used other people's fax machines a fair amount. When people ask me for my own fax number, I generally say that I haven't a fax machine but intend to get one as soon as my telephone implant is completed. More often than not, people neither laugh nor ask me what I mean.

The assumption of the new information society seems to be that more is better. I find that more information tends only to weigh more heavily on me. That part of information known as the news has long ago begun to pall; the following headlines from a recent daily edition of the *New York Times* may, technically, be information, but I'm far from clear about the purposes to which they might be put: "Peace Once Again Vanishes in Sarajevo," "Japan Opens AIDS Forum," "A Catholic Mother of 5 Children Is Shot Dead in Northern Ireland," "Rwandan Doctor's Journey Through Horror and Death." Local television news, at least in my city, is all heartbreaking, anxiety-making, and nightmarish: stories of child abuse, juvenile gangs, murder, and rape. This too, I guess, is information.

Living in Italy and writing in the eighteenth century, Lady Mary Wortley Montagu, who wrote such splendid letters, would wait for as long as five months for information about her family in England. Such was the slowness of the mails in Europe, and in time of war they were even worse. Lady Mary was a woman of towering curiosity, and it must have pained her to wait so long to receive quite vital personal information, but there was nothing for it. Apart from letters from her daughter and a small number of friends, she learned about English life from novels, not all of them first-class novels, either. Writing to her friend Sir James Steuart, Lady Mary remarked: "It is true a very small proportion of knowledge is allowed us in this world, few truths permitted, but those truths are plain; they may be overseen or artfully obscured from our sight, but when pointed out to us it is impossible to resist the conviction that accompanies them."

Henry James filled in the blanks left by Lady Mary here, when, in *The Princess Casamassima,* he wrote: "The figures on the chessboard were still the passions and jealousies and superstitions and stupidities of man, and thus positioned with regard to each other at any given moment could be of interest only to the grim invisible fates who played the game — who sat, through the ages, bow-backed over the table." That, folks, remains the news, though I don't think Dan Rather likely to read it some Wednesday evening at 6:30, EST.

Plowed under by too much information, I have, from time to time, felt that I had all the information I could use just now, thank you very much. If there is a minor malady called information fatigue, I believe I have it. Not long ago I picked up one of the monthly magazines I subscribe to, and, scanning its table of contents, I discovered I didn't give a rat's rump about people serving prison time for smoking marijuana, or about the sex bias in medicine, or why good olive oil costs so much, or why Islamic government may be in the future for a number of Middle Eastern countries, or why tourists in Russia manage to have fun there despite the absence of amenities. The only piece in the entire magazine I thought I might read was one on pool hustlers, but, somehow, I never got around to it.

With the information revolution closing in, I ask myself whether it isn't possible to live deeper down, at some more genuine, less superficial level of life than that promised by an endless flow of still more and then yet again even more information. It has taken me a good while to understand this, but it turns out that the only information I am seriously interested in is that about the human heart, and this I cannot find any easy way to access, not even with the best of modems, fiber-optic cable, or digital technology. Pity, though, to have to miss out on another revolution.

I Like a Gershwin Tune

YOU MAY NOT have caught my act at the old Pratt-Lane Hotel. Brilliant stuff. A knockout, take my word for it. I came on and sang one number, and one number only: "Any Bonds Today?" Maybe you'll recall the song's most powerful line, which — modesty won't do here — I belted out gloriously: "Bonds of freedom, that's what I'm selling, any bonds today?" The crowd — my parents and their friends — went wild. The year was 1942, the war was on, and I was five. I retired as a singer later that same year, when I was told in nursery school not to sing so loudly, especially since I sang off-key. Knowing when to quit — that, I'd say, is the name of the game.

I admire people who know when to quit, especially singers, many of whom go on much too long. "I always wanted to sing as well as Frank Sinatra," someone I know reported five or six years ago of the great crooner, "and now I can." Julie London, the torch singer, must have recognized that, beyond a certain age, carrying that torch can only singe a woman's no-longer-lush eyelashes. Another singer whose retirement I regret is Tom Lehrer, whose musical parodies, though much dated, still amuse. A friend tells me that he asked Lehrer why he stopped writing and performing his comic songs. "Since Henry Kissinger won the Nobel Peace Prize," Lehrer replied, "nothing seems funny anymore."

In the America of the 1940s and 1950s, when I was growing up, popular music was everywhere; and it was not of interest only to the young, as popular music is today. Singers were great heroes, bandleaders famous personages. At a neighborhood delicatessen in Rogers Park called Ashkenaz, there was a sandwich called the Lou Breese, named after the bandleader at the Chicago Theater. I don't recall the contents of that sandwich, but I feel confident it must, by today's standards, have been powerfully life-threatening: chopped liver and pastrami, perhaps. I do know, though, that I would rather have a sandwich named after me than receive an honorary degree from any university in the Western world.

Radio shows not only featured singers, but many had a singer as part of the regular cast — Jack Benny had Dennis Day, Bob Hope had Frances Langford. A bandleader named Kay Kyser had a radio show that he called, in a kind of subtitle, "The Kollege of Musical Knowledge." Ozzie Nelson, of *The Adventures of Ozzie and Harriet,* was another bandleader. Jokes about the drunkenness of musicians, a specialty of Phil Harris, who was also on *The Jack Benny Program,* were also endemic. In the early years of television, singers of popular songs were still thought necessary: Arthur Godfrey had Julius LaRosa, Steve Allen had Steve Lawrence and Eydie Gorme. Any singer who had a big hit song was certain to be booked on *The Ed Sullivan Show.* Bing Crosby and Frank Sinatra were more widely known than any American athlete or politician except the president. Popular music was part of the national (as opposed to teen) culture in a way that it has not come close to being ever again.

Mine was far from a musical family. No one played an instrument, and the phonograph, as it was then called when it wasn't called the Victrola, was not at the center of our family life. The only records I remember being played in our apartment were an album of 78s of Stephen Foster songs sung by Bing Crosby that my father liked to nap to and an album of fast-talking Danny Kaye songs, "Minnie the Moocher" prominent among them. My father would occasionally hum a tune while shaving — "Anybody Here Seen Kelly?" was in his extremely limited repertoire — but my mother never sang in my hearing. I probably got my off-key singing voice from her.

But even in this relatively unmusical home I could not avoid the sheer musicality of life. Singing was part of grade school life; every year in grammar school, one's class would prepare programs to sing at semi-annual assemblies. Music lessons as well as tap dancing lessons were offered through the public school system at very low rates. In high school, one had to take a course in music, which, along with art, was known as a minor subject. Our music teacher was a lovely woman: a spinster more than six feet tall who dressed in tailored suits, Miss Adele Burke played great rolling arpeggios on the piano while singing Jerome Kern and Rodgers and Hart songs in a florid style. Every other movie seemed to have singing in it; José Iturbi or Oscar Levant was regularly seated at a piano near a swimming pool or in a marvelously suave Manhattan apartment; and it was not uncommon for the male lead in these movies to croon into the ear of his inamorata, which, in reality, couldn't have been all that pleasant from the standpoint of the inamorata.

So pervasive was song in middle-class American life, and so tied up with the notion of romance, that a regular activity of midwestern college fraternities was serenading sororities. When a member of a fraternity gave his pin to a member of a sorority, not only was a serenade called for, but during the serenade the boy was expected to step forth and sing, solo, directly to the girl. I spent a semester in such a fraternity, and I still remember the serenade of a boy named Ronald Kaplan to Janey Weinstein, an heiress to a funeral-parlor fortune. Ronnie Kaplan, large and rather lumpy, was a boy with the gift of perpetual middle age — how easy growing older must have been for him! At the appropriate moment during the serenade, he stepped forth to allow, in a quavering voice, that yes, Janey, though both the Rockies and Gibraltar might crumble and all the rest of it, his love, hey! no question about it, his love was here to stay. It turned out he was right, for they later married and, as far as I know, have lived happily ever after.

I don't mean to imply that I grew up in a limitlessly rich era of songwriting. Throughout my boyhood a flow of entirely junky novelty songs kept popping up, among them "Mairzy Doats," "I Like Chewing Gum," "Chickery-Chick, Cha-la, Cha-la," "Come On-a My House," "Mañana," "(How Much Is That) Doggie in the Window," "Behind the Green Door," and the immemorial "Purple People Eater." As a kid, I was swept up by these songs quite as much as so many of my countrymen. I have a painful memory of standing before a mirror caressing into shape an ambitious pompadour I wore at fourteen and singing a little number titled "Cincinnati Dancing Pig" (we were, I seem to recall, invoked to witness him do "the barnyard jig"), when my learned and immensely dignified grandfather walked into the room. At that moment, gazing upon his idiot grandson, he must have felt that his leaving Bialystok fifty-odd years before had been a grave mistake.

A number of the famous male singers of my youth were notably cheesy and tended to sing songs about their quite hopeless enthrallment by love. Such singers as Don Cornell, Al

Martino, Tony Martin (whose real claim to fame was his marriage to the beautiful dancer Cyd Charisse), and particularly Frankie Laine specialized in the big heartbreak numbers. The torment caused Frankie Laine by a woman named Jezebel (whose "eyes promised paradise") was almost more than one could bear to contemplate.

Laine, a Chicagoan of Italian ancestry, had some of the greatest record hits of my adolescence. Along with "Jezebel," he scored with two western songs — "Mule Train" and "The Cry of the Wild Goose." This was before television, and so one had to imagine what Laine looked like. Whips cracked while this man sang, rhythms pounded like the heart of a miser in a French restaurant in New York, and I imagined Frankie Laine to be a darker and perhaps more muscular Gary Cooper. When he appeared at the Chicago Theater, which in those days — the late 1940s and early 1950s — had stage shows as well as movies, I betook myself there to see him in person. A profound letdown doesn't begin to describe what happened. Frankie Laine was a thickset man with a large nose who wore a pretty obvious toupee. This "brother of the old wild goose," as he styled himself in one of his songs, seemed more fit to own a Chrysler agency or a State Street jewelry store than to drive the mule train that he kept screaming about in his hit song. Not the last of life's little disappointments, I fear.

The Chicago Theater was something of a hangover from vaudeville days, and the headliners of its stage shows were almost always singers. I saw there a flash-in-the-pan singer named Johnnie Ray, who after two big hits, "Cry" and "The Little White Cloud That Cried," disappeared. On its stage I saw the elegant Billy Eckstine, wearing one of his famous high Mr. B. shirt collars and singing "Everything I Have Is Yours." Joni James, a singer who had had a hit during my high school days called "Let Me Go, Lover," stopped off to play the Chicago Theater on her way to obscurity.

The Four Aces, my favorite group in those years, also appeared at the Chicago Theater, singing their heavily stylized songs, which contained such lines as "as we danced the night away, my heart said she's for me." They wore gold-colored tuxedo jackets and their hairdos made them look as if they came straight from the *Exxon Valdez* oil spill. The Crew Cuts, another foursome, this one from Toronto, sang at one of our high school dances at the Edgewater Beach Hotel; they, surely it cannot so soon have been forgotten, gave the English language the phrase "sh-boom, sh-boom."

By the time I saw Nat King Cole — again at the Chicago Theater — he had already entered his hit-record and therefore high-popularity phase. I heard him sing his signature songs from this period, which included "Mona Lisa," "Dance, Ballerina, Dance," and "Walkin' My Baby Back Home." Melodramatic and a little foolish as these songs are, Nat Cole lent them some of his own considerable dignity. He was a very elegant man, with a diction and timbre (if I am using that word correctly) that were like no one else's. Because he sang love songs without seeming to want your girl, he was the first black singer to break through and find himself in the empyrean of popularity wherein dwelt such singers as Bing Crosby, Perry Como, and Frank Sinatra. For a time in the 1950s, he had his own television show.

I came a little late for the young Frank Sinatra, who drove bobby-soxers bonkers, but I do remember that the movie *From Here to Eternity* put him back in business as a big-time draw. He was a marvelous singer who was not without a flaw or two as a human being. He was known for flares of terrible temper, during which he might do something humiliating to a studio musician; later, to make it up to him, he might, bighearted guy that he was, buy the musician's parents, say, the town of Kenosha, Wisconsin.

My own sense is that the late-night hours Frank kept may have made him cranky. This is a man, after all (if we are to believe the evidence of his songs), who was regularly out in the wee small hours of the morning, when it was a quarter to three, no one in the place but the bartender and he; and even when he went to bed he kept imagining some girl dancing on his ceiling, from "underneath his counterpane." (Go figure people's taste in bedding. You don't suppose Frank slept in a canopy bed, do you?) Doubtless these bad habits were reinforced by the mood indigo that he suffered, which first came upon him when his baby said good-bye. But he, Frank, could sing, no doubt about that. In a novel by Willie Morris, the hero thanks Frank Sinatra and Nat King Cole for what little sexual success he had in high school.

Fred Astaire, whose singing I have come to like more and more (and for whom Irving Berlin said he enjoyed writing more than for any other singer), hadn't Sinatra's problems. His songs, like his movies, are pure, sweet fantasy, and on the whole charmingly upbeat. Apart from having to undergo the mild depression of a foggy day in London town, when even the British Museum appears to have lost its charm, most of the difficulties Astaire encountered took place on the dance floor, as when a woman he admired danced every dance with "that same fortunate man" — not, alas, him. Yet Astaire did log more than his share of time dancing cheek to cheek, which, you might say — actually he did say it — is nice work if you can get it, which he did. As made plain, in another song, he was dancing and he couldn't be bothered now.

Fred Astaire's indomitably cheerful songs, implying days

spent in ascots and buttery cashmere jackets and nights spent in white ties and tails, always suggested urbanity and suavity, with only occasional dips into self-pity ("A Fine Romance," "Let's Call the Whole Thing Off"). In this, Astaire was anomalous. Self-pity has been the keynote emotion in much of American popular music. You have either lost or cannot obtain the affection of the one you love; your innate qualities of sensitivity, constancy, and profound affection are not appreciated. Songs pledging undying affection — "I'll Never Stop Loving You" is one that comes to mind — were big. George S. Kaufman was probably closer to capturing the truth of the matter when he said that he would have preferred it if Irving Berlin's song "Always" had been instead titled "Thursday," so that its clincher line would go, "I'll be loving you, Thursday."

Self-pity is probably the only authentic emotion that adolescent boys and girls feel, which partly explains the preeminence of popular music in my era. I know I felt self-pity myself, though I'm not sure that I didn't have to whip myself into it artificially. Even though I must have felt young love — "They tried to tell us we're too young" was a line in a hit song of my adolescence — my youthful existence lacked genuine romantic drama. As a boy, I surely yearned, but never can it be said that I pined — I didn't really have the attention span for extended pining. I should have liked to have been the kind of fellow who could drive women mad with longing, even the worthless kind that stimulates certain women. But I soon enough sensed that these were not the roles Central Casting had put me on earth to play.

In 1953, when I was sixteen, Raymond Chandler, complaining about the low quality of public education in America, wrote to a friend that "about all they teach there is the increasingly simple art of seduction." I for one could have used that course, but — damn — it wasn't offered at my school. I left no string of broken hearts, paternity suits, or attempted suicides in my wake. As a youth, I was a less than fully convincing seducer.

In my lifetime I have felt jealousy and I have known sexual envy, but even as an adolescent, I never felt the need to devote myself full-time to the great sex chase. The world, in Ira Gershwin's rather mortal phrase, never had to "pardon my mush," though, as a boy and young man, I had many a crush. Yet I don't believe I ever made a complete fool of myself in pursuit of a woman — perhaps only a third or half a fool. This left a fair amount of free time for reading, sports, and popular music.

Popular music is, of course, almost entirely about the sex wars: about yearning and love unrequited, about betrayal and consummations left at the stage of devout wishing. It is music to fantasize by. None of this is to say that popular music didn't stir me — or doesn't stir me still. When Louis Armstrong asks for "a kiss to build a dream on," allowing how his imagination will build upon that kiss, I do believe I understand him. But perhaps the last time I took this music altogether seriously was in high school, in the age of sexual awakening.

A friend at dinner not long ago claimed that he considered most fish as no more than a vehicle on which to convey sauce to the mouth. In a similar vein, when I was in high school, music was, through dancing, a way to get close to girls. Mine was the last generation that went in for what is now called slow, but would more accurately be called close, dancing. Our dancing came just after the jitterbug, danced to swing music, and before the twist — the first of the non-touching dances that began in the early 1960s — and all the autoerotic solo dancing that followed.

Every so often at a wedding or other large party where a band has been hired, a couple in their late fifties or early sixties will hit the dance floor to do a jitterbug. What great fun it looks! The last jitterbugging couple I remember from high school days was Frankie Sommers and Nancy Shaffner. Frankie, a couple of years older than I, was one of the golden boys of my youth. He could throw a football sixty yards, and nothing ever got past him in his position in left field. His voice had a charming rasp, and his smile could light up an alley in a terrifying neighborhood.

Nancy, like Frankie, was small. She wore braces and had a slight lisp. Frankie and Nancy — they seemed a perfect couple, and they went on to marry. I gather that they, too, stayed married. They were a smash on the dance floor, bopping away to a Count Basie or Duke Ellington tune. So good were they that, once they began, everyone else left the dance floor the way dancing couples cleared the floor for Fred Astaire and Ginger Rogers in the movies. Frankie, who had the build of a gymnast, would toss Nancy in the air, or dip her across his hips, or swing her between his legs. Fantastic!

The rest of us, more earthbound, slogged away at our slow dancing. "Graduation's almost here, my love," with the preceding line, "should the teacher stand so near, my love," was the kind of lyric to which we vibrated. "I wanna be loved with inspiration" was a line in a song in which the singers — the Andrews Sisters — went on to make plain that they were in "no mood for turtledoving." Neither, let me say here, was I, who was ready at all times to get "On a Slow Boat to China," firm in my belief that "Love Is a Many Splendored Thing."

Intellectuals don't dance. Or so, accused of acting out of character, I was told as I came off the dance floor with my wife a few years ago in San Francisco. Clearly I am an exception to an entertaining, but less than fully sound, generalization. I have always thought dancing a fine thing, wish I were better at it, and admire those who can beautifully glide around a dance floor.

In my last year of grade school, at the age of thirteen, I was sent to something called Fortnightly — though I could swear it met every Saturday afternoon — where some of my classmates and I were taught dance-floor etiquette and many intricate dance steps, almost all of which I have long since forgotten. I have retained the handy, all-purpose box step, the basis of the waltz and other dances, which has kept me from being the otherwise perfect wallflower. For a time in high school, I fancied myself a rumba king (also based on the box step) and doubtless made a considerable jackass of myself. In the 1950s, Latin American dances were big stuff; even the sedate Perry Como sang a hopeless tune called "Papa Loves Mambo." All I wish to say in my own defense is that, in a life marred by many sins, large and small, of commission and omission, at least I never danced the cha-cha. I hope this will be recalled in my favor on Judgment Day.

Social life at my high school, Nicholas Senn, was organized around dancing. Not only were there school and club dances, but records were played during the three lunch periods in our large assembly hall, and kids could dance there if they wished. There was even a goofy little jog step called the Senn Walk, in which the boy held his left hand far away from his body, making dancing couples look slightly contorted.

Disc jockeys were important figures in the Chicago of those years. One among them, a man named Howard Miller, who died not long ago, was a towering figure. He was said to be able to launch a song into popularity through main force — main force being the playing of a song over and over, which is to say plugging it ruthlessly, on his own show. He was married to a singer named June Valli, who had a weepy hit titled "Crying in the Chapel," now justly forgotten. Miller was also notable for giving optimistic weather reports, falsifying the temperature by as many as ten degrees — this in the undramatic days before the advent of wind-chill factors — so that, after getting his rosy report, one would step out on a winter's day and be blown off the sidewalk. When rock 'n' roll came on the scene, Miller himself was blown away as a disc jockey and began a blustery political talk show.

But the great disc jockey for young pseudo-sophisticates like me was a man named Jay Andres. He played light classics — such as "The Story of Three Loves," taken from the powerful theme of Rachmaninoff's "Rhapsody on a Theme of Paganini" — along with much Sarah Vaughan, Ella Fitzgerald, Mel Tormé, Nat Cole, Dick Haymes, and other, cooler, more understated singers. His show was on at night, late-ish. The highlight of many a date came when an adolescent boy, driving his father's clunky Buick northward on the wonderful Outer Drive, turned to his date and, his hand hovering over the radio dial, asked, "A little Jay Andres?" The question retains its magic for me even now. "A little Jay Andres?" ranks up there with "A little champagne?"

The next stage in my popular-music life came at the University of Chicago, where the music of choice seemed to be folk music. I gave this a shot, went to a concert or two, and heard an impressive woman named Odetta, a young man named Bob Gibson, and a number of others whose names are now lost to me. The charms of a folk music hootenanny did not entirely escape me, though if the truth be told, I had a bit of trouble identifying, as the kids say, with "John Henry." Whenever I heard the song, I replaced the name John Henry, a steel-driving man, with that of Al Rabinowitz, a cab-riding man among my contemporaries. But it was no go.

Two albums dominate the musical recollections I have of my days at college. One was Harry Belafonte's *Calypso* album, with its red background and picture of the devastatingly handsome Belafonte in a green shirt on its cover. "Day-O," "Jamaica Farewell," "Brown Skin Girl," and "Come Back Liza" were some of the songs on the album, and no greater music for singing in the shower was ever devised ("Come Mr. Tally Man, tally me banana"). I later saw Belafonte in performance, and unlike Frankie Laine, he was in no wise disappointing but rather one of those extraordinary performers whom you still don't want to leave the stage, even after a two-hour show.

The other album that I listened to over and over was *The Misty Miss Christy,* torch songs by June Christy, who sang for the Stan Kenton band. Her songs about loneliness, desertion, betrayal, and general mistreatment at the hands of men made Ovid, in the *Heroides,* seem, in the crying-the-blues department, strictly bush league. The cumulative impression the album conveyed was of a beautiful woman alone at a bar — smoking a cigarette and two drinks ahead of everyone else in the room — who had gotten a very raw deal. The fantasy that it allowed to college boys was that, with a bit of luck, one might meet such a woman and make her — and oneself — well. The questions about her — why had so many men left her in the lurch, and was there something fundamentally wrong with so habitually unhappy a woman — were, of course, best left unanswered. In musical romance, only the unexamined life is worth living.

At twenty and twenty-one, I spent a bit of time in Rush Street nightclubs hoping to meet such a woman. I heard the beautiful

Fran Jeffries, who was married to Dick Haymes, sing at the smart (as it would then have been called) club called Mr. Kelly's. At the old Black Orchid I heard Peggy Lee, whose marriage to an alcoholic musician gave her sufficient reason to sing her own sad songs, which she did exceedingly well. I would occasionally drop in at the lounge at the Maryland Hotel, also on Rush Street; and, on the city's South Side, I heard Miles Davis at the Sutherland Lounge.

Sad to report, I never met either June Christy or the June Christy–like woman, who might have called me baby, or implored me to drink up and order anything I like, or asked me to come to the party and leave my blues behind. Instead, one day at Mr. Kelly's, I began a conversation with Mort Sahl, who invited me to walk back with him to his hotel. Along the way we traded jokes, and one that he told me — the year was 1956 — was that President Eisenhower and Adlai Stevenson were supposed to meet to discuss the state of the country before the election, but the meeting had to be canceled because Eisenhower's interpreter never showed up.

Music pervaded even the military. One of the first things a number of soldiers did with their initial army paycheck was buy a portable radio. I remember the barracks in basic training at Fort Leonard Wood, in Missouri, flooded with music. The hit song of the time was "Tom Dooley," sung by the Kingston Trio. A bit of a downer, that song — Tom, you may recall, was invoked to hang down his head, poor boy he was going to die. Jukeboxes at the PX blared lots of Elvis. The year was 1958, and Elvis himself was then a private at Fort Hood, Texas. Two bunks down from mine, an Appalachian fellow named Bobby Flowers, who was drafted because his ex-wife turned him in for failing to make alimony payments, used to sing about flying over these prison walls but for the want of angel's wings, and he made lots of jokes about his ex-wife while menacingly cleaning his M-1 rifle.

For the clichémeisters, the decade of the fifties is musically lashed to Elvis Presley. Not quite true. First, the King, as his fans now call the old boy, came rather late in the decade; and second, you had to be an adolescent when he came along to get worked up about him. For those of us who came of age earlier in the decade, popular music meant an elegant club singer such as Julie London, with whom every man must have been in love (I know I was); it meant an extremely rich period for jazz; and it meant the end of the great era of musical comedy. For us, the fifties had nothing whatsoever to do with hound dogs, heartbreak hotels, and blue suede shoes.

Presley was many things, not least among them a southerner. As everyone now acknowledges, his songs combined black rhythms with a country-western outlook. In the army and later, while living in the South, I heard vast quantities of country-western music, and I came to like it, though I always, perhaps I should confess, felt rather superior to it. My pedantry seemed to get in the way. A song such as "Everybody's Somebody's Fool" seemed to me badly in need of qualification; and that God made honky-tonk angels seemed to me, as a reader of Thomas Aquinas, theologically dubious. Still, as a young man, I put in my hours in a few Arkansas and Texas honky-tonks (no angels sighted), where the atmosphere seemed to bristle with potential bottle-breaking violence every time the band took a break.

I don't remember when *The Hit Parade* — which was first on the radio, then on television, and always, I believe, sponsored by Lucky Strike, L(ucky) S(trike) M(eans) F(ine) T(obacco) — ceased broadcasting, but over the years, in the back of my mind, I have kept a little list of songs that are on my Hate Parade. On this list appear: "Begin the Beguine" (Desi Arnaz), "My Way" (Frank Sinatra), "I Gotta Be Me" (Sammy Davis, Jr.), "I Left My Heart in San Francisco" (Tony Bennett), "Oh My Papa" (Eddie Fisher), "People" (Barbra Streisand), "Leaving on a Jet Plane" (Peter, Paul & Mary), and "There's No Business Like Show Business" (by anyone). If there is a jukebox in hell, these will be the only songs it plays, relentlessly.

At the same time, there are some songs less than Schubertian in quality that, when I hear them, continue to give pleasure. Vaughn Monroe's "Ghost Riders in the Sky," which I haven't heard in years, is such a song. I find a good many of Dean Martin's songs — "Houston," "That's Amore" — always make me laugh, perhaps owing to the utter casualness with which he seemed to sing them. I like "You've Got to See Momma Every Night" both for itself and because it reminds me of an old Groucho Marx story, the punch line of which is "You've got to order sea bass every night, or you can't order sea bass at all." I adore Jimmy Durante singing "September Song" and George Burns singing the Lennon/McCartney song "When I'm Sixty-four." Sometimes a wildly goofy line or two can put a song permanently in my mind, such as the song that, inquiring into the name change of Constantinople to Istanbul, asks why did the former name "get the works" and then responds that this is "nobody's business but the Turks'."

Some songs stir up memories more surely than M. Proust's petite madeleine. Sarah Vaughan singing "Make Yourself Comfortable" takes me back to lengthy necking (what a funny word!) sessions in a living room on a shady street named Mozart, but pronounced in Chicago *Moe-zart*. The song "Fascination" recalls Gary Cooper, in the Billy Wilder movie *Love in the Afternoon*, sweating it out in a steam bath in Paris while four violinists, in tuxedos in the steam bath with him, schmaltzily play that tune to comfort him in his sadness about losing the love of Audrey Hepburn. Every time I hear "Send in the Clowns," I think of taking my father-in-law, a very stylish man then dying of cancer, to a matinee performance of *A Little Night Music*. "Imagination," as another song says, "is funny."

Reading an article in *Esquire* about David Letterman, I learn that "he prefers music to stoke him, never to soothe." The music of Letterman's choice, it shouldn't surprise us, is rock 'n' roll. The comedian is, musically, of the rock generation. B.R. or A.R., Before Rock or After Rock, is one of the great, perhaps uncrossable, divisions of humankind. Those of us who came before cannot hope — and, let us speak candidly, do not all that much wish — to understand the musical tastes of those who came after. I, unlike David Letterman, prefer music that soothes me, for the world stokes me rather more than I like as it is, thank you very much.

Listening to Louis Armstrong sing almost anything makes me happy and reminds me of life's vibrant possibilities. Armstrong was a musical genius, a wonderful singer, and the best jazz trumpeter the world has known. "A man blowing a trumpet successfully," wrote the Welsh writer Rhys Davies, "is a rousing spectacle." But it's Louie the singer who really knocks me out. When he sings, in the divine rasp that was his voice, that it's not the pale moon that excites him, I almost have to leave my chair, so ready am I for bopping around the room. I wish I could do what I do one-twentieth as well as he did what he did. But even if I could, I shall, in my line of work, never be able to say, as he did: "Take it, Ella. Swing it!"

Certain phrases from the songs I love still send me: "the very thought of you"; "see the jungle when it's wet with rain"; "it never entered my mind"; "Argentines without means do it"; "no kick from champagne"; "hates California, it's cold and it's dark";

"diamond bracelets Woolworth doesn't sell, baby"; "see the pyramids along the Nile"; "the world will always welcome lovers"; "still I can't get started with you"; "that's the story of, that's the glory of love"; "nights were sour spent with Schopenhauer." I admire the general culture and wit that allowed Ira Gershwin to write that last phrase. Sad to think there is no one around today likely to write anything to equal it. "Oh, baby, say you'll be mine / we'll acquire a cozy cottage / and I'll read you Wittgenstein." Not, this attempt of my own, nearly so fine. Many of those phrases were written fifty and more years ago.

During the first three decades of this century, a remarkable generation of songwriters arose — what other verb can one use to explain the presence of even minor genius — most of them Jewish guys with names such as Irving, Ira, Larry, Harold, Gus, Oscar, Sammy, and a few brilliant non-tribesmen named Cole, Noël, Harry, Johnny, and Hoagy. (My favorite songwriting name is Irving Caesar; he wrote the lyrics for "Tea for Two" when woken by Vincent Youmans in the middle of the night and claimed that most of his songs were written in fewer than fifteen minutes.)

S. N. Behrman, in a fine memoir titled *People in a Diary,* claimed that the figure in Manhattan and Hollywood during the 1920s who seemed to outshine everyone else in sheer vitality and effulgence of talent was George Gershwin. Gershwin possessed, according to Behrman, "the quality of joy" — joy unimpeded, as he points out, by modesty. Of his mother, Gershwin once remarked: "You know the extraordinary thing about her — she's so modest about me." Behrman recounts having to bring Gershwin the bad news that a woman he claimed to love was secretly married. "Do you know," he said, "if I weren't so busy, I'd feel terrible."

Ira Gershwin, the younger brother and generally thought the

junior partner, was, in his quiet way, quite as impressive. He was intensely, though unpretentiously, literary, and in his late adolescence, as he reports in his autobiography, he "fooled around with French verse forms, such as the triolet, villanelle, and especially the rondeau." He had an interest in etymology and was a reader of the *Oxford English Dictionary.* Fred Astaire said of George Gershwin that "he wrote for feet," while Ira wrote for the head. "You reading Heine, I somewhere in China," appears in the same song, "Isn't It a Pity?," as the Schopenhauer allusion.

George Gershwin died at age thirty-nine. "He lived all his life in youth," Behrman notes, adding that "his rhythms were the pulsations of youth; he reanimated them in those much older than he was. He reanimates them still." George had the gorgeous musical vitality, Ira the splendid literary sophistication, and together they gave people who could spare a few moments to listen a sense of what lies behind the phrase *joie de vivre.* Gershwin's last word, on his deathbed, was "Astaire."

But if the Gershwins and others wrote songs that had about them the spirit of youth, it was youth of a different kind than we have come to associate with being young. It was youth untroubled, full of promise, agonizing over nothing greater than winning that boy or girl. "Moon and June and roses and rainbow's end" runs a phrase in a Blossom Dearie song titled "Down with Love." Ah, all those lovely, lilting rhymes: caressing/blessing, breeze/memories, arms/charms, sighing/crying, tree/bees . . . do it, even chimpanzees do it.

Why do so many of these lyrics remain in my mind when I worry that the four numbers I need to use the cash machine at my bank won't stay in my memory? They are more amusing, for one thing; but, more pertinently, they are also part of my own youth. I'm glad I grew up in a time when "writers who knew better words" had not begun to use four- or even no-letter words. I feel a debt, a positive obligation, to remember some of those words, just as I owe all those female singers — "vocalists," as they were then called — a letter of thanks for all those daydreams. "So here's to the ladies, God bless 'em," as the Victorians used to say. "Thanks, Billie, Ella, Sarah, Peggy, Julie, June, Judy, Jo, Lena, Lee, Rosie, Anita, Chris, Dinahs (Washington and Shore), Doris, Keely, Eartha, and Blossom. Thanks, I wish I could say, for the memories, but let me say instead, thanks for the sweet fantasies.

I find myself listening more and more to the best of this music. The pleasure, far from decreasing, seems greater than ever. A few months ago I memorized, for my own diversion, the lyrics to "Stars Fell on Alabama" and "Softly, as in a Morning Sunrise," which I now retain as mantras. I suppose I ought to be grateful that I can neither play the piano nor sing, else I should spend most of my waking hours sitting at the piano playing and singing this music. Instead I walk around with all these tunes in my head. At my stage in life, where mild depression would seem only to make good sense, they provide a regular and by no means artificial boost.

The Art of the Nap

INTELLECTUAL SERENITY in the United States, I have heard it said, consists in not giving a damn about Harvard. Having been in Cambridge recently, I sensed — no, actually, I knew — I had achieved it. Bopping about Harvard Square, peeping into the Yard, popping into a building or two, I felt not the least yearning. I did not wish to be the Seymour Boylston Professor at Harvard or even to give the Charles Eliot Skolnik Lectures — not now, not ever. I have no children whom I wished to be admitted to Harvard. Yes, Harvard could continue to get along nicely without me, as it seems to have done over the past 350-odd years, and I, in the time remaining to me, can get along nicely without it.

With such serene thoughts, I set myself on my back on my comfortable bed at The Inn at Harvard, the hotel where I was staying. I had on gray wool trousers, a blue shirt, and a four-in-hand knit tie, which I didn't bother to unloosen. My hands were folded together on my chest in the corpse-in-the-casket position, and I hadn't bothered to turn back the bedspread. It was three-thirty on a cold and gray February afternoon. My next appointment was at five o'clock. There was nothing, at that moment, that I was eager to read. Into the arms of Morpheus I slipped, and for the next half hour I slept, I won't say like a baby, or like a log, or like a turtle, but like what I now prefer to think myself — a man who has mastered, in all its delicate intricacy, the art of the nap.

I did not move, I did not stir. I woke, as planned, without a wrinkle in my shirt, trousers, or cheek, not a hair out of place. A most impressive, if I do say so myself — and at that moment I did say so to myself — performance. Really quite brilliant. The term *control freak* is almost never used approvingly, I know, but I felt myself at that moment a control freak entirely happy in his work — that is to say, in perfect control. I carefully slipped off the bed and walked into the bathroom, where I gazed at my clear eyes in the large mirror. Another fine nap successfully brought off. I was rested, perhaps a touch less than radiant, and ready to continue not giving a damn about Harvard.

I don't ordinarily nap on a bed or on my back. As a nap-master, I fear too much comfort and the consequent difficulty of pulling myself out of the pleasures of too deep sleep to go back into the world. I also wish to avoid rumpledness, the toll that a nap on one's back on a couch often takes. Most of my napping therefore is done sitting up, on a couch or chair, shoes off, with my feet resting on a low footstool. Having one's feet up is important.

Most of my naps — and I usually get on the average of three or four a week — take place late in the afternoon, around five or five-thirty, with the television news playing softly in the background. As the reports of earthquakes, plagues, arson, pillaging, and general corruption hum on, I snooze away, a perfect symbol of the indifference of man in the modern age. These naps last from twenty to thirty-five minutes. ("A nap after dinner was silver," says old Prince Bolkonsky in *War and Peace*, "a nap before dinner golden.") Should the telephone ring while I am in mid-nap, I answer it in an especially clear and wide-awake voice that I don't usually bother evoking when I am in fact wide awake. Some of these naps leave me a touch groggy, though this soon enough disappears. Usually, they all do the job, which is to help get me through the evening.

Taste in naps differ. I not long ago asked a friend, an Englishman, if he naps. "Whenever possible," he replied. Supine or sitting up? "Supine." On a bed or couch? "Bed." Trousers on or off? "Generally off." And for how long? "That depends," he said, "on when the cats choose to depart." Joseph Conrad wrote that his task was "by the power of the written word, to make you hear, to make you feel — it is, before all, to make you *see*." The picture of my friend with his cats napping atop him is almost too easily seen.

I nap well on airplanes, trains, buses, and in cars and with a special proficiency at concerts and lectures. I am, when pressed, able to nap standing up. In certain select company, I wish I could nap while being spoken to. I have not yet learned to nap while I myself am speaking, though I have felt the urge to do so. I had a friend named Walter B. Scott who, in his late sixties, used to nap at parties of ten or twelve people that he and his wife gave. One would look over and there Walter would be, chin on his chest, lights out, nicely zonked; he might as well have hung a Gone Fishing sign on his chest. Then, half an hour or so later, without remarking upon his recent departure, he would smoothly pick up the current of the talk, not missing a stroke, and get finely back into the flow. I saw him do this perhaps four or five times, always with immense admiration.

Certain jobs seem to carry (unspoken) napping privileges. Writing in 1931, H. L. Mencken noted that one of the tests of a good cop was the talent of "stealing three naps a night in a garage without getting caught by the roundsman." Surely, movie projectionists get to nap to their hearts' content. Cab and limousine drivers must nap. Napping on the job can scarcely be unknown to psychoanalysts and other workers in the head trades. ("Uh-huh," mumbles the dozing psychiatrist in the caption of a cartoon that shows the feet of his patient who has just jumped out the window.) The only job in which I ardently longed to nap was guard duty in army motor pools on cold nights in Missouri, Texas, and Arkansas. Ah, to have slipped into the back of a deuce-and-a-half and ZZZ'd-out for a quick half hour! But fear, that first goad to conscience, won out and, difficult though it was, I stayed awake.

At a job I held one summer in college at a phonograph needle factory, one of the maintenance men regularly slipped up to the fourth floor for a forty-minute shot of sleep. I have seen lots of people nod off at corporate meetings and at conferences. One steamy summer day in Washington, at a meeting of the National Council of the National Endowment for the Arts held at the Old Post Office Building on Pennsylvania Avenue, I noted an entire half table of council members, heads nodding, necks jerking, eyelids drooping, effectively sedated by a slide show on city planning. I envied them, and doubtless should have joined them but for the fact that I had myself only recently awoken from a delightfully soporific lecture on the meaning of the avant-garde.

I have always slept reasonably well during lectures and never better than when a lecturer is foolhardy enough to darken the room for slides. Lecture and classroom naps tend to be of the variety I call whiplash naps — the ones where your head seems always to be snapping to. At the University of Chicago, I slept through the better part of the Italian Renaissance, or at any rate through a course in the history of its art. As a teacher myself, I am now being justly repaid by having students fall asleep in my own classes. I don't say that they drift off in droves, but I have — how to put it? — relaxed a respectable number of students in my time. At first, I found myself resenting a student falling asleep in one of my classes. But I long ago ceased taking it personally. I have come to look upon it avuncularly: poor dears, they may have been up all the previous night doing I prefer not to think what. My view of students sleeping in my classes is that, what the hell, if they cannot arise from my teaching inspired, let them at least awake refreshed.

My own youthful naps were owing, as I hope are those of my students, to happy excess. My current napping, I regret to report, is all too much part of the machinery beginning to break down. Not that I long for a nap each afternoon; if I am out in the world, I do not think about napping. My condition certainly does not yet begin to approximate the eponymous hero of Goncharov's novel *Oblomov:* "Lying down was not for Oblomov a necessity, as it is for a sick man or for a man who is sleepy; or a matter of chance, as it is for a man who is tired; or a pleasure, as it is for a lazy man; it was his normal condition." Still, if an opportunity for a nap presents itself, I find I take it.

I live in an early morning household. I generally rise by 4:45 A.M. I like the early morning; it is, for me, the best part of the day. I used to joke that one met a better class of person (namely, oneself) at that hour, but, in fact, what I enjoy about it is the stillness, the absence of interruption it provides, the gradual awakening of life around me. I make coffee, I begin reading; sometimes, if what I am reading is not all-demanding, I turn on a classical music station. And life seems under control, flush with possibility, hope-filled.

I have become, no doubt about it, a morning person. I was not always thus. As a young man, I used to come in around the time I now wake up. Weekends I slept till two or three in the afternoon, resting up to return to the sweet fray. So much was I a night person — a player in all-night card games, a dropper-off of dates at three or four in the morning — so congenial did I find the night that, one quarter at university, when all my classes met in the morning, I decided to sleep days and stay up nights.

Time has never again seemed so expansive as it did during that quarter. I would return from my classes, eat a light lunch, and sleep till six-thirty or seven. After arising, watering and feeding myself, I searched for distractions: movies, television, ball or card games. Not the least pressed for time, I schmoozed with all and sundry. Generally, I socialized till eleven or twelve and then I returned to my room with its hot plate, box of tea, small record collection, and books.

I might study for two or three hours. Then I found myself alone, no one else up in the student quarters in which I lived, at three in the morning, with nothing to do but read or listen to music, or both, till roughly eight in the morning. I went to a school where only great books were taught, so these free hours allowed me time to read some merely good books, for which I was hungry. I read, as I recall, chiefly novels: Christopher Isherwood and John O'Hara and Truman Capote and Evelyn Waugh; also lots of Edmund Wilson's literary criticism, which I had just discovered. I drank dark tea till my nerves achieved a fine jangle; I greeted the rising sun with a slight palsy of the hands: wired, happy, ready for class.

After my classes, I returned to bed and began the entire cycle again. This period of time lasted ten weeks and, from my present perspective, is something of a blur, but it was, it seems to me, time deliciously well spent. It also gave me the first evidence of my taste, and even minor talent, for solitude.

Something there is about being awake for sunrise that gives pleasure. The only exception to this that I can recall are those times, also at college, when I decided to stay up all night to cram for an examination. My junior year at school I discovered, through a friend, the stimulating effects of the pill known as Dexamyl (or was it Dexedrine?). These little pellets allowed me to stay up round the clock while mastering narratives of English history. They also, toward sunrise, set my heart pounding at a furious clip. I can recall my heart clanging away in my chest as I sat in a classroom giving three significant effects of enclosure on British politics and five reasons for the bloodlessness of the 1688 revolution. By the time I got back to my room, my heart was playing a very up-tempo version of "Take the 'A' Train." I used to think of it as studying English history with only a slight threat of death behind it. Nothing, though, that twelve or four-teen hours of sleep couldn't cure, and always did.

I have been fortunate in my sleep life. For one thing, the night, from as far back as I can recall, never held any terror for me. Not even as a small child did I imagine monsters in the corner, snakes under the bed, spiders on the spread, or anything else that might go bump in the night. The chief reason for this, I suspect, was that when I was a child my family lived in fairly small urban apartments and my parents were always nearby, so the element of fear was largely removed, as it wasn't for children who lived in large two- and three-story houses. I have no memories of nightmares. I had the reverse of nightmares — sweetmares, night-delights? I remember often dreaming of being in possession of marvelous things — elaborate electric trains, splendidly realistic metal cap pistols, vast quantities of bubblegum — that weren't available to children during World War II. Toward morning, I regretted having to wake and, alas, give them up.

So well do I generally sleep that, when I roll round in bed for more than fifteen minutes or so before falling off, I consider it a troublous night. Occasionally, and at no set intervals I can make out, I will hit a dread night of insomnia. Usually, this comes about less from anxiety than from the condition I think of as a racing mind. Too much is flying loose in my skull: words and phrases for things I am writing, obligations, trivial yet nagging memories, and (the last step, the nail in the mattress) fear that, owing to not being able to sleep, I shall be tired and blow the next day. I roll, I turn, I mutter, finally I surrender and get up. Less than an hour's bleary reading or listening to the idiot chatter of a late night television talk show often does the trick, and I slog back to my bed, where Somnus almost always agrees to treat me more hospitably.

True insomnia of the relentless night-after-night kind must be absolute hell. Such a torture is it that I don't for a moment believe Bertrand Russell, who said: "Men who are unhappy, like men who sleep badly, are always proud of the fact." I have a number of friends who have suffered from insomnia. One walked about with the dark-rimmed eyes of a raccoon to prove it. Another friend suffered insomnia and (non-clinical) paranoia, which allowed him to stay up most of the night and think about his enemies. Once, in Florence, I suffered an extended — that is, roughly two-week — bout of insomnia, not at all helped by a too soft bed and an almost continuous flow of motor-scooter traffic vrooming past my hotel window. I tried to concentrate on pleasant things: small animals I have loved, tennis courts in the rain, giraffes cantering off into the distance. None of it worked. All I was finally left to think about was the longing for sleep itself — a topic always guaranteed to keep one awake.

Insomnia has its own small place in literature. Ernest Hemingway deals with the subject in his story "Now I Lay Me," which is about a wounded soldier in World War I who is recovering in a military hospital but unable to sleep. He is afraid that, should he fall asleep, "my soul would go out of my body." The soldier, who tells the story — and it seems a very autobiographical story — remembers every trout stream he fished as a boy and invents others, he says prayers for all the people he has known, he imagines what kind of wives the various girls he has met would make. He allows that some nights he must have "slept without knowing it — but I never slept knowing it," which is exactly what the sleep of insomnia often feels like.

F. Scott Fitzgerald cites Hemingway's story at the outset of "Sleeping and Waking," his essay of 1934. Fitzgerald himself suffered insomnia, beginning in his late thirties, and became something of a connoisseur of the illness, if that is what it is. He tells of a friend, awakened one night by a mouse nibbling on his finger, who never slept peacefully again without a dog or cat in the room. Fitzgerald's own insomnia began with a battle with a mosquito, which he won, though only in a Pyrrhic sense, for ever afterward he was haunted by what he called "sleep-consciousness," which meant he worried in advance whether he would be able to fall asleep. With an imagination for disaster, he prepared for sleeplessness, setting by his bedside "the books, the glass of water, the extra pyjamas lest I wake in rivulets of sweat, the luminol pills in the little round tube, the notebook and pencil in case of a night thought worth recording."

Fitzgerald's insomnia took the not uncommon form of dividing his sleep into two parts. He slept, that is, until roughly two-thirty, then woke for a cruel ninety-minute or so intermission during which pleasant fantasies (of playing football at Princeton, of wartime heroics) availed him nothing. He was left, awake against his own desires, to think of the horror and waste of his life: "what I might have been and done that is lost, spent, gone, dissipated, unrecapturable. I could have acted thus, refrained from this, been bold where I was timid, cautious where I was rash." And so he tortured himself, until, like a reverse mugger, sleep beautifully snuck up on him, and his dreams, "after the catharsis of the dark hours, are of young and lovely people doing young and lovely things, the girls I knew once, with big brown eyes, real yellow hair."

Vladimir Nabokov was another insomniac, though he referred to himself instead as "a poor go-to-sleeper." (That *iac* suffix has something sad or reprehensible about it: hemophiliac, hypochondriac, paranoiac, kleptomaniac, none of them jolly conditions.) Easy sleep was a matter of amazement to him, so much so that he found something vulgar about people who slept easily: "People in trains, who lay their newspapers aside, fold their silly arms, and immediately, with an offensive familiarity of demeanor, start snoring, amaze me as much as the uninhibited chap who cozily defecates in the presence of a chatty tubber, or participates in huge demonstrations, or joins some union in order to dissolve in it." The fact is, Nabokov not only didn't like but rather resented sleep, which put his endlessly inventive mind temporarily out of commission. He calls sleepers, in *Speak, Memory,* "the most moronic fraternity in the world, with the heaviest dues and crudest rituals."

Perhaps if one had a mind as richly stocked, as assailed by perception, as happily imaginative as Vladimir Nabokov's, one wouldn't wish to turn it off either. But enough writers have suffered from insomnia to make it seem almost an occupational disease. De Quincey, Nietzsche, Jorge Luis Borges, who once referred to the "atrocious lucidity of insomnia," all knew its horrors. Borges is the only one to write his way to a cure — specifically, through "Funes the Memorius," his wonderful story about a young man who dies from what one can only call a memory overload.

Does insomnia inflame the imagination? Or is an inflamed

imagination the cause of insomnia? But then, too, life can deal out punishment of a kind that allows no easing even in sleep. After his wife's death, Raymond Chandler reported: "I sit up half the night playing records when I have the blues and can't get drunk enough to get sleepy. My nights are pretty awful." Sufficiently awful, it turned out, for Chandler, during this period, to attempt suicide.

Even as a middle-aged adult I have known the condition of not wishing to turn off my mental machinery and retire to sleep; and I have also known the pleasure of awakening eager to turn it back on. Most nights, though, I am ready to close up shop, pack it in, send up the white flag, not of surrender but of cease-fire. Sleep on such occasions seems a marvelously sensible arrangement. But on other nights sleep seems an inconvenience, a drag, even something of a bore.

What removes some of the boredom is that one can never be sure what awaits one in sleep. "But she slept lightly and impatiently," writes Robert Musil in his story "The Temptation of Quiet Veronica," "as someone for whom the next day there is something extraordinary in store." Sometimes it seems there are quite as many states of sleep as of wakefulness: light sleep, troubled sleep, restless sleep, wakeful sleep, deep sleep, well-earned sleep. People talk, walk, snore, and emit semen in their sleep. They may be more receptive of the truth when asleep than when awake. "To sleep:" as the man with the notably receding hairline said, "perchance to dream. . . ." Not much perchance about it.

Envy has long ago begun to desert me, but I admit to feeling it for people who seem not to require much sleep. Those who can get by, indefinitely, on four or five hours of sleep a night have a small jump on the rest of us. I myself require six or seven hours of sleep, which beats by a bit the line from the old song that runs: "I work eight hours, I sleep eight hours, that leaves eight hours for fun." Still, the prospect of sleeping roughly a third of one's life away is more than a little dismaying. But then who among us would like to be presented with a careful accounting of how he has spent his time on earth? My own might look something like this: sleep — slightly less than one third of total; watching men hit, chase, kick, and throw various-sized balls — eleven years, seven months; reading — thirteen years, four months; following the news — three years, six months; eating and activities connected with digestion — four years, eleven months; daydreaming and hopeless fantasizing — five years and seven months; gossiping, sulking, talking on the telephone, and miscellaneous time-wasting — undeterminable but substantial. . . .

As a fellow mindful of time, I tremendously dislike the notion of losing any of this valuable substance. Worry about the loss of time must kick in at a certain age. I know that it has been more than two decades since I have been able to stay abed later than seven in the morning with a good conscience. When I have, I feel as if the day has quite escaped me. Yet I recall reading with admiration, in *Howards End,* about the character Mrs. Wilcox, who spends entire days in bed, paying bills, answering letters, taking care of the small but necessary details in her life as well as recharging her batteries. I have also heard, as doubtless we all have, about people who in defeat, or more often in depression, repair to their beds and do not emerge for days, sometimes weeks. Not getting out of bed for weeks at a time — there's something, I find, rather enticing about that. My guess, though, is that I could not last more than an eight-hour stretch, and then I would lose to guilt whatever I gained in rest.

Sleeping in some beds, of course, is more pleasurable than sleeping in others. From childhood memories, doubtless by now nicely coated with nostalgia, I recall the comfort of sleeping on trains, with the clickety-clack of the tracks beneath, the stars above, the occasional lights from towns passing by. I have only read about sleepers on airplanes, which were in service, I gather, during World War II; or at least I recall A. J. Liebling remarking that, trying to sleep in a bed on a military transport, he heard his watch and pen, in a bedside table, rattling around "like dice in a crap-shooter's hand." It would have been nice, though, I imagine, to have watched the sky pass as one awaited sleep. As a boy, I would have been delighted to have slept in a bunk bed; I only did so later in the army. I have never slept in a hammock. The idea of camping out-of-doors, which I also had a taste of in the army, could be made tolerable to me today only if I could find a campsite where room service was included. Sleeping in the cramped quarters of a submarine wouldn't be easy for me. Sleeping alone in a hotel in a king-size bed, on the other hand, gives me the willies.

I often go to sleep with music playing. My bedside clock radio has a sleeper function, which allows the radio to play for a specified amount of time before it clicks off automatically. Usually I go to sleep listening to classical music. Cello music is perhaps most soporific. Opera music, with only rare exceptions, doesn't work: too much blatant emotion. Most modern music is hopeless for sleeping. (Glenn Gould also slept with his radio on and said that sometimes the news got into his dreams.) But nothing puts me out faster than Chicago Cubs games broadcast from the West Coast. When heard late at night lying down, the droning of the announcers, who with their impressive assemblage of clichés are describing a game in which there is nothing whatsoever at stake — a Mickey Finn could not be more effective.

It is four-fifteen in the afternoon, and, owing to my having had less sleep than usual the night before, I am beginning to grow a bit tired. So I walk out to mail a few letters, and on the way back I stop at the public library a block or so away to pick up a copy of Freud's *Interpretation of Dreams*. The brief walk in the fresh air has put me in the perfect mood for a little nap.

I betake myself to the couch on which I do my serious napping. I remove my glasses, loosen the belt on my trousers, slip out of my shoes, rest my feet on a small black leather-covered footstool, and set my head against the back of the couch. I call out to my cat, who chooses not to join me (she is napping elsewhere in the apartment). I am, for the next thirty minutes, history — sleeping with my head back and, I believe, my mouth open. I am now fortified for the longish drive I have to make out to the western suburbs to meet with cousins for dinner. A bit of water over the eyes, a rinse of mouthwash, and, yo! I'm on my way.

I do not recall having had any dreams, but if I did they must not have been worth remembering. I tend not to dream, at any rate not very vividly, when napping. My dreaming during the night seems to me, if I may say so, rather commonplace, even a bit drab. By setting us to the task of interpreting our dreams, Sigmund Freud put us all on the road to being both novelist and critic of our own sleep life. Beginning well before Freud, though, there exists a lengthy literature on the meaning and function of dreams. To what extent one's dreams provide the key to one's unconscious and subconscious still seems to me very much, after all these years, in the flux of controversy. From time to time — less often than I would like — people I love who are dead show up in my dreams; I long for them not to leave, but, like the electric trains, cap pistols, and bubblegum of my childhood, they, too, inevitably depart. Many of my own dreams are sheer whimsy. The other night, for example, I dreamt about a bespoke suit that cost only $150. When I asked the woman in whose shop I saw it how she was able to produce such a suit at so low a price, she authoritatively answered: "Simple — low quality material and poor workmanship."

When I have nightmares, I find I am able, after only a brief spell, to turn them off, rather as if I am changing television channels. In fact, sometimes I will gain semi-consciousness during such nightmares and quite lucidly announce to myself, who needs this? and then turn over and await another dream. In sleep, if not in actual life, I seem to have something akin to a satellite dish with almost endless channels available to me.

Along with the whimsy channel, I seem fairly often to find myself on the anxiety channel. My dentist informs me that I am a man who grinds his teeth at night, a sufferer from the dental problem known as bruxism, which these anxiety dreams must help along. One of these dreams, in fact, which comes up perhaps once a year, is about losing my teeth, or at least a few key teeth. Occasionally, I have a mugging dream, in which I find myself in a hallway or on a deserted street confronting two or three young guys, one of whom has a knife, who want my money. Usually I am able to change channels, or I simply awake, before any violence is done.

My more common anxiety dreams, though, have to do with my making a great fool of myself in public. The setting here is invariably pedagogic. I have agreed to give a lecture or to teach a course on a subject about which I know absolutely nothing: Persian literature, say, or astrophysics. Screwup follows hard upon screwup. I cannot find the room; I have lost my notes; I need frightfully to make water. "Persian literature," I begin, before a large crowd well stocked with Iranian faces, "is extremely rich." And then I realize that I do not know the names of any Persian writers apart from Omar Khayyám. I hem. I haw.

I wonder what extraordinary hubris propelled me into agreeing to deliver this lecture in the first place. "Persian literature," I continue, "is more than extremely rich — it is highly varied. Take the case of Omar Khayyám. . . ."

When young, I had a student variant of these anxiety dreams in which I walk into a final exam of a course I have not attended all quarter long. The course is inevitably on a subject that is abstract yet also specific — Boolean algebra, say, or eighteenth-century musicology — something, in other words, that I cannot bluff my way through with stylish writing. Particular knowledge is needed, and, in these dreams, particular knowledge is exactly what I never have. Now, thirty years later, as a teacher rather than a student, in my dreams I still don't have it.

I occasionally have more ordinary nightmares: squirrels or possums or other animals with sharp claws are crowding in on me. A thief is at the window, but I cannot muster the energy to shut it as he begins to crawl in. I am traveling to Europe by plane, and I cannot locate my luggage, my tickets, my wife. Time is running out. I am never going to make it. As I say, all these seem to me fairly commonplace dreams. I have had only a single dream in which the Nazis figured, and it was connected, as I remember noting, to no recent book or movie or discussion of the subject I had encountered. It just came up arbitrarily — out of the dark, one might say. I am just not much of a world-historical dreamer.

Unlike Graham Greene, who kept a dream diary that has recently been published under the title *A World of My Own,* and whose dreams had a richness that make my own scarcely worth changing into pajamas for. Greene regularly dreamed of popes and heads of state and dictators. He dreamed of spying; in one dream, he helped capture Hitler. His dreams have a political line — they are reliably anti-American. Living and dead writers drop in with some frequency. Kim Philby recruits Ernest Hemingway to work for the Communists in Hong Kong. Evelyn Waugh, in another dream, shoots W. H. Auden. Henry James joins Greene on a river trip to Bogotá. T. S. Eliot queries a line of a poem he has written and turns out to be wearing a mustache. Greene's nightmares have to do with birds and spiders and urinating *crevettes* and *languoustines*. But in a darker, a true writer's, nightmare, his publisher cannot be talked out of praising the novels of C. P. Snow.

Graham Greene refers, in this book, to his dreamworld as "My Own World," in contradistinction to "the world I share," which is his designation for the real world. Impressively rich though the world Greene shared was — filled with mistresses, politics, intrigue, literary success, religious crises, and the rest of it — his Own World is even richer. With dreams of the kind he records, I should imagine he could hardly wait to get to sleep at night.

But then artists have always been dreamers. Maurice Ravel felt that because they do spend so much time dreaming, even when awake, it wasn't fair for artists to marry. In my own case, though much of the material of my youthful fantasies — world fame, sexual conquest, appalling riches, enemies nicely discouraged — has lost its allure, I still manage to spend a goodly portion of my waking hours in a semi-dream state. I wish I could tell you more precisely than I can what it is I daydream about, but so vague, not to say misty, are these little sallies on which I float off that they are quite unmemorable and insubstantial. I am in a gentle clime; I drive along a blue coast in a convertible with a grandchild seated next to me; I have written something immemorially beautiful.

Many years ago, I read in a biography of Hannah Arendt that Miss Arendt set aside an hour every afternoon during which she lay on a couch in her Manhattan apartment and did nothing but think. I kitchen- or rather couch-tested this procedure and found I was unable to concentrate that long when on my back; in fact, engaged in concentrated thinking, I soon dozed off. Most of my thinking, if thinking it really is, comes in inconvenient spurts while daydreaming: in the shower, at the wheel of my car, with a book in my hand, while napping, just before falling off to sleep at night. For me, stray — and occasionally useful — thoughts, if not responsibilities, begin in dreams.

I was of that generation of children who said their prayers before going to sleep. I cannot recall whether doing so was my parents' or my own idea. But the prologue to the prayer I said was the standard one that ran:

> Now I lay me down to sleep;
> I pray the Lord my soul to keep.
> If I should die before I wake,
> I pray the Lord my soul to take.
> God bless my mother, my father . . .

Looking at these words in cold type, this little prayer seems quite terrifying — at least for a small child — holding out as it does the distinct prospect of imminent death coming in one's sleep. Beyond a certain age — nowadays I suppose it is eighty — it is thought extremely good luck to be allowed to die in one's sleep. *She just slept, and slipped, away,* one reports of some deaths, usually with a suggestion in one's voice of the mercifulness of the arrangement. Departing thus does deprive one of the drama of possibly uttering profound last words — "More light!" "What is the question?" "Trade Kingman!" "Is it a little hot in here, or do I imagine it?" — but most people, I suspect, would be willing to forgo those last words for a calmer because unconscious departure.

Shelley refers, in the opening lines of *Queen Mab,* to "Death and his brother Sleep!" Sleep itself has been called "little death." It's not a bad description of the phenomenon of sleep. To fall asleep, after all, entails a letting go, a giving up of consciousness, a journey to one knows not where. As with death, so with sleep, no one knows with certainty what awaits on the other side: nightmares, sweetmares, brief (one hopes) oblivion.

I have described my prowess at napping, or the art of napping in action. What I have not gone into is the secret behind the attainment of this prowess. In no small part, it has to do with wanting a time-out — with wanting out of life, not deeply, not permanently, but at least for a while. The English writer A. Alvarez, in a book titled *Night,* allows that he has become addicted to sleep — that he finds it no less than, in his own word, "sensual." He remarks that in his adolescence and twenties he chiefly thought about sex; once he married and that department of his life was in order, in his thirties "the obsession with sex was replaced by an obsession with food"; and now, in his sixties, this has been "usurped by a new obsession: sleep."

I wonder if the larger meaning of the obsession with sleep isn't a slow, albeit unconscious, preparation for closing up shop. I wonder, too, if this is such a bad thing. I know many people will despise this notion, arguing that one must never give in, give out, give up. They will claim, with much right on their side, that life is too precious a gift for one to permit it to slip away of one's own volition — in effect, for one to welcome death. Stay in the game, turn up the music, keep fighting, they will argue, plenty of time for napping in the grave. And they are, again, right.

Yet there is something marvelously seductive about sleep, and especially about a nap, which might best be viewed as a lovely and harmless touch of cheating, comparable, if one wishes to talk about sleep in terms usually reserved for sex instead of for death, to an afternoon tryst. As an artful napper, a nap remains, in my mind, one of life's fine things just so long as, when napping, one doesn't dream that one has been made some fantastic, some really quite impossible to refuse, offer by Harvard.

A Nice Little Knack
for Name-Dropping

I WAS A name-dropper before I knew what name-dropping is. What name-dropping is, to put it in a quick formulation, is using the magic that adheres to the names of celebrated people to establish one's superiority while at the same time making the next person feel the drabness of his or her own life. Name-dropping is a division of snobbery, and one of the snob's missions is to encourage a feeling, however vague, of hopelessness in others. A small but quite genuine art, name-dropping, an art that requires the right, consummately light touch, for the least heavy-handedness in this line, as in so many of the fine arts, can destroy everything.

My own early efforts as a name-dropper had less to do with encouraging hopelessness in others than with inflaming hope in myself. The scene of my initial foray into name-dropping was an immense amusement park in Chicago called Riverview. Torn down in 1968 and now the site of an industrial park and a shopping center, Riverview contained an Aladdin's Castle fun house, a tunnel of love, a motorcycle hippodrome, a tower of terror called the Pair-O-Chutes, a delightful plunge into water known as the Chutes, roller coasters named the Bobs, the Greyhound, the Fireball, the Blue Streak, and other entertainments called the Flying Turns, the Boomerang, the Flying Scooters, the Dodge 'Em, along with cat games, free-throw shooting, a freak show, and much else besides.

At sixteen, my friends and I, middle-class flaneurs, would take ourselves to Riverview on steamy summer nights, there to view the passing scene. The part of the scene that interested us most was high school girls, whom we tried to pick up — with, let me say straightaway, a pathetically poor success rate. In this operation I led the way, and I did it through name-dropping. We would come upon three or four girls, and I would ask them, in my most earnest fashion, where they went to school. If they answered, say, Steinmetz, I would reply, "Then you must know my cousin Jack Pully." If they answered Von Steuben, I would reply, "Then you must know my cousin Hershie Carl." If they answered Lake View, I would reply, "Then you must know my cousin Ron Youngblood."

Lest anyone think I belong to an impressively multi-ethnic extended family, let me say that Jack, Hershie, and Ron were not in fact my cousins. They were star basketball players at, respectively, Steinmetz, Von Steuben, and Lake View. My (false) relationship with these talismanic names unfailingly impressed these girls, and though my friends and I were not very good at what is nowadays called "coming to closure," my phony name-dropping earned us, at least conversationally, a foot in the door. The larger lesson to be learned here, of course, is that to Shakespeare's question "What's in a name?" the correct answer is, "Used properly, quite a bit, actually."

To this day, more than forty years later, I continue to drop names. I think of myself as an occasional and, I'll allow, inveterate, if not, I hope, habitual name-dropper, in no way resembling the man whose name-dropping Edmund Wilson described as "like the rattle of rain on the roof." I recently caught myself saying: "Paul McHugh, a friend of mine who is the head of psychiatry at Johns Hopkins, thinks that sex-change operations are likely one day to be viewed as the lobotomies of the second half of the twentieth century." I have said more than once: "George Will, with whom I talk from time to time, has a son who went to Northwestern on a baseball scholarship." I mentioned to someone the other day: "Judith Martin, who writes the 'Miss Manners' column, told me that you never want to wear a white dinner jacket to a wedding unless you are planning to bring along a full set of drums." And then a few years ago, in teaching a course on Henry James, I inquired about the possibility that the character Quint in "The Turn of the Screw" may represent pure evil. When a student asked what I meant by evil, I found myself replying: "I hope you will forgive a bit of name-dropping, Mr. Koenig, but I mean, very precisely, the work of the Devil."

It shouldn't be any surprise that people are impressed by even mildly famous names. I find I'm as susceptible to celebrity as the next person, maybe a touch more so. The other day, for example, at lunch in a neighborhood restaurant, I saw a dark, still very fit-looking man, dapperly turned out, maybe a decade older than I, sitting two booths in front of me. My lunch companion pointed out that this was the old Chicago White Sox outfielder Orestes "Minnie" Minoso. Minoso, a Cuban, was a more than respectable, though just slightly less than great, player. I felt no need to go up and thank him for the pleasure his play had given me over the years; the people who ran the restaurant knew who he was and accorded him the attention properly owed the locally famous. But I felt pleased to be in the same restaurant with — if I may — Minnie, whose aura added more than a touch of tarragon to my own food.

Years ago, in New York, at a Chinese restaurant called the Pearl, I felt distinctly distracted when Paul Newman and Joanne Woodward walked in. (Funny, an hour later I was hungry for fresh celebrities.) One evening at La Guardia I saw Floyd Patterson, once heavyweight champion of the world, and, because no one else seemed to notice him, I went up to him and said that I thought him a great boxer (he wasn't, quite, but what the hell!). At ten years old or so, I met Tony Zale, then the middleweight champion of the world, and I was duly impressed. Several years ago I had dinner in Los Angeles with six other people, one of whom was the television actress Barbara Eden, who, it pleased me to discover, required little in the way of extra attention. But, as name-dropping goes, all this, I fear, is small change.

Let us now consider someone handling larger denominations. The screenwriter and novelist John Gregory Dunne was among those recently asked by the editors of *Esquire* magazine to name a woman he admired. His choice was Katrina vanden Heuvel, currently the editor of the *Nation* and the granddaughter of the powerful Hollywood agent Jules Stein. Mr. Dunne recalls for us his memory of Miss vanden Heuvel at parties at her grandparents' house, where "one mixed with Gregory Peck and Warren Beatty and Jennifer Jones and the odd maharani arriving from India." He also recalls a slightly older Miss vanden Heuvel for us at her mother's Central Park West apartment, "where all the nobility of arts and letters regularly congregated" — toot your kazoo here for some rather debased nobility — "William Styron and Norman Mailer and Gore Vidal and Woody Allen and Lillian Hellman and Robert Rauschenberg." The subtext here, as the kids in literary criticism say, is represented by that balding gentleman with the paunch, one Mr.

Dunne — and not Finley Peter Dunne either — happily mixing with all these names. Ah, sure, and it's a glorious and glamorous life, that lived among the famous.

John Gregory Dunne's is name-dropping by indirection, which is one way of going about it. Another, more direct way is what is called "the secondary name-drop." A specialist in the secondary name-drop, according to his son, was Ben Sonnenberg, the public relations man, who used to claim he was in the business of erecting very large pedestals for very small statues. Sonnenberg was a man who could claim, "I know the difference between Irving Berlin and Isaiah Berlin, and I know them both." The secondary name-drop, as he practiced it, entailed making plain that one not only knew the famous but had a kind of kitchen intimacy with them. When asked if he knew George Gershwin, for example, Sonnenberg would reply: "Know him? I used to play gin rummy with his mother."

I love that and only wish I could find occasions to put it to use. Did I know Diaghilev? Know him? I used to play racquetball with his brother Irwin. Did I know Louis Armstrong? Know him? He sold me his old *Oxford English Dictionary*. Oscar Levant was once asked if he knew Doris Day. "Know her?" Levant is supposed to have replied. "I knew her before she was a virgin."

Another refinement on name-dropping is to drop not the name but the nickname or diminutive or private name of the famous person. This needs to be done with a studied casualness. In literary circles, here are some of the possibilities: Red (Robert Penn) Warren, Bunny (Edmund) Wilson, Archie (Archibald) MacLeish, Cal (Robert) Lowell, Kitty (Katherine Anne) Porter, Freddy (A. J.) Ayer, Joe (A. J.) Liebling, Wystan (W. H.) Auden, and Lizzie (Elizabeth) Hardwick.

One of the technical difficulties of name-dropping is that one cannot always be sure that the person one is talking to will be suitably impressed with the name one has dropped. This is a concern if one has a wide range of acquaintances. A name that will capture attention in one circle may achieve no more than empty looks in another. All the literary names in my last paragraph are unlikely to cut much ice at a Bears-Packers game. Few things are sadder than a name-dropper carrying the luscious load of a name he cannot drop.

Alan Bennett, the English comedian and playwright, who, so far as I know, is not at all a name-dropper, nonetheless neatly illustrates the point. Mr. Bennett's father was a butcher in the city of Leeds, and among his customers was a family named Fletcher. The Fletchers had a daughter named Valerie, who married a man named Eliot, a poet — T. S. Eliot actually. Bennett's mother was one day introduced to Eliot on a street in Leeds and had no idea who he was. Bennett tried to explain to his mother, but, as he recounts, "*The Waste Land* not figuring in Mam's scheme of things," he didn't have great success. "The thing is," Bennett finally said, "he won the Nobel Prize." To which his mother, not overly excited, replied: "Well, I'm not surprised. It was a beautiful overcoat."

In most circles T. S. Eliot is a fine name to drop. So, I should say, is Winston Churchill. Stravinsky isn't at all bad, though Picasso is probably better. Balanchine is nice. Various of the Kennedys might ring the gong, excluding Ted and Joe the father. Vladimir Nabokov is an excellent drop. Isaiah Berlin gives good value; best, though, to refer to him by his first name only, getting that pronunciation, with two long *i*'s, right. Kingsley is another first-name-only drop; besides, someone once said that his full name, Kingsley Amis, sounded rather like the name of an English village. In his day, Somerset Maugham's name dropped with a lovely ping. Someone dropped Cary Grant on me a few months back and, truth to tell, got my attention.

Is it a sign of the leanness of our times that there are fewer and fewer living names that seem worth dropping? If I tell you that I had lunch with, say, Steven Spielberg, would you be impressed? Somehow I don't think so. What about Barry Bonds or Joe Montana? Great athletes both, yet neither seems very exciting. Gloria Steinem? Mike Nichols? These names don't bang the bong, at least not on my block. "Spent last night in the company of Madonna and Mick Jagger. Haven't had so much fun since that lunch I had in Tangier with Yo-Yo Ma and Dennis Rodman." Sorry. No fireworks. The earth refuses to move.

Every generation, every social group, every interest group has its own set of approved names. In certain circles in Chicago, a long night with Mike Ditka might be as the French Revolution was to Wordsworth: "Bliss was it in that dawn to be alive." I don't think dropping Mike's name would have gone over big with Red, Cal, Bunny, and the boys. In Washington, the best names to drop are those of politicians — chiefly, make no mistake, those of politicians in power, the more powerful, the more resonant the name — with that of an occasional Supreme Court justice to leaven the loaf.

At 6:30 one spring morning in Washington, on my way to the airport, I was picked up by a heavyset black cabdriver in front of the Cosmos Club. A man filled with bonhomie, comfortably seated in his cab with a mug of coffee in hand, he announced that he had just dropped off Franco Harris's nephew. He assumed that I would know who Franco Harris is, and he was correct: Harris is the former great running back of the Pittsburgh Steelers who in a playoff game against the Oakland Raiders made the famous touchdown catch known as the "immaculate reception." We discussed that catch at some length, and then he went on to tell me he used to work the lights at a once famous nightclub in Atlantic City, where he had been friendly with the singer Billy Daniels (drop) and the comedian George Kirby (drop). A very agreeable fellow, this cabdriver was establishing himself as someone who had shaken many an important hand.

"May I ask," he inquired as we approached National Airport, "if you are someone whose autograph I ought to have?"

"Not yet worth having," I answered.

When I asked him why he would ask such a question, he mentioned that a fair number of famous people in government and journalism come in and out of the Cosmos Club, where he had picked me up, and he wondered if I might be one of them. I thanked him for a pleasant ride, overtipped him — a man in touch with so many famous people, to my way of thinking, deserves more than an ordinary tip — and flew home.

That cabdriver's name-dropping seemed to me not at all invidious or otherwise unpleasant. In dropping his few names from sports and show business, he was merely making plain to me that his hadn't been all that dull a life. This was name-dropping with a friendly face. Most of us, after all, would much rather hear about the celebrated than the obscure. It is only the unbearable sucking up to them that sickens.

Ten or so years ago I found myself knee deep in the Big Namey when I was asked to be a member of the National Council of the National Endowment for the Arts. A small number of moderately famous people in the arts were among my fellow council members: Martha Graham, Robert Joffrey, Helen Frankenthaler, Celeste Holm, Robert Stack, Marvin Hamlisch (briefly), and Toni Morrison.

At first, I felt myself pleased to be among them. Here I am, thought I, a simple lad from the Midwest sitting amongst these famous artists. How grand! But then, in time — and not very much time, either — I noted their flaws and their various shortcomings. Some were spectacularly narrow in their interests and as spectacularly broad in their ignorance. Some clearly had received too much attention for too long — what I would call altogether too much love outside the home. Few things, by the way, are more pleasing than feeling superior to a celebrated person. It gives one a heightened sense of the world's injustice and folly, which, when one isn't especially wounded by that injustice or stung by that folly, can be a considerable comfort.

Finding the famous a little disappointing seems to be a fairly common experience. A friend of mine, an art critic, tells of being introduced to Edward G. Robinson at an art exhibition. He admired Robinson's acting as much as that of any movie actor then alive, and when Robinson asked my friend if he might join him as he made his round of the exhibition, he said yes indeed, he would be honored. And so he was, for roughly fifteen minutes, until Robinson's rather platitudinous conversation about art — he was, you may recall, a collector — led my friend to wonder, "How do I get rid of this guy?"

If the celebrated do not turn out to be disappointing, they are likely to prove, alas, all too much like the rest of us. An acquaintance recently told me about stepping into the men's room after a dinner at the Pierre Hotel in honor of a retiring magazine editor and finding himself trough-by-trough between Henry Kissinger and Rupert Murdoch. He was a touch dizzy to find himself mingling (not quite the precise word) with the famous, until he noted that, like himself, his trough-mates, being in their sixties, seemed less interested in their intrinsic glamour than in the mechanics of the task at hand.

My father used to tell a story in which one day at lunch his boss, noticing a boy at a nearby table, became very excited, grabbed my father by the elbow, and announced that there was someone he wanted him to meet. He then introduced my father to the boy, and they engaged in a bit of empty chatter. Upon returning to their own table, my father asked who the boy was. "Oh," said his boss. "You don't know? [*Dramatic pause — wait for it*] He's the batboy of the Chicago Cubs."

When the only celebrities one really longs to meet are no longer alive, it is a sign that one is growing old. I would love to have met Babe Ruth, but I could pass on meeting just about any major league ballplayer of the current day. Someone told me the other day that he went to see Wayne Gretzky play before his retirement. I can understand that — Gretzky may be the greatest hockey player in the history of the game. But I long to meet Gretzky, my guess is, roughly to the extent that he longs to meet me. I should have liked to lunch with Fredric March or Myrna Loy (whom I actually did once meet, if I may be allowed a little name-dropping), but I shall leave the planet with the same equanimity with which I arrived if I never meet Barbra Streisand or Al Pacino.

Had I known him, I would have dropped Fred Astaire's name, and dropped it often, with the exquisite, happy confidence that it would have gotten the attention of most people. "What you have just said reminds me of something Fred Astaire once told me," I might have inserted into conversation. Or: "Fred — Fred Astaire, that is — would probably agree with what you just said." Or, a forced drop: "Apropos of nothing, Fred Astaire always used to say . . ."

I like to think that Fred Astaire in person had a natural elegance of the kind he demonstrated in all his movies. I assume he wore wonderful loafers and socks of some astonishingly subtle color, suitable raiment for the world's most deserving feet. Had I met him, he would have put me immediately at ease. He'd have been kind to the waiter. He'd have ordered something light and wonderfully simple, a chicken sandwich on white toast, perhaps, and a split of champagne. His talk, though witty, would have been radiant with common sense but would not touch on politics. "My politics," he would have said, "are let Paris be gay, in the old sense, of course. Say, how about another glass of champagne, kiddo?" After ninety minutes or so of dazzling talk — filled with charming anecdotes told with a pleasing and altogether benign irony and at appropriate intervals touching on the profound — he would have graciously allowed me to pick up the check. "Fred, my pleasure and small recompense for all the enjoyment you have given me over the years," I'd have said. "We'll do it again, kiddo," he'd have said, putting on his hat outside the restaurant, shaking my hand, and going off in a jaunty walk that seemed awfully close to a dance.

The first place I'd have dropped Fred Astaire's name would have been in my journal, where over the years I have made a number of private drops. One of the reasons I read other people's published journals and diaries is to be let in on this game of private name-dropping. My own, in this regard, is rather thin. On even a quick spin through *In the Twenties*, the one-volume diary of the German publisher Harry Kessler, one gets a true taste of what serious name-dropping looks like. "Lunched with Jean Cocteau. . . . To tea with Albert Einstein. . . . Visited Frau Foerster-Nietzsche. . . . In the morning a discussion with Ramsay MacDonald in his room at the Commons. . . . Mrs. Harold Nicolson, Virginia Woolf and her husband, Leonard Woolf, came to tea. . . . After lunch I drove him [Maillol] to Marly and then visited Paul Valéry. . . ."

Count Kessler's little visit to Valéry is to the point here. The purpose of the visit was to invite Valéry to do a translation of Virgil's *Georgics*, which Valéry chose not to do, claiming he knew nothing about agriculture. So ignorant of it was he that, would you believe, Mallarmé once had to explain to him what corn is. An eye for an eye, a name-drop for a name-drop — here is Paul Valéry, an eminently droppable name himself, dropping the name of Mallarmé in conversation with Count Kessler, who will duly record it in his diary and thus obtain two drops for the price of one.

This little incident also brings up the question — the problem, really — of whose names the truly famous get to drop. What names did Vladimir Horowitz, Samuel Beckett, or Bing Crosby — all handsomely droppable names — get to drop? Most of their dropping had to be in the past tense: great people they once knew. In a television interview, Horowitz — how I wish I could refer to him as Volodya — dropped the names of Rachmaninoff and Scriabin. "I first met Yeats in 1934," Beckett told Robert Craft. I suppose Crosby must have dropped the names of long-dead bandleaders or, possibly, deceased professional golfers.

The celebrated, even the mildly celebrated, do at least get to drop their own names, and some learn to do so artfully and in a way that gets a response. I went to a basketball game a while back with a movie reviewer who has a national television show, and dinner was planned after the game. From his car phone, he called a restaurant, and even before asking if it was open for a late dinner, he announced his name, which clearly got the manager's attention. The restaurant, it turned out, was closing, for which the manager all but apologized, and he asked the movie reviewer to please try the restaurant again. This anecdote reinforces a story told in an *American Scholar* letters column about Ira Gershwin's failing to get a table in a popular restaurant but his friend's succeeding because he told the maître d' that his name was Ira Gershwin. What's in a name? At the very least, it would seem, a good table.

Eccentric behavior, or simple oddity, combined with genuine

talent is one way to get one's name dropped. W. H. Auden furnishes the best example here. Everyone who has ever met Auden seems to have at least two stories about him. He is a diarist's delight, a name-dropper's dream. With his rumpled clothes, his drinking habits (martinis before dinner, wine during, whiskey after), his odd footwear, above all his comic, often amusingly catty remarks, Auden ("Wystan," alas, not to me) comes near to stealing the show in Robert Craft's diary, *Stravinsky: Chronicle of a Friendship, 1948–1971.* "Wystan Auden for dinner in the I.S.' suite. Besides the glittering jewels of his intellect, he wears a dark brown flannel shirt, black necktie, wicker beach shoes, and — on departure, shortly before midnight — very dark glasses, like a jazz musician." When asked that evening if he believes in capital punishment, Auden replied: "Well, there have been people on whom I can picture it being carried out. Brecht, for one. In fact, I can imagine doing it to him myself. . . . Still, you must admire the logic of a man who lives in a Communist country, takes out Austrian citizenship, does his banking in Switzerland, and, like a gambler hedging his bets, sends for the pastor at the end in the event there could be something in that, too."

Here we get not only the good names of Wystan and Bert (if I may, and since both are dead, who is to stop me?), but also an extra little fillip of gossip. It is pleasing to know that Auden had a correctly low opinion of Brecht. But then name-dropping and gossip have always been sister arts. For those of us who have become a bit jaded, the sweet tintinnabulation provided by a good name is no longer sufficient without a touch of gossip attached to it. The dirt, the lowdown, the true gen about the famous — now here is something with which one can work.

The true professional name-droppers have always been the gossip columnists. Walter Winchell, Leonard Lyons, Earl Wilson, and others brought the two — name-dropping and gossip — together to high perfection in New York as did Hedda Hopper and Louella Parsons in Los Angeles. In Chicago, a man named Irv Kupcinet had the reigning gossip column when I was a boy. "Kup's Column," as it was called and still is nearly fifty years later, set out names from show business, politics, and sports in boldface type. After the sports section, Kup was the first thing I turned to in the *Chicago Sun-Times*. The astonishing thing about this column was that it dished very little dirt and contained no malice whatsoever. One would drop one's eyes down the column in search of interesting names — Ginger Rogers, Sinatra, the Deans Acheson, Martin, or Rusk, Sid Luckman, Harry Belafonte, Adlai Stevenson, Zsa Zsa Gabor — next to which one would find some quite useless tidbit of information. Why a fourteen-year-old boy needed to know that "Ole Blue Eyes" (one of Kup's cliché names for Sinatra) was thinking of canceling his forthcoming engagement at the Riviera Hotel in Las Vegas I cannot explain, except to ascribe it all to the magic inherent in famous names. Somehow it gave comfort. Zsa Zsa is about to take another husband, and all's right with the world.

None of the Mesdemoiselles Gabor is present in the bountiful index of *Remembering My Good Friends,* the autobiography of the Austrian-born English publisher George Weidenfeld, but almost everyone else is. Mr. Weidenfeld is celebrated, I think it fair to say, for being friends with the celebrated. His book is a nearly five-hundred-page "Kup's Column," but without the boldface type and with a much higher quality set of names. I read it with breathless avidity.

The Gabors may be a bit *de trop* for Mr. Weidenfeld. His international name-dropping runs from the socially prominent to the intellectually distinguished to the plain bloody rich, from the Agnellis to Bernard Berenson to David Ben-Gurion to Oscar de la Renta to Yukio Mishima to Picasso to the Rothschilds to the Whitneys to Lord Solly Zuckerman. Fame provides the water in which Mr. Weidenfeld most happily swims, and he has managed to stay joyously afloat, as one reviewer of his book has it, on four different continents. Buying a house, Mr. Weidenfeld has to tell about its well-known previous occupants. He takes the social weight of any room he enters. "Loelia, Duchess of Westminster, whom I had met through Grace Radziwill, invited me to join her for Christmas at Russborough, the palatial house of South African financier and philanthropist Sir Alfred Beit and his wife Clementine, a cousin of Nancy Mitford." That trailer, "a cousin of Nancy Mitford," is the tip-off, if any be needed, that Mr. Weidenfeld is able to squeeze all the juice possible out of any name he drops. "For years," he notes, "I tried to persuade Herbert von Karajan to write his memoirs." That "for years" suggests a long acquaintance and hence an intimacy. Mr. Weidenfeld, one suspects, makes his own intimacy; wherever the famous gather, there precisely is he at home.

I not long ago had occasion to be introduced to George Weidenfeld, whose name I hope he won't mind my dropping. It was at a dinner attended by a fairly large number of writers, intellectuals, and politicians, some mildly famous. As he heard my name, I could see him quickly run it through his own personal social register and I noted that it didn't click for him. The happy anticipation in his eyes faded. Ping! Ping! — where two eyeballs once were, two small *x*'s were now, for the lights went out in his mind. Without further word he ambled off, hunter after bigger game. Quite right, too.

I may seem to mock George Weidenfeld — Lord Weidenfeld as he now is — but that doesn't mean that I don't also admire him. I admire his knowing what makes him happy and going out to get it without any false hesitation. He is not without courage; he takes political positions; he is not above criticizing the famous; he does not truckle; he is no sycophant. I admire, too, his consistency. A man who acts true to type is a fine thing. George Weidenfeld is a type, a pure and beautiful type, a man who has made himself fit for Proustian portraiture, which, in our non-Proustian days, is no small achievement.

At the same dinner at which I met and didn't register with George Weidenfeld, I was seated next to a woman whose specialty seemed to be not name- but place-, or educational-institution-dropping. Whenever she mentioned anyone to me, she would always give that person's, so to say, institutional affiliation. "My daughter, who is at Princeton," she would say. Or, "My son-in-law, whom my other daughter first met at Oxford . . ." "My nephew, who is now at the Yale Medical School . . ." Everyone she knew seemed to be at or to have been recently released from some absolutely O.K. college or university. "Daddy was at Leavenworth," I wanted to say to her, "and Mum, Mum was of course at Bellevue."

I remember a rather brittle period when the children of my contemporaries were about to enter college. At certain times, one felt as if one were in a high-status bridge game, with prestige-laden schools as trumps: Yale, Harvard, Princeton, Brown, Stanford, Berkeley, Duke — the cards slapped down on the table. A mug's game, but everyone holding a strong hand felt he had to play.

This is the sort of thing that has given name-dropping a bad name, and it's a pity, for there is a positive side to name-dropping. Famous people on occasion are extraordinary; their achievements, if genuine, can give them an extra dimension. Fame, along with sometimes serving as an aphrodisiac, has its own intrinsic fascination. In a room with a famous person, one is inclined to feel a bit of added electricity in the air. If the famous person isn't a dolt, creep, or shmegegge, one is also inclined to feel a bit elevated by his fame.

At a party at a restaurant in Oak Park, Illinois, a beautiful, large whitefish was dedicated by the chef to Pierre Boulez and to me. The chef, gracious man, announced that he was carving and cooking this fish in honor of two artists, Pierre Boulez and Joseph Epstein. So you are reading a man who has shared dedication of a whitefish with Pierre Boulez. The only thing I have to report about M. Boulez is that he is delightfully old shoe, everything you would expect a contemporary avant-garde artist *not* to be: kindly, sweet-tempered, a swell guy. I justify my name-drop to myself by saying that Pierre Boulez's good nature is something worth reporting.

Had he turned out to be unpleasant, would I have told stories, if not in print at least to friends, about his unpleasantness? Probably. Boulez's fame, I suspect, would have held my audience's attention. Certainly more so than if I announced that I met this guy last week, I don't know what line of work he's in, but what a jerk he turned out to be.

Besides, Pierre Boulez's seems a nice name to drop; it has something of the equivalent feel of quoting Paul Valéry in an essay — something understated and Frenchly elegant about it. As drops go, it has the correct feel, the right weight. Nothing blatant about it, unlike Ned Rorem's drops in his *Nantucket Diary*, where he boasts of having slept with four *Time* cover subjects.

On the other hand, why not let my casual and pleasant meeting with Pierre Boulez go unremarked? Wouldn't it be much nicer to be known as a man who knows all sorts of famous and grand people but feels no need to advertise the fact? It would, but I cannot always do it. I seem to be a man who lives to tell, which is one — if not the only or most noble — definition of a writer.

Having met someone famous whom I admire, I am somewhat in the condition of the man in the joke cast adrift on a small island with a famous model. One thing leading to another, before long the two begin sleeping together. After a few weeks, the man asks the woman if she would mind putting on a pair of his jeans, one of his shirts, and his baseball cap. When she does so, he suggests a walk around the island. He then asks her if she would mind if he called her, just for now, Bruce. When she says not at all, he turns to her and announces: "Bruce, you'll never guess whom I'm sleeping with!"

Highly conscious of the human weakness known as name-dropping, I hope not to overdo it. I attempt restraint. I sometimes tell what I think is a fine joke about how artists lie about crowds, royalties, fees, and almost everything else having to do with worldly success. When the joke receives a kindly response, I want to say that it was told to me by Robert Stack, but more often than not I hold back doing so, lest I be thought to ruin a fine story with the stain of name-dropping. Sorry, Bob, no acknowledgment, not even a footnote.

Behind much name-dropping is a desire for distinction. Look, the name-dropper implies with each fresh drop, I am distinguished, at least by association. If this were not so, why would all these senators, movie stars, athletes, artists, and the rest put up with my company? The desire to be taken for distinguished seems all but universal. Robert Mapplethorpe, who, one would have thought, had plainly thumbed his nose at society, confided sadly to his biographer shortly before his death that he wouldn't be alive to "reap the benefits of his celebrity."

Ancestor worship is another form of attaining distinction through association, and dropping the names of one's own famous relatives, even if they are still alive, can provide its own comforts and comedy. I was not long ago at a dinner with a man named Milton Himmelfarb, a writer on Jewish subjects who will always be honored by me for once writing that — I paraphrase — the Jews are the only people who live like Republicans and vote like Puerto Ricans. Someone introduced Mr. Himmelfarb as the brother of the historian Gertrude Himmelfarb. "No, no, no," he said. "Actually, I now think of myself as the uncle of William Kristol," the Republican Party intellectual who at that moment was getting a vast amount of publicity.

Of course, if one could only be certain of one's own distinction, the whole matter of name-dropping might never arise in the first place. I hope someone will let me know if I ever arrive at being distinguished, so that I can knock off all this nonsense. Am I, I ask myself, anywhere near close? I keep turning out books. I have friends in what are known as high places. I know a Nobel Prize chappie or two. Publishers ask me to drop my own name on the backs of other people's books in the form of blurbs. I am asked, in other words, to drop my own name, if only in ink. What does it add up to? Not enough, I fear. But if I were ever to become a name, don't, please don't, hesitate to drop me.

So to Speak

FINDING THAT one has been walking around during a day full of crucial appointments unaware of the noticeable fleck of broccoli lodged between one's upper front teeth — that, roughly, is the despairing feeling that discovering one has been mispronouncing a word or a name gives. Only at the death of the Romanian writer E. M. Cioran did I learn that I had been mispronouncing his name over many years and before lots of students. I had always referred to him as *SEE-or-an;* in his obituary, I learned that it is properly pronounced *TCHAW-rahn.* For a good stretch, I didn't do much better with the Alexandrian poet C. P. Cavafy, whose name I pronounced *CAV-a-fee,* until a friend, who knew better, politely said, "I think it's *Ca-VA-fee.*" As a mnemonic device he suggested I hum the tune "You're the kareem in my Ca-VA-fee."

Why does it feel so foolish, so ketchup on one's white shirtfront, so absolutely fly open at the senior prom, to know one has been mispronouncing a word? La Rochefoucauld may have supplied the answer when he noted that people would rather have their opinions questioned than their taste criticized. A mispronounced word or name has to be considered a lapse in taste, but, unlike normal poor taste, it is brought about by genuine ignorance. It also represents a self-puncturing of one's own pretensions, assuming one has any, and I happen to have quite a few. When I first saw the word *banal,* I took to pronouncing it *BAY-nul.* I have long since switched to the more Frenchified *bu-NAHL.* Between *flutist* and *flautist,* I chose the latter, but only a few days ago I heard a woman with much greater musical culture than mine refer to a *flutist,* and I also found that H. W. Fowler, my household god in these and allied matters, also prefers *flutist.* Only moments before I taught a full course on the novels of Willa Cather did I learn that her name is pronounced to rhyme with *rather.* The other day I suggested to a woman that she might just have a Copernican complex — in which one believes that all the planets revolve around oneself — and I pronounced the word *Co-per-KNEE-can* (to rhyme with *Puerto Rican*), to which she replied that she always thought the word was pronounced *Co-PER-ni-can* — without, that is, the knee that I had placed in its stomach.

Until age eighteen, when I began college, pronunciation, speech, and language generally were not matters of any concern. I am an American, Chicago born — that's *Shu-CAW-guh,* pal — and, like Mr. Augie March, I went at things my own way. I of course knew about the comedy of accents, especially the greenhorn accents of immigrants (radio shows and their characters, such as *The Life of Luigi,* Mr. Kitzel on *The Jack Benny Program,* and Mrs. Nussbaum on *The Fred Allen Show,* emphasized the comic possibilities of butchered language). From the movies I picked up the lovely lilting English accents of Ronald Colman, Douglas Fairbanks, and Deborah Kerr and the elegantly alluring European-accented English of Ingrid Bergman, Sophia Loren, and Rossano Brazzi.

My own speech was without pretension. I wouldn't, frankly,

have known to what to pretend. Nor was the speech of any of my classmates at all noteworthy. Among the kids with whom I grew up, there were no stutterers. I don't recall that we mispronounced any words in those days, though my range of words — apart from the standard boy's ample stock of profanity — was much less ornamental than it is now. I spoke freely and easily, full, I am sure, of every kind of error but that of self-consciousness.

Just about everyone I went to grade school with was in the same social class — lower middle to middle. It was a less mobile America than we have now, and no one came from the East or the South or any other place where he or she might have picked up a regional accent (with one exception, a sweet-natured boy named Ben Rosenberg, a displaced person from Europe). Speech snobbery had not raised its stupid and largely disapproving head.

Only at university did pronunciation become a matter that required attention. I hadn't a clue about how to pronounce *Thucydides* the first time I saw it: *THUCK-a-dieds* may have been a first stab. English words of any complexity made me nervous. *Posthumous,* I recall, was among them; I kept seeing it as *post-humorous,* which the condition also is. Even the simplest French — about which more later — seemed surrounded by barbed wire and bear traps: I wasn't all that certain about knocking off the *s* in pronouncing *Camus.* I spent a fair amount of time as a college student disguising my ignorance.

But once I had determined to join the so-called educated classes, I had to take up the American version of what one Professor Henry Wyld, quoted in H. W. Fowler, calls "received pronunciation." By "received pronunciation" Wyld meant "the pronunciation of the great public schools, the universities and the learned professions, without local restriction." The sensible

Fowler claimed that, in matters of pronunciation, "the right rule is to speak as our neighbors do, not better." The problem, though, is to establish in just which neighborhood one wishes to live. And this problem is compounded by that buzziest — not to say fuzziest — of all buzzwords, *elitism*.

Received pronunciation is that which is used by those who are deemed the best speakers among us. Who these might be is a question in the flux of controversy — with *controversy* pronounced, in the English way, with the accent on the second syllable: *con-TRAH-versy*. Irritating though it is to say so, I suppose that the "best" speech in America is made up of the amalgam of academic, broadcasting, and what remains of upperclass speech. It is an English accent without the mellifluousness, if you can fancy that.

English political power has more than dwindled, English quality in consumer goods seems largely a thing of the past, but American envy of the English accent has not much lessened. For a time in New York corporate life, having a secretary with an English accent was a perk for powerful executives. In academic life, an English accent, at the full-professor level, has been worth, by my estimate, an extra $10,000 to $30,000 in salary. There may not always be an England, but there always will be snobbery, and English speech, or at any rate the speech of southern England, continues to bang the snobbery gong.

The English have us doubly over the barrel in that they establish pronunciations that are even more arbitrary than ours. Some English pronunciations are merely more beautiful, owing to the sound of the vowel (the British short *a* instead of the American long *a* in *charade*) and the syllable that is accented (the last in *tirade* in England as opposed to the first in America); *lehzure* beats *leesure* all to hell, and so, for my money, does *DIN-asty* beat *DIE-nasty*.

Only fairly recently did I learn that in England the name Maurice is always pronounced *Morris*. (I suppose one ought to be grateful that Morris isn't in turn pronounced *Maurice*.) Many another English name gets its odd, less than logical twist. P. G. Wodehouse's name is pronounced *Woodhouse*. Christopher Isherwood used to pronounce Aldous Huxley's first name *ALL-deuce*. The novelist Anthony Powell can become a bit touchy, or so I have been informed, when Americans do not know that his last name is pronounced *POE-ul*. The star of *I, Claudius* prefers his name to be pronounced Derek *JAY-co-bee*, not *Ja-CO-bee*. I not long ago heard, on television, Clive James, an Australian, pronounce the word *urinals* as *your-EYE-nals*, which sounds a bit like a Swedish toast: In your eye, Nels. But, then, if *Cholmondeley* is pronounced as *Chumli* and *Magdalen* as *Maudlin* and *Caius* as *Keys*, all of which the English do, how is one to get one's bearings? Simple: if one is not English, one never does, quite.

Out for a drive one evening, a young daughter of friends earnestly inquired: "Why doesn't Mr. Epstein speak American?" She was, I take it, registering her mild astonishment at the hodgepodge accent I have apparently acquired over the past forty years since going off to college. What I hear in my own speech are a light New York accent, a slight whininess, and every so often an oddly overpronounced patch, as if I am trying with my voice to supply lots of italics. An acquaintance not long ago told me that my pronunciation of the words *roof* and *root* identify me unmistakably as a middlewesterner, which was a setback. I used to do a respectable imitation of Elmer Fudd, and some days I wonder if I oughtn't to stick to it as my regular way of talking and let it go at that.

Some words I regularly forget how to pronounce, possibly because their exact spelling slips my mind: *incunabula* is one. (Who was it that said that spelling is to pronunciation as reading is to writing?) There are other words that I wish I could say all the time because they are such a pleasure to sound out. *Deliquescent* is such a word. *Excursuses* is a word I would find amusing to say, though I don't think I've ever said it. *Post-exilic* is the only *post-* word that lights my fire, and *Eliotic* seems to me pretty nice, too. I do believe I would enjoy saying *Antiochenes, Diodorus,* or *Cassiodorus of Helicarnassus* but shall probably never have the occasion. A name I do have occasion to say, whose mere utterance gives me pleasure, is Arnaldo Dante Momigliano — a name to which, with another two or three syllables added, one can almost dance.

I once knew a pleasant fellow who pronounced Dostoyevsky's name *Dos-TOR-ev-sky,* but I hadn't the heart to correct him. *Proust* is a name that seems to give people trouble, and many who have not heard it said tend to pronounce it *Prowst.* People seem to have a tough time, too, with *Turgenev* and *Nabokov.* It took me a long while to remember to put the accent on the second syllable: *Tur-GAY-nyef* and *Na-BO-kov. Nietzsche* is another notable elocutionary hurdle. The tendency of the underconfident is to mutter "Nitsey" or "Nitsky" and play on through.

As a schoolteacher, I feel a part of my job is to correct the faulty pronunciations of my students. I do not do so gleefully. Actually, I do not do so at all, at least not directly. I know it would have wounded me when I was young to have been publicly corrected. If, say, the word *assuaged* is pronounced *ass-WAGED* early in the class, I make a note to reuse it later in the hour and give it the full-fathom-five French, *uh-SWAHGED.* I do the same, of course, with other shaky or plain-wrong pronunciations: Evelyn Waugh's first name pronounced as if it were the standard female name (*EH-ve-lyn*), for example, instead of

EVE-lyn. Whether my students pick up on this, I am not at all certain.

Mispronunciation can lead prettily into malapropism. "I want to buy kike," the Russian-born Tatiana Liberman is supposed to have said, when she meant *kite.* A friend reports that he regularly hears the phrase "take it for granite," though I have not heard it myself. Another friend tells me that at his health club he has heard the treadmill machine referred to as the "thread mill." The confusion between *prostate* and *prostrate* generally gets as good a workout as the thread mill. "Strike while the metal is warm," Inspector Poirot says. "All the money's in egg roll," an immigrant woman noted, when reporting that her husband's will was going through probate; that she didn't top it off by saying "going through prostate" is a shame.

I feel nothing but sympathy for those who have to learn English in midlife. The barriers to mastering the language, at any rate in its spoken version, are impossibly high. In English, as Fowler notes, there are six different ways to pronounce *al-* followed by a consonant, and no fewer than nine different ways of pronouncing *-ough:* as in *bough, though, cough, rough, through, ought, hough, lough, borough.* Fowler adds that *hiccough* might be a tenth if it weren't a misspelling.

I have European friends of great brilliance who have become masters of English prose but who, after decades in this country, still struggle with the language as it is mysteriously spoken. I remember a lunch with two friends — one a Romanian mathematician, the other a Czech literary critic — who described their terror (the exact word they used) when they found out they would have to learn English.

What, I ask myself, would I do if forced to survive in Hungary — Hungarian, I am told, being a notably difficult language?

The first thing I would do, I suspect, is cease laughing at a story I was recently told about the Hungarian-born Arthur Koestler playing Scrabble. In this game, Koestler set out five letters that hooked up with three other longish words, all with lots of *q*'s and *x*'s and *z*'s, thus giving him a vast quantity of points. The five letters formed the word *vinch*. As Koestler was happily counting up the points he had scored, an embarrassed silence gripped the three other players, one of whom was his English wife. "Darling," she said with some hesitation, "are you quite certain that this is a word?" "Of course, angel," Koestler is said to have replied. "You know, *vinch*, angel, to shrink from or recoil, as if from a blow."

In *Pnin*, Vladimir Nabokov, who himself spoke English with an international accent and a universal understanding of puns, took on the subject of the nightmare of the foreigner having to negotiate the world in English. In this novel the English word doesn't exist for which the Russian émigré Professor Timofey Pavlich Pnin cannot find a mispronunciation. "If his Russian was music," Nabokov writes, "his English was murder." Larynx, tongue, lips, and soft palate all conspire in poor Pnin to make every word so *diffishool*. *Whiskey and soda*, for Pnin, come out *viscous and sawdust*, *afternoon* as *afternun*, the name *Thayer* as *Fire*, and *catastrophe* as *cat-a-stroph*. Nabokov's is a heart-crushing story that makes one realize how absolutely cut adrift one is from friendship, from society, from reality itself without control over language. I can, as the psychobabblists say, identify; in fact, I "vinch" at the mere thought.

Joseph Conrad, in spoken English, came closer to Professor Pnin than to his creator. Everyone who met the great novelist noted the rough quality of his spoken English; the discrepancy between it and his beautifully written English was too obvious to go without mention. The sculptor Jacob Epstein, who did a bust of Conrad, wrote in his autobiography: "At a few of the sittings Conrad dictated letters to the secretary. His English was strongly foreign with a very guttural accent, so that his secretary frequently failed to get the right word, which made Conrad growl." In his story "Amy Foster," Conrad dealt with the awfulness of being a foreigner, whose language renders him even more a stranger, and with the loneliness and despair that can result. The story is about a castaway whose "quick, fervent utterance positively shocked everybody" and left him like "a man translated into another planet, . . . separated by an immense space from his past and by an immense ignorance from his future." There can be little doubt that the psychological provenance for this story was in Joseph Conrad's own struggles with spoken English.

Like most Americans, I am without any gift for speaking another language. I could, I suppose, hide behind George Bernard Shaw's probably self-justifying remark that anyone who has a lot to say in his own language hasn't got time to master a foreign one. But the truth is that I should be pleased to speak foreign languages for all sorts of reasons, among which is the prospect of hiding out mentally every now and then in another language.

I would have thought that mastering foreign accents would not have posed any great difficulty for me. As a perhaps too indefatigable teller of jokes, I am a pretty fair mimic: I do Englishmen, Australians, Irishmen, East Indians, Germans, Mexicans, Italians, and the Jews in a thousand voices. I have a modest Yiddish vocabulary. I read French, though never without the aid — increasingly more necessary — of a dictionary. I once thought that I was picking up Italian but discovered that I had acquired only enough to get on the wrong train to Milan. Late for my plane, I had to pay an Italian cabdriver eighty dollars to speed out to the Milan airport. On the way we spoke about Frank Sinatra in our equally atrocious French.

Many people learn foreign languages through necessity: émigrés, people from what I think of as lesser-known-language countries (Romania, the former Czechoslovakia, Hungary, etc.). Some people have the sweet gift of easily acquiring speaking knowledge of foreign languages. In Cathleen Schine's novel *Rameau's Niece*, the heroine's husband knows "seven languages, and accepted with only the poorest grace that he could speak just one of them at a time." Just how many polyglots walk the streets is apparently a matter of some dispute. My guess is that there are not all that many such characters around.

John Weightman, the excellent English critic of French writing, thinks that "monolingualism may well be the norm for the human mind." He goes on to report that he has heard "bilingual or trilingual colleagues complain of uncertainty about their personal identity through the conflicting pulls of two or more linguistic atmospheres." If true, this, to people locked in my monolingual condition, is good news comparable to that of learning that the very rich are all desperately unhappy.

I should still someday like to be able to speak Italian, the babbling of whose words gives such musical pleasure. Is it, by the way, the Tower of long-*a* or short-*a* Babel? I must find out for certain right after I learn whether *Hiro-SHE-ma* or *Hir-O-shima* is correct. Then I must go back to check the correct pronunciation of the name of the Russian writer Isaac Babel.

I have sent up the white flag on ever speaking French with ease and confidence. I used to half claim that I could speak French through little demonstrations of false modesty. "Do I speak French?" I would say when asked. *"Je parle français comme une vache espagnole.*" Or I would suggest that, in French, I sound something like this: "Excuse me, boody boy, but maybe for me the time you can tell?" In fact, I don't believe my French sounds quite that good. Certainly, it isn't that fluent.

In his essay "On Speaking French," Max Beerbohm publicly confesses to a fraudulence similar to my own. He, too, would modestly claim his French was wretched, allowing his was "French *pour rire.*" Because of his general impeccability, it was assumed that Max had perfect French, and so at dinner parties he was not infrequently seated next to French guests. He recounts one such occasion when a French woman launched a fusillade of (to him) perfectly incomprehensible French, to which he responded with his usually successful riposte of "*C'est vrai.*" Only later did he learn that the woman was asking him who among the young French novelists the English critics thought important, and she had to admit her surprise at never having heard of this fellow Sévré.

"To be shamed as a talker is bad enough," Max notes; "it is even worse to be shamed as a listener." Although I think I have a decent ear, I, too, don't really hear French very well. The soft stress the French put on their syllables and the tricks that elision plays cause spoken French ultimately to elude me. Max Beerbohm, who rightly says that French is a more elegant written language than Italian, compares spoken Italian to a violin and spoken French to a flute. To most foreign ears, he adds, English has "a rather harsh sound" (a kazoo, perhaps?).

In my car, I have been listening to a tape of the immensely cheering songs of Charles Trenet. I pick up only words (*fenêtre, bonheur, printemps*), sometimes phrases (*que rest-à-t'il, le soleil et la lune, il pleure dans mon coeur*), but, alas, I cannot put an entire lyric together. How I wish I could, so that I could join the old boy in, say, his rousing rendition of "La Mer" while spinning down the Outer Drive, my own *mer,* Lake Michigan, on my right. Sometimes I join him by substituting the title "My Hair" and making up lyrics of my own.

My own mistakes in pronouncing French words that everyone else seems confident about continue to crop up. I have only very recently discovered that the *s* in the name of the extravagantly expensive French shop Hermès is indeed to be pronounced. I remain edgy about attempting those French words or names with lots of vowels: Pouilly-Fuissé, Marie-Laure de Noaille, *gouailleuse.* Odgen Nash wrote a poem about nobody's being able to pronounce the name Saint-Saëns correctly; I wish he had written others about the violinist Eugène Ysaÿe and the composer Ernö von Dohnányi.

Edmund Wilson, a bull in many china shops, is said to have taken himself by the horns and pronounced French with no regard for its silent letters, elisions, or any other of its fundamental rules of pronunciation. This is certainly one method, the Wilson method, of speaking French: just not giving a damn about how you sound. Another is to treat the entire question of French pronunciation as comedy. The novelist Josephine Herbst, friends of hers have told me, always deliberately pronounced the word *milieu* as *ma-LOO,* which I of late have taken to doing, if only to deflate some of the pretentiousness implicit in an English speaker's using the word.

Two recent books by Americans, one a Francophile, the other a recently converted Francophobe, convince me that learning to speak French well is probably a hopeless project and one I should probably cease even fantasizing about. In *French Lessons,* Alice Kaplan recounts an almost lifelong engagement with French. As a girl, she went off to French summer camp in Maine where campers were given *mauvais points* for reverting to English, she attended school in Switzerland, and she later spent long stretches in France. She explains how long it took her to master the pronunciation of the French *r*. When she finally achieved it, with the aid of something called the Capretz Method, it was, evidently, one of the great moments in her life. Catharsis! Eureka! The earth shook.

An academic, a teacher of French language and literature at Duke University, Miss Kaplan also recounts the unending pressure that American teachers of French are under lest they make a mistake — assigning the wrong gender to a noun, say — before their French-born colleagues. "There is invariably trouble," she writes, "when a tyrannical or insensitive native speaker rules over a department where all the assistant professors are Americans, forever on guard against the telling mistake that might cost them a promotion." An important American critic of French literature, whom Miss Kaplan doesn't name, likes to "tell how he was denied tenure at another elite college because of his French *r*, which smelled of New Jersey."

A scholar specializing in Descartes, a middlewesterner, a man with a white beard, Professor Richard Watson, who is thoroughly at ease with French on the page, was invited to give a paper on Descartes in French in France. He knew his spoken French to be wanting and so decided that, before giving his paper, he ought to put himself through a course of instruction in spoken French, which he did, during a sabbatical year, at the Alliance Française in Paris. There this highly intelligent American academic, owing to his inability to get his mouth to form many of the subtler French sounds or his ear to hear the cascades of the language pouring from his indifferent instructors' lips, sadly failed his course.

The experience, as we *américains* say, has left Professor Watson steamed. No doubt a translator into French would make this phrase ". . . has left Professor Watson dry-cleaned." The novelist Louis Begley, going over a French translation of one of his novels, discovered one of his characters waiting at the curb for a large lemonade, and, unable to remember having written this, he returned to his English text where he discovered he had originally written that his character was awaiting "a stretch limo." Seeking vengeance, for him a dish best served hot, Watson attacks French pedagogy, the French people, the snobbery and inconsideration he feels inherent in so much teaching of French. But his real rage is against the French language itself.

In *The Philosopher's Demise,* his book on attempting to learn to speak French, Watson concludes that, while he loves to read French and especially to read French philosophers, he intensely dislikes the sounds of spoken French. The French, he avers, can't even swear properly, *mon Dieu!* He carries on amusingly about the awfulness of the word *l'oiseau:* "It cannot be pronounced without simpering," one cannot say it without making a prissy face, no, it is quite unspeakable. There is something amusing about watching a man rail against an entire language — at least at its spoken version — that is, if you have a taste for watching a grown man fighting a Bozo doll that keeps popping back up at him.

Enjoying Richard Watson's scorched-earth attack on the French language has not cured me of my longing to be impeccably correct, beautifully precise, absolutely fluent in French. Even though French no longer dominates diplomacy, commerce, or anything else, except perhaps international snobbery, I am still hostage to the notion that an educated person ought to be able to speak the language with ease. Hostage, however, I shall remain. Perhaps in the next life I shall speak perfect French; then, too, many say that French is likely to be the official language of hell. A rumor has it that, for their snobbery about their own language, a number of neighborhoods in hell have been set aside especially for the French, where they will be allowed to hear only Americans confidently mispronouncing their language.

In this life, meanwhile, there remains the continuing work of mispronouncing English, a nearly full-time job in itself. Take the often awkward matter of names. Correct pronunciation of so many names simply cannot be known until one hears them pronounced by someone else. For nearly everyone whose name ends in *stein*, for example, there is the great *steen* or *styne* problem. The origin of the difficulty is the anti-German feeling in the United States during World War I that caused many people with *stein* in their names to give it the less-Germanic-sounding pronunciation *steen*. In later years, Leonard Bernstein, going the other way, insisted on a *styne* ending for his own name.

Some mispronunciations are charming. Winston Churchill pronounced *Nazi* as if it rhymed with *snazzy*, and, as far as I am concerned, he was richly entitled to do so, having defeated the bastards. Sam Weller, in *Pickwick Papers,* pronounces all his *w* words with a *v* sound, which gives him, a charming man to begin with, added charm. Yet certain simple mispronunciations set my teeth, as Professor Pnin might say, on ledge. I used to teach J. S. Mill's *On Liberty,* and inevitably some students would pronounce Mill's name *Mills.* Mill is a simple enough name — as well as a famous one — and they ought to get it right, damn it. I came to believe dogmatically that anyone who mispronounced Mill's name had no hope of ever understanding him. I'm afraid that I still believe that.

Possibly the J. S. Mill screwups are connected with a propensity I have noticed on the part of people to botch simple four-letter names. In the army, two of my friends were Dick Delp (rhymes with *yelp*) and John Fike (rhymes with *Mike*). Everyone seemed to want to call Delp "Delph," "Delt," or "Dorph"; he was lucky, I suppose, that the slang word *dork* had not yet come into being. Had they the foresight, his parents probably should have changed the family name to Delphi. As for Fike, everyone called him either "Fink" or "Fikey"; no one, so far as I know, ever called him "Fichte," but then the sergeants I came across in Missouri, Arkansas, and Texas tended to be notably weak in German philosophy.

English pronunciation seems to be especially difficult for Germans. I read the other day that Thomas Mann, as intellectually sophisticated as he was, used to pronounce *movies* as *moovings*. The German professor sputtering his way through English was a stock bit for Sid Caesar and other comics. It had its source in reality. I once sat in a meeting next to the Austrian-born conductor and opera director Kurt Herbert Adler, as Viennese a gent as one can imagine, who whispered something to me of which I could make out only what I thought was the word *lozenges*. As it happened, I had a package of Life Savers in my pocket and promptly offered him one. "No, no, no," he protested. "I zed Los Ang-elees."

My using that "zed" reminds me that I don't much care for fiction that makes fun of regional or foreign accents by using phonetic spellings. Only Mark Twain, Stephen Crane, Finley Peter Dunne, Ring Lardner, and Rudyard Kipling seem to get away with it — but even their work doesn't always avoid giving the sheer irritation that deciphering phonetic spelling exacts. On the other hand, the real thing, actual unconventional speech in real life, served up in unreceived pronunciation, is almost always a delight. I enjoy regional accents, affected pronunciation, and almost all speech that comes, so to say, with a twist.

I also enjoy people who toss an extra syllable or two into their pronunciation. Kenneth Tynan, in his days as a drama reviewer, remarked of the performance of Donald Wolfit in a Shakespeare play that it was worth seeing "if only to hear Mr. Wolfit giving the hapless word 'Nature' its full eight or nine syllables." Stendhal is said to have pronounced *logique* with three syllables. I have heard certain Reform rabbis give the word *Israel* what seemed like twelve or thirteen syllables. Goldsworthy Lowes Dickinson said that he had heard that the philosopher C. E. M. Joad had discovered God and imagined he pronounced His name with a soft *g* and a long *o*.

Owing possibly to television, regional accents may be slowly disappearing. I have students from southern states who speak without clearly discernible southern accents. New York accents — "I've an idear. Why don't we get a vodker?" — seem on the wane. Mary Cantwell, in a memoir, refers to a Connecticut accent entailing a strangling of vowels that she calls "Locust Valley Lockjaw," and she distinguishes it from the West Hartford accent; from her days working on women's fashion magazines, she also mentions café-society snarls and "well-syllabled women." I imagine those women as in the room they come and go, talking of Michelangelo, in T. S. Eliot's poem, as extremely well syllabled.

In my view, you can't cut these things too fine. The more accents, oddities, goofinesses, the better. I believe I can distinguish a North from a South Carolina accent. A Boston Irish accent seems to me a fine thing. I am also partial to Maine accents. The old Chicago working-class accent — *dese, dem,* and *dose* for *these, them,* and *those* — is less in evidence than formerly. No one can say that it ever hurt anyone's career, at least not in Chicago politics. It was the accent of the late Mayor Daley, and it still creeps into the speech of his son, the current Mayor Daley. One of the things that make California less interesting is that it has produced no distinctive language, unless you count psychobabble.

The sheer delight of pronunciation in and for itself ought not to be overlooked. Splendid pronunciation, as Kenneth Tynan once noted, "demonstrates command: the ability to make words perform for you, skip, leap and gyrate, or, in Max Beerbohm's phrase, 'tread in their presence, like kings, gravely.'" As a drama critic, Tynan was attentive to pronunciation. He once criticized Peggy Ashcroft, performing the part of a Chinese woman in the Brecht play *The Good Woman of Setzuan*, for her "telltale Kensington vowels." He found another actor, Clive Brook, able to suggest "centuries of decadence behind every syllable he utters." He praised the technical versatility of Danny Kaye's voice, noting that "fastidiousness gleams blindingly in his sheer power of pronouncing." Hermione Gingold, "the best female impersonator of our time," had a voice that "is a delectable plummy rasp, emerging from her as from a cement mixer." He loved Maurice Chevalier, not least for the delicious way he mangled English: a love affair, in the French singer's version, was "churst worn of thoz krezzy theengs."

Perhaps Kenneth Tynan admired elocutionary achievement to the extent he did because he was himself, at least early in life, a horrendous stutterer. A journalist named Alan Brien once wrote about Tynan's own speech that "the stutter starts as a nervous spasm in the solar plexus and leaps to jaw muscles . . . then he will make four or five snapping sounds like a man taking quick bites from an apple and produces a long balanced sentence in which pun cannons into pun in a verbal break at billiards." That is very good — perhaps too good. But it does remind one of how serious would be the deprivation of the pleasures of easy pronunciation.

For a piece of journalism, I once attempted to interview a six-foot eight-inch forward for the Chicago Bulls named Bob Love, who stuttered so badly that a true interview wasn't really possible. Bob Love couldn't communicate; instead he could make the most delicate, dead-on jump shots I have ever seen. All poor Ken Tynan could do was write some of the most consistently interesting prose of his time. Compensation, you might say, sometimes has its compensations.

The more one thinks about it, the more pronunciation itself seems "churst worn of thoz krezzy theengs." Our way of pronouncing is in good part set by our environment: by family, region, friends, education. Yet much room exists to remake ourselves in the way we wish to seem by remaking the way we pronounce words. To sound tough, refined, elegant, confident, yes, even natural — "People don't understand," Ravel once complained, "I am naturally artificial" — these are only a few of the multitude of choices pronunciation makes available.

Which brings me to what I have been told was Ira Gershwin's favorite story. It has to do with a young woman trying out for a Gershwin musical. On the audition stage she announces that she would like to sing a song from a Gershwin musical and goes promptly into "Let's Call the Whole Thing Off." In singing "You say either, I say either, you say neither, I say neither," she pronounces all the *either*s, the *neither*s, the *tomato*es, the *potato*es exactly the same. Presently, the casting director calls out: "That will do. Thank you Miss Le-VEEN, thank you very much. We'll be in touch with you, Miss Le-VEEN." Gathering up her music, she looks out into the seats. "Oh, by the way," she says, "the name is pronounced Le-VINE."

A Real Page-Turner

*. . . be admonished: of making many books there is
no end; and much study is a weariness of the flesh.*

— ECCLESIASTES, 12:12

I N W H A T I S S A I D to be the shortest book review on record,
Ambrose Bierce once wrote: "The covers of this book are
too far apart." I have not been able to discover the title
of the book that occasioned this model of concise criticism,
though I myself have read books of fewer than two hundred
pages to which the same criticism applies. Actually, had they
been between covers, I have known reviews, office memos,
sonnets, notes to milkmen to which it would also apply. Bierce,
it turns out, may not have been the perfect author for that
review. Near the end of his life, he allowed a friend named
Walter Neale to persuade him to bring out twelve bloated volumes of *The Collected Writings of Ambrose Bierce*. Talk about
covers being too far apart!

Lengthy books are not everyone's notion of a good time.
They become less so, I fear, as one grows older and hears the
clock ticking all too obstreperously in the background. Still, if
one is committed to the reading life, if one has decided to think
of oneself as a cultivated person, then there are certain lengthy

books that one ought to have read. Notable among these multivolume works are Proust's *Remembrance of Things Past*, Gibbon's *Decline and Fall of the Roman Empire*, *The Memoirs of the Duc
de Saint-Simon*, Macaulay's *History of England*, Frazier's *Golden
Bough* . . . But I had better stop here, for I see that, of the five
works I have mentioned, the latter two I have failed to read, at
least in their entirety.

The Macaulay is a depressing case in point. I acquired a
five-volume set of *The History of England* in 1962 in a used-book
shop on Fourth Avenue in New York. I cannot recall the price,
but my guess is that it was less than fifteen dollars. When, not
long afterward, I left New York, having sold my small library to
save the expense of transporting it, this set of Macaulay was
among the twenty or so books I chose not to sell. I later supple-
mented it with the two-volume *Life and Letters of Lord Macaulay*
by Macaulay's nephew G. Otto Trevelyan. The seven volumes
have since lived with me in two houses and five different apartments. I made one mad rush at reading *The History of England* —
and brilliant stuff it seemed, too — but I was put off by the press
of other work before completing even the first volume and
never returned to it. Only the other day, in an activity I don't
generally go in for called facing reality, I sent the five volumes
off to a younger friend. Let them, I decided, sit in his house
unread for thirty or more years. Having them out of my own
apartment, at least I won't, as Ozymandias says in rather a
different context, have to "look on [these] works . . . and despair."

About a shortage of despair on this count I need never worry,
for other multivolume works in my possession that have for
years gone unread pop up all over the joint. Sharing the intimacy of my bedroom, there is H. A. Taine's *History of English
Literature* in four volumes, which I purchased many moons ago

because I read that Taine was an important influence on Edmund Wilson. He has exerted no influence whatsoever on me, since I have never cracked its covers (a previous owner cut the pages). Five small, green and blue volumes of *Makers and Finders,* Van Wyck Brooks's history of American literature, sit in the upper corner of a bookcase that is itself in the corner of my living room. I have read in these volumes from time to time, but the books' cleanliness shows their obvious disuse over the decades. I am missing three of the six volumes of Elie Halévy's *History of the English People in the Nineteenth Century,* which I must make a mental note to begin reading once I acquire those three missing vols, though not a moment before. I own a boxed, three-volume set of *The Muqaddimah* of Ibn Khaldun (whom A. J. Liebling used to quote to such amusing effect), which, as the punch line from an off-color joke I heard more than forty years ago had it, "ain't even been out of the box yet."

In a hallway bookcase sit sixteen volumes of *The Works of William James,* like a New England virgin, which is to say, practically untouched; Jane Austen's six slender novels fill out the rest of the space on that particular shelf; those at least have been read. In the same bookcase is the six-volume George Birkbeck Hill edition of Boswell's *Life of Johnson,* which I really do hope to read through one more time before my shot clock is used up. About the thirteen-volume *Cambridge Modern History,* squatting on the lower shelf of this bookcase, let us not speak.

I am talking here about tomes. A tome is, technically, a volume forming part of a larger work, or a large or scholarly book. I myself think of a tome purely in terms of heft, and a book doesn't have to be scholarly to qualify. Tome-dom sets in, in my opinion, somewhere around 550 pages. The first tome I can remember reading is James Jones's best-seller *From Here to Eternity* (1951), which I devoured in high school in its closely printed 860 paperback pages. I read *From Here to Eternity* straight through, at no point slowed by a critical sense, an interest in style, or a concern about what I (not yet thinking myself a writer) could steal from it for my own purposes. Pure pleasure, it was the literary equivalent of wolfing down a box of chocolates, all with nougat centers. When it was over, I was a bit sated, a bit sad, but otherwise a perfectly satisfied customer.

The first serious tome I read was John Dos Passos's trilogy *U.S.A.* The three novels comprising that work run to 414, 473, and 561 pages, respectively, and I was so swept away by them that I shouldn't have minded a fourth. I read the trilogy in its Modern Library Giant edition, with rather proletarianized drawings by Reginald Marsh. Even now I can remember many of the details surrounding my reading of that book. I was eighteen; it was a hot summer; I took it to a nearby park called Indian Boundary, and day after day, sitting on the grass, I read it. This was the first book that I felt, even as I was reading it, had a powerful influence on me. It inflamed me with the idea of social justice; it formed and set my political viewpoint for the next twenty years of my life.

The odd thing about this, I suppose, is that by the time I read it, John Dos Passos's politics had radically changed. What hadn't changed was his decency as a human being. At thirty-three, I had the notion of writing Dos Passos's biography. I sent him some things I had published and asked if he would be willing to cooperate with me in writing his biography. He wrote back, working on an obviously aged typewriter, saying that he wouldn't mind my writing such a book, so long as I agreed to "put the liberal ideology in mothballs," promised never again to use the word "explicate," and understood that he wouldn't have all that much time to give me since he had a lot of work to get done while he still retained "a few of his marbles."

I took a publisher's advance for the book. Dos Passos and I exchanged a few more letters, and then, not long thereafter, he died. I am glad I never wrote the book. The fashion for great thick biographies had begun not long before with Mark Schorer's life of Sinclair Lewis, and my guess is that I probably would have turned out a book of similar tonnage, for Dos Passos had a long and full life. When I began to plan my Dos Passos biography, I established a folder for each year of my subject's life; there were seventy-four of them. The world is no worse off for my not having written such a book; and so, probably, is the reputation of John Dos Passos. I returned the publisher's advance.

Big biographies have become a problem for me, whose belief in the finitude of time becomes ever more pressing. Theoretically, one could write a biography of a man or woman that is quite as long as his or her life — and maybe a bit longer, since there is the aftermath to be dealt with. Some lives really do seem to support multi-volume effort. When I read Jacques Barzun's elegantly lucid two-volume *Berlioz*, I did not feel it in the least too lengthy. I had no complaints, either, about Leon Edel's full-fathom five vols on Henry James, and later I even read the excellent single-volume abridgment of that work, but then I am a sucker for Henry James.

More recently, however, I found I could not get through Brian Boyd's two-volume biography of Vladimir Nabokov, though it is clearly written and I have genuine curiosity about Nabokov's life. I have read only one of the four thus-far-published volumes of Joseph Frank's biography of Dostoyevsky; it is superior stuff, and I tell myself that I should like to read through the whole thing but wonder if I ever really shall. I have already decided to take a pass on David McCullough's 1,117-page biography of Harry Truman. As for Robert Caro's multivolume, still-in-the-works biography of Lyndon Johnson, I tap my knuckles on the table and mutter, as at the poker table, "By me."

Another part of my difficulty with long biographies is that I have come to have genuine doubts about biographical truth. I am not sure I believe that any outsider can really get inside the life of another person, at least in a persuasive way. I know I carry around too many secrets of my own for anyone to have a chance to discover them, let alone their crucial pattern, which I myself haven't quite figured out. As for autobiography, I continue to read and be amused by it, but increasingly for its lies, evasions, and elaborate self-duplicities.

In biography, longer does not necessarily mean more penetrating. Recently in the *Times Literary Supplement* the reviewer of an 874-page biography of the economist Alfred Marshall, after citing John Maynard Keynes's brilliant essay on Marshall, reports: "What Keynes says in seventy pages, Professor Groenewegen says in 700. It has taken him ten years to write. It is full of interesting detail, exhaustive in its research and exhausting to read, sensible and sensitive in its judgments. It could have been better done, but having been done is unlikely to be superseded." In other words, it seems to me, the reviewer is all but saying that they should have saved the trees.

One of the services of criticism is to tell a normally busy person what not to read. I recall, roughly three decades ago, Edmund Wilson performing that important service for me when he put down, with a thump, Carl Sandburg's more than 4,500-page, six-volume biography of Abraham Lincoln. Wilson not only found it coarse, sentimental, and vulgar, but added that "there are moments when one is tempted to feel that the cruelest thing that has happened to Lincoln since he was shot by Booth has been to fall into the hands of Carl Sandburg." Before reading Wilson, I felt a slightly guilty tug whenever I saw one or more of Sandburg's volumes in someone's house or in a used-book store. Not anymore. What a gift Wilson bestowed upon me — no fewer, by my rough calculations, than three months of my reading life.

I no longer require Wilson's, or anyone else's, authoritative judgments in such matters. In recent months, a more than 1,200-page biography of James Thurber has been published, as has the first of two large volumes devoted to Tennessee Williams. More than 1,200 pages for Thurber, two volumes for Tennessee Williams? Where does that leave biographers of Beethoven, Rembrandt, and Dickens? It leaves me saying, "Thank you very much all the same." Shorter, in biography, may be better, forcing the biographer into greater efforts at finding the essence of his subject.

Sorry to mention all these page totals, but I am someone who cannot begin any book without first checking the number of its final page. I know people who never do this, who just read blithely away, heedless of how far they have to travel, and I envy them. I seem to be one of those people who are on some unwritten schedule. To go where and to do what has never been quite clear. Perhaps I want to know the number of pages in the book I am reading so that I shall have some idea of when I can begin the next book that I want to read.

Many of the tome-ish books of my youth were available, like *U.S.A.*, in Modern Library Giants. These books were as wonderfully inexpensive — my memory has them costing $2.45 — and conveniently available as they were ugly and difficult, because of their small, cramped print, to read. Sometimes they included a writer's entire oeuvre — as in the case of Lewis Carroll or Charles Lamb — and sometimes they were devoted to a single great book. I read *Moby-Dick* and *Anna Karenina* in Modern Library Giants. The very name "Giant" gave a book imprimatur and gravity. In those days, many still-living writers were in the Modern Library — Faulkner, Malraux, Gide — but to have one's works buried in the box of a Modern Library Giant you had to be dead: a tomb for a tome. Being a Modern Library Giant seemed to me easily worth the price of death.

Apart from *Anna Karenina,* most of the Russian novels I read were in Penguin editions. This was when Penguins still had elegant plain covers, with differently colored borders for the different national literatures: in my memory, green for French, orange for English, red for Russian, purple for Latin. All ample works of Russian fiction — those of Gogol and Chekhov excepted — seemed tome-ish, but who cared? Henry James called these books "baggy monsters" — as opposed, one gathers, to his own well-tailored monsters — yet all I remember, as I worked my way through Dostoyevsky and Tolstoy, was feeling an immense affinity for a world I would never know but to which I felt marvelously drawn. To this day, whisper the words *troika, steppe,* or *Nevsky Prospect* in my ear and I will follow you anywhere.

I hope to have yet one more go-round with the great Russian novels. My heart lit up some years ago when the late Alexander Gerschenkron, the economic historian at Harvard, noted that he had read *War and Peace* fully fifteen times, and on no occasion did he "fail to discover something new in this inexhaustible store of observations, insights, ideas, and images that the previous readings have failed to reveal. . . . A book like this is rereadable *senz' altro,* and at least twice I began rereading *War and Peace* at once, starting again after having read the last page." I have read *War and Peace* only once; but if someone told me that I wouldn't be able to read it again, I should be profoundly sad.

Just before his death, my friend Erich Heller went into the hospital with a volume from Thomas Mann's tetralogy, *Joseph* and His Brothers, a work I shouldn't have been surprised to learn he may have read ten or fifteen times. My English one-volume edition runs to 1,207 pages. It is the only novel of Thomas Mann's I haven't read, and it occurs to me that I'd better get around to doing so. I also haven't read Ford Madox Ford's Parade's End, a work of 836 pages, slender for a tetralogy. I have read all twelve books of Anthony Powell's sequence of novels, A Dance to the Music of Time, and I read them at a more leisurely pace than I can recollect reading any other novels. Perhaps this was owing to the lack of any urgency in the plots of the books. So amusing were Powell's narrator's generalizations and the rich comedy of his characters that one scarcely cares what happens to any of them, so long as they return from time to time, which, decent chaps, they generally do.

I own the three volumes of Solzhenitsyn's Gulag Archipelago, but I've read — and was quite blown away by — only the first. Magnificent as the first volume is, I suspect that I may never return to read the other two because of my increased nervousness about reading large quantities on the subject of human cruelty. In the early 1960s, I did a lot of reading about the Holocaust, and I now shy away from this subject, too, telling myself that the enormity of it is more than my mind can accommodate. I have read somewhere that people who immerse themselves in the literature about the Holocaust emerge prone to suicide, which seems perfectly believable to me.

I devoted a good part of this past summer to reading a work of triple-tome weight, Robert Musil's The Man Without Qualities, which has long had the status of an unfinished classic. Brilliant though long stretches of it are, I finally found it more unfinished — and hence disappointing — than classic. But perhaps, à la Dr. Strangelove, I ought to learn to stop worrying and enjoy the longueurs, at least if I plan to continue reading books of such girth (*The Man Without Qualities* is nearly 1,800 pages in two volumes). I read the first two volumes of Naguib Mahfouz's Cairo trilogy but have let so much time elapse that I have all but forgotten the characters, who, I trust, reappear in the final volume. Why didn't I read the third volume straightaway? I can't recall, but, clearly, as a once popular song has it, it's too late baby now, it's too late.

I have read only one of the novels — *The Masters* — in C. P. Snow's *Strangers and Brothers* sequence, and though I admired it at the time, I feel no need to read the others. I have never read a word of *The Forsyte Saga* and, in a way I cannot quite explain, feel I am missing something by not having done so. I have not read all the novels that comprise Balzac's *Comédie humaine,* and only a few of the novels in Zola's *Les Rougon-Macquart* series. I have read *Remembrance of Things Past* twice, in two different English translations, and would like to spin through this book just once more.

Of all the various gaps in my reading of thickish books, the largest, easily, is the Bible. I have of course read *in* the Bible, but I have never read *through* the Bible. On a few occasions, I have made a charge at it; once I fell back when they began the begats. Other times I have read separate books — Genesis, Exodus, Psalms — and the Gospels. I have discovered that the Bible is not easy to read if one doesn't go at it, so to say, religiously. I was once asked if I wished to contribute to a book on the Old Testament in which various writers were asked to write on their favorite biblical book. The fee was $1,500. I declined. Had there been a book of Pharisees, I might have accepted.

This lacuna in my reading is serious even apart from the saving of my blasted soul. As a literary man, I should be sufficiently aware of the Bible, Old Testament and New, to be able to pick up many of the allusions with which the English and

American literatures of previous centuries are rife. I take cold comfort here from the fact that most people I have asked — literary men and women chief among them — have also admitted to not having read the Bible straight through.

Now that I have passed sixty, it occurs to me that I ought to read those key books I haven't read, re-read those I read badly because I was too young, and re-read again those books that I cannot bear the thought of having read for the last time. Inevitably, these tend to be preponderantly thick books. I would like another shot at *Moby-Dick*. Maybe I ought to re-read *Tom Jones,* which, on my last reading, at twenty, I remember lapping up with sheer pleasure. I'd like another go at certain novels by Dickens. I've not read anywhere near enough Trollope. Alexander Herzen's *My Past and Thoughts* is a book I read too quickly the first time around, having agreed to write for a newspaper 1,500 words about its perhaps three quarters of a million. Another binge of Balzac is a treat I feel I owe myself. (This one's for you, little guy.) *Don Quixote* is a stout volume I wish to revisit — Rosinante, to the road again! Alas, I remember few of its details, only a permanent blur of delight.

At the University of Chicago in my day, English majors were presented with a junior- and senior-year reading list of important books — not offered in regular courses — on which they were tested. The list, as I remember it, was a brilliant compilation of precisely those books — tomes, a vast number of them — that, if one was normally lazy, one would most certainly avoid reading: Samuel Richardson, Hobbes's *Leviathan,* lots of John Locke, *Paradise Regained* (of *Paradise Lost* Samuel Johnson rightly said that no one ever wished it longer; of *Paradise Regained,* he might have added that no one ever wished it existed). A friend recalls during this period finding me in my pajamas, unshaven, books all over my bed, a little uncertain about what time of day it was or what country I was in. I recall staggering my way through this load, reading every book on the list but drawing a thick line at *The Faerie Queene*. I couldn't read the bloody *Faerie Queene*. I decided to bet against the test's including any questions about Spenser's horrendously long (as it seemed to me then) poem — and, hallelujah! I won. I haven't read it yet. Moreover, I have no intention of reading it. You don't suppose, do you, that it's on Saint Peter's list?

I re-read Montaigne's *Essays* a few years ago, in M. A. Screech's new translation, and I can't imagine not peeking back into it from time to time, though I'll probably never read it straight through again. I read Montaigne chiefly in the early morning hours, between five and six-thirty, generally with my cat on my lap, taking notes on pertinent passages, of which there are a plethora. Fat books present physical problems. They are not easily manipulated. One hesitates to travel with them, because they weigh one down and cause one's luggage to bulge. Nor does it seem appropriate to carry them out on an errand — to the bank or post office, for example — where one might, while standing in line, have a chance to read a page or two, because they make one seem too much the bookworm. Better, for this purpose, to tote one of the six-by-four-inch Oxford World Classics volumes, though the fear here is that these little dark blue books might make people think one is studying for the ministry.

I admire people who have had the stamina and patience to write lengthy books — admire them, that is, without much wishing to emulate them. Apart from various collections of essays, literary criticisms, and stories, I have written only two full-length books — one of 318 pages, the other of 312. In the middle of writing a long book, I find myself generally at sea, confused about direction; I put a fresh piece of paper in the typewriter and type some number like 273 at its top, certain that it's too late to turn back. At the end of writing a long book, my paramount emotion has been a combination of relief and regret, brought on by the feeling that I now know how the book *ought* to have been written and I would do so if only there were time to write it all over again, but there isn't.

Sitzfleisch is required not only to write but to read thick books. Historically, this capacity may be undergoing change. Sainte-Beuve, as a young man, read the *Nouvelle Héloïse* in a day. In *The Razor's Edge*, Somerset Maugham has his protagonist, sitting in an English club, not move out of his chair until, again in the course of a single day, he had read through William James's *Principles of Psychology*. This shows powerful concentration, *sitzfleisch,* the real thing. A friend who teaches Russian novels to undergraduates tells me that, in the current day, one cannot expect students to read more than two hundred pages a week for each of the four courses they are taking. The national attention span, it may well be, has diminished.

In more recent times, I have heard it said that the formula for a certain kind of booming bestseller includes writing it to a length that allows readers to get through it in a single sitting. *Jaws, Love Story, The Bridges of Madison County* are a few titles that seem to bear this out. Those particular books are not much to my taste, but the notion of a slender book is increasingly becoming so, even though I am almost never able to read anything in a single sitting. I prefer the weight in my hand of a book of learned yet elegant lectures published by, say, the Clarendon Press, or a volume of verse designed by Harry Ford at Knopf. *Watermark,* Joseph Brodsky's little book on Venice, approximates my ideal; most of Max Beerbohm's books realize it.

I have of late been reading a charming book titled *Why I Have Not Written Any of My Books* by Marcel Bénabou, which is its author's explanation for his impressive infecundity over the years; it is a book of the quite perfect length of III pages. I wonder if I shouldn't put in a call to Random House to see if there is any interest in a new series of books, over which I would serve as general editor, to be called Modern Library Pygmies.

And yet, despite this new penchant for brief books, I find that the writers I most love have been hugely productive. My pantheon of writers, all of whom combine exceptional energy with exceptional talent, includes Samuel Johnson, Edward Gibbon, Marcel Proust, and Henry James. What unites them is that all were beings organized for literature. (I also have a genuine weakness for Winston Churchill, though I would rather read about him than actually read him; and I fully expect to leave the planet without ever having stuck my nose into the four volumes of his *History of the English-Speaking Peoples* or the six volumes of *The Second World War.*) None of these men exactly worked in miniature, and two of them, Gibbon and Proust, devoted the major intellectual and artistic efforts of their careers to single if voluminous works. Not only do I never tire of reading these men, but everything about them interests me. Their writing and their lives give me an enhanced sense of human possibility.

As the literary equivalent of a bulimic, without the throwing-up part, I have lately been bingeing myself on Gibbon, reading him and reading about him; and, I must report, the older I get, the more my admiration for the little fat boy grows. I say little fat boy because I can never think of Gibbon apart from his physique — five feet tall and more than two hundred pounds. In a silhouette of him cut by a contemporary named Mrs. Brown, he has a body resembling nothing so much as a figurine: an enameled little man with an enameled prose style. "Fat and ill-constructed," wrote Fanny Burney, "Mr. Gibbon has cheeks of such prodigious chubbiness that they envelop his nose so completely as to render it in profile almost invisible." Now there is a detail that sets a face, permanently, in concrete.

Reading Edward Gibbon, one feels one is looking on as an immensely bright and imaginative boy is playing the world's most astonishing game of toy soldiers, only he is using real soldiers, also emperors, popes, barbarians, eunuchs, sultans, emirs, and other key pieces that he moves around the board more brilliantly than anyone had ever done before or has done since. I also think of Gibbon as one of a very small number of human beings who seem to have accomplished in life exactly what they set out to do. Macaulay, who is said to have wished his history to have a place on the bed table of every educated woman in England, which it soon did, is another. Gibbon, whose book "was on every table and almost every toilette," topped Macaulay in earning the praise of David Hume, which he, Gibbon, claimed "overpaid the labour of ten years."

There is something invigorating about reading *The Decline and Fall of the Roman Empire* — invigorating and inspiring — something that makes you believe, while you are reading it, that the panorama of life, in all its complication, has been mastered, at least intellectually. I am far from alone in feeling this. Winston Churchill, Lord Moran reports in his diaries, also felt it: "And when, as a subaltern in India, he began to read Gibbon, already he knew what he wanted to do in life" — which was to become a great orator and handler of words.

"Another damned thick, square book — always scribble, scribble, scribble! — eh, Mr. Gibbon?" said the Duke of Gloucester when, in 1781, the second two volumes of *The Decline and Fall* appeared. But a more definitive judgment has been that of Walter Bagehot, who wrote that "there is no more solid book in the world than Gibbon's history," adding that "if the Roman empire *had* written about itself, this was how it would have done so."

Edward Gibbon was what today we might call, in the poverty of our language, a "control freak." I should say that no one had a keener sense of his own limitations or demonstrated how impressively those could be stretched. "My unfitness to bodily exercise reconciled me to a sedentary life," Gibbon writes in *Memoirs of My Life*. Of his own finances, he notes: "I am persuaded that had I been more indigent or more wealthy, I should not have possessed the leisure or the perseverance to prepare and execute my voluminous history." Later in his memoirs, he notes, accurately, that "few works of merit and importance have been executed either in a garret or a palace," and, besides, he himself had money "sufficient to support the rank of a gentleman, and to satisfy the desires of a philosopher." Even his incomparable prose style was formed by habits of control: "It has always been my practice to cast a long paragraph in a single mould, to try it by my ear, to deposit it in my memory, but to suspend the action of the pen till I had given the last polish to my work."

Gibbon knew, too, that his somewhat detached and mannered personal style was not to everyone's taste. Boswell detested him. Horace Walpole, while praising him to his face, mocked him behind his back. "I had not," Gibbon noted, "been endowed by art or nature with those happy gifts of confidence and address which unlock every door and every bosom." George Colman, who met both Samuel Johnson and Gibbon on the same memorable evening, when he was only fourteen, later remembered that "Johnson's style was grand, and Gibbon's elegant. . . . Johnson marched to kettledrums and trumpets; Gibbon moved to flutes and haut-boys."

The interior Gibbon was of course much more interesting

than the exterior. What a plentifully vivid imagination he must have had, this man who could truthfully say "that I was never less alone than when by myself." He was greatly aided in his ambition by knowing early in life that he "aspired to the character of a historian," the only question being a historian of what. He considered writing a history of the liberty of the Swiss; he considered writing the history of the Republic of Florence under the Medicis — what a book that would have been! It was on October 15, 1764, in Rome, "amidst the ruins of the Capitol while the barefoot fryars [of the Franciscan Order] were singing Vespers in the temple of Jupiter, that the idea of writing the decline and fall of the city first started to my mind." Although it would take him nearly eight and a half years before he got down to the actual composition — a work that, when it was done, would comprise more than a million and a half words and eighteen thousand footnotes — the rest, it has perhaps never been more precisely said, is history.

Gibbon apparently talked with no other scholar when writing his great history. Neither did he leave disciples or found a school. He was intellectually isolated, spiritually alone, *sui generis.* One of nature's bachelors — as are most men given to producing vast, multi-volume books — he withdrew from his one chance at marriage (to Suzanne Curchod, the future mother of Madame de Staël) when his father opposed the match: "I sighed as a lover," he notes in his memoirs, "I obeyed as a son." Yet he seems not to have felt anything like loneliness or regret and near the end of his days could remark, "When I contemplate the common lot of mortality, I must acknowledge that I have drawn a high prize in life's lottery."

But the prize, for those of us who have an unending taste for his polished periods, is ours. I find reading Gibbon has a calming effect on me. Under the spell of the confident cadence of his prose, I thrill to his lovely, lilting ironic generalizations. Superior athlete in prose that he was, Gibbon had every rhetorical move: startling phrasings, fine formulations, delicious rhythms, and, most pleasurable of all, flat-out subtle good sense: "But the power of instruction is seldom of much efficacy," he writes, apropos of Marcus Aurelius's attempt to educate his son Commodus, "except in those happy dispositions where it is almost superfluous."

Unsurpassed in historical writing are Gibbon's wonderfully economical accounts of the characters of the Roman emperors, from the Antonines — "possibly the only period in history in which the happiness of a great people was the sole object of government" — to Caracalla — the "common enemy of mankind" whose "life disgraced human nature" — with splendid sidebars for such as Gordianus's son, whose "twenty-two acknowledged concubines, and a library of sixty-two thousand volumes, attested the variety of his inclinations; and from the productions which he left behind him, it appears that the former as well as the latter were designed for use rather than for ostentation." Gibbon knew early in his history of the Roman Empire that, for a writer of his temperament — ironic, cool, detached — he was sitting on a mother lode: "The annals of the emperors," he wrote in his third chapter, "exhibit a strong and various picture of human nature, which we should vainly seek among the mixed and doubtful characters of modern history."

Gibbon thought himself the historian of Rome in her decline, but he is quite as justly thought to be among the best students of human nature, that most elusive of subjects. He was, it oughtn't to surprise anyone to learn, a persistent reader of novels. It is a shame that he was born too early to read the novels of James or Proust. James read Gibbon and quotes him in one of his stories; whether Proust read him, I do not know. I have begun *The Decline and Fall* again; it is only my second time through. As I said, I'd like to read through Proust once more. Stop me before I begin *The Golden Bough,* though not if I begin (again) *The Golden Bowl.* Borges says somewhere that it is "tiresome and laborious folly . . . to write lengthy tomes, to expound in five hundred pages on an idea that one could easily propound orally in a few minutes. Better is pretending that the books exist already and offering a summary or commentary." Quite so — but only if you happen to be Borges.

The rest of us have no choice but just to keep on reading. Behind all this reading and re-reading, especially later in life, is the notion that we are smarter now, better able to plumb the depths and discover the secrets buried in wise books, better able to take them to heart and make superior use of them. I at any rate continue to operate under this no doubt illusory assumption. No one has ever said about anything I have written that it is, in the cant phrase of the day, a real page-turner, but in the end a real page-turner may be the best description of me yet.

Ticked to the Min

TICKED TO THE MAX, kids say, or at least used to say, a nice shorthand phrase meaning mad as hell, angry to the highest power, gorge risen to its utmost height. I haven't myself been ticked to the max in many years — I mean really ticked, plate-throwing, fist-through-the-window, strangle-the-bulldog ticked. A single observation has helped to keep my anger down. It is that one must never be enraged when people one takes for creeps act like creeps. In these, my sunset — make that my dusk — years, I have become a calm, gentle fellow, a relative pussycat, almost comatose. Save the ticking, hold the max.

What I do find, however, is that I am more and more ticked to the min. Small things irritate me: lots of them. Minor events bug me. The other night, at Orchestra Hall in Chicago, I was greatly enjoying myself while listening to an attractive, mostly youthful group called the Brandenburg Ensemble. It was playing one of the Brandenburg concerti with great vivacity when I noticed that the first violinist and leader of the group, a youngish man named Todd Phillips, was wearing, along with his tuxedo, red and green argyle socks. Why would he do that? Why did it distract me so much that his socks were not black? I

spent the better part of the second half of the program contemplating those argyles. I was, I think it fair to say, ticked to
the min.

Someone mentions that she has had a "fun time" at a party,
and this use of the word *fun* as an adjective ticks me to the min.
A fun person, a fun couple, a fun place — I want nothing to do
with any of them. Years ago an English acquaintance, the late
Vernon Young, asked me, in perfect deadpan, what I thought
Americans meant when they instructed one, on parting, to
"have fun." I have put that phrase in quotation marks, but the
typographic support needed to make plain Vernon Young's drip-
ping contempt doesn't exist, except perhaps in smoking red
neon. I suppose there must also be fun cities, fun states, fun
countries — who knows, fun continents or even fun funerals.
Don't get me wrong. I do not wish to stand in the way of anyone having a "fun time"; I just don't want them around me.

For a couple of decades now, I have been a bit nutty on the
subject of language. Every five or so years, another word sets
off my perhaps too hair-triggered tickeroo. Frequent use of the
word *impact* used to get to me. Then the ardor for *impact* cooled
and *process* was the hot word; people seemed to feel that every
damn thing in life was a bloody process. I guess the word made
its users feel they were deep thinkers. *Intriguing* in place of *interesting* or even *fascinating* followed; *intriguing* should go right
back into the worlds of spying and diplomacy where it belongs.

Now the word that registers on my tickometer is *focus*. A
metaphor from the world of cameras, microscopes, and tele-
scopes, it must be the most endemic — and silly — word of our
day. People are invoked to "stay focused." Athletic teams that
lose their focus are in serious trouble. Every student paper, no
matter how diffuse, begins by talking about its focus. Tin-eared
academics even go in for the odious *foci,* and may they find joy

in it. Let's get back to such quite sound words as *concentrate* and *emphasize*. I'm ticked, I tell you, ticked to the min.

I also have a strong aversion toward all botanical metaphors. I don't like the notion of people "growing"; I don't much fancy "nurturing" anybody. "Fermenting," too, is not my idea of a good time, and put a hold on "replanting." All this botanizing of human experience is a lot of fertilizer, in my view. But, then, I may be alone in this; for the majority of people it may make no "differential," as the sports announcers are wont to say.

I see myself making quotation marks with my fingers around the word *differential*. I see myself doing this in a nightmare, of course. If I were ever to use what I think of as "finger quotes," I hope some decent citizen will grab my fingers and bend them back, fiercely. Once a sad, old device of academic lecturers, finger quotes have come to be used by non-academics, too. When I've noted their use, I've wanted to ask whether the person using them also does ellipses. "Have you," I want to add, "a sign to denote irony — a nice little back flip perhaps?" Ticks me, baby, knock it off.

Ticks me perhaps as much as what I have come to think of as dumbing-down footnotes. "Dandiacal means 'inclined to be a dandy,'" reads a footnote on page 26 of *John Betjeman Letters*. "No kidding," I answer, in my happy habit of talking back to print. And in the Penguin edition of Joseph Conrad's *Under Western Eyes*, the editor, helpful fellow, tells me who Jean-Jacques Rousseau was and explains that a samovar is a "copper urn for boiling water and keeping tea hot." Penguin's edition of Henry James's *The Europeans* informs me who George Washington was. (Thanks, dude.) A recent reviewer in the *Times Literary Supplement* referred to a book "so meticulously annotated as to be fully comprehensible to readers unfamiliar with western civilization." A good deal of this, apparently, is going around.

This dumbing down ticks me off, but not quite so much as historical bloopers in movies. By this I mean the increasing use in period movies of words and phrases that had not yet historically come into being. In Woody Allen's *Bullets over Broadway,* a movie set in the 1920s, the following phrases are found in the dialogue: "conflicted," "a real page-turner," "I try to factor it into my work," "the difficulty of relating," and "she's so charismatic." What ticks me off here is the inability, or unwillingness, to get small things right — especially at those prices. But, then, perhaps I ought to be grateful that God, after Moses thanked him for parting the Red Sea in *The Ten Commandments,* didn't answer, "Hey, no problem."

I go to the movies less and less and have become chiefly a VCR man. My taste in movies is broad; I tend to be of the view that a bad movie isn't going to destroy my virtue, though I do prefer a bad movie to cost only three dollars instead of fifteen or sixteen dollars, as it does for two at a movie theater. The inexpensiveness of movies on videotape has probably lowered my own taste, making me tolerant of less-than-respectable movies. But I still find it difficult to take heavy sex scenes, especially what I think of as slow-motion sex scenes. When I am watching with someone else in the room, I don't quite know where to put my eyes — I am embarrassed to the point of being mildly, minimally, but still genuinely, ticked. Am I being prudish here, or am I only offering in myself an illustration of the La Rochefoucauld maxim "We do not so much desert our appetites as they desert us"?

I've never had an appetite for violence, at least not one that went beyond slapstick comedy. I cannot abide much in the way of bloodiness in movies or television shows. I watch no hospital dramas, lest my dreams be interrupted by the specter of blood-drenched rubber gloves. The ghastliness of the local news has caused me to cease watching it. All those body bags, photographs of battered wives and children, interviews with relatives of the freshly murdered — just who is it that requires a continuous flow of such monstrous information?

I don't really know, but, like the old Persian kings greeted by bad news, I say let's put out the messenger's eyes. Or, in the case of all these television Johnnies and Janes, I say let's put out their hairdos. My tolerance for television newsmen and newswomen is exceedingly low. My notion of hell would be to have to eat all my meals with the on-camera cast of *60 Minutes*. ("Please pass the beets, Andy.") Something about the gathering of news diminishes a human being, leaves him without dignity, and doing it on a daily basis, in front of a television camera, can make him positively detestable. I dislike the people who do it even more when they engage in the false banter known, I believe, as "happy talk," in which they attempt to give their best but never quite persuasive impression of human beings.

I find I quickly grow tired of celebrities, or those people whom the media tend to vaunt, highlight, attack, or otherwise italicize. Increasingly, the media like to turn their attention to their own, which adds a note of piquant self-aggrandizement to the whole affair. My fatigue with celebrities, I note, doesn't take long to turn into general impatience, which elides into disapproval, a form of free-floating ticked-off-edness. I wish to hear no more, for example, about the comedian David Letterman, a man I once thought amusing; the same goes for his mother. I have heard enough about Emma Thompson to hold me for a good spell. My own celebrity, it seems to me, is just about right: I am, much to my surprise, mildly famous and quite thankful that almost nobody knows about it.

I still find myself a little ticked when I watch people go gaga over those ultimate American celebrities, the Swiss Family Kennedy, our very own substitute for a royal family. None of this has much to do with politics, for I can think of good reasons for not thinking much of Jack and Bobby Kennedy from either the left- or right-wing perspective. No, what I think ticks me is the inability of people to see through such thin pretensions as the Kennedy family provides to being great or even greatly stylish to the sadness, squalor, and, in the case of Joseph Kennedy, the so-called Founding Father, the deep corruption and downright meanness that lie behind it all. Put an ad in the *Chronicle of Higher Education:* A better royal family wanted. The current one ticks me.

Almost all forms of telemarketing tick me off — and some of them register slightly beyond the min on my tickometer. I don't like to get these calls during the day, I don't like to get them at night, and I especially don't like to get them while at dinner, when most of them seem to arrive. Of late I have been getting early morning calls from brokerage firms, from guys with New York accents and very knowing voices wanting to put me on to a good thing. I find I don't in the least mind telling these rebarbative types to kiss off. I feel rather differently about women trying to get me to take a J. C. Penney or Sears credit card; they, clearly, are trying to make a few extra bucks to keep things afloat. (In my twenties and briefly out of work, I once tried to sell newspaper subscriptions over the telephone. I lasted two nights and never went back to pick up my check for eleven dollars.)

Yet my tolerance is short-circuited if the telemarketers address me by my first name. I take it that more and more of them have been trained to do so. Why it is thought good salesmanship I cannot say, for what person wishes to be called by his or her first name by a stranger likely never to be encountered again? I even read a mild contempt into this first-name business, comparable to the old habit of calling men Mac, Ace, Chief, or Buddy, or calling women Honey, Sweetie, or Doll.

If the person on the other end of the line sounds especially young, I will sometimes say that I am in my early nineties and that I wonder, given my elderliness, if perhaps I ought not to be addressed as Mr. Epstein. On a few occasions, I have lectured people who have addressed me over the phone by my first name. Invariably, doing so has been a mistake, because the caller had something useful to offer: a job for a former student, kind words about something I have written, a message from a common friend. I have ceased to lecture.

Still, all this phony informality is, I suppose, part of a tendency toward the informalization of public life generally. In fully half the restaurants I frequent, the waiters tell me their first names, and some of them tell me that they have already tasted the food I have just ordered. Such informality goes along with the gradual elimination of neckties and jackets, dresses and heels from the regular wardrobes of adults, or what used to be called — quaint term as it now seems — grown-ups. Perhaps it is my own tendency, once I discover the way the wind is blowing, to turn around and march directly into it, but I have come to appreciate formality more and more.

As a sometime university teacher, I have always addressed my students, at least in class, as Mr. Newton or Miss Quinn. If I get to know the student better, I may use his or her first name outside of class, but I never allow students to address me by my first name. I am pleased to report that it has never occurred to any of them to do so, which leads me to believe that I am giving off the correct fumes of formality.

When I began teaching, twenty or so years ago, I wasn't sure how I would deal with the great first-name or last-name question. I remember calling the roll on the first day in a freshman class and coming to the name — last name first, on the enrollment sheet — Pipal, Faustin. In response to my calling it out, a redheaded kid with a winningly open face asked, "Excuse me, sir, but would you mind calling me Frosty?" It took me only a nanosecond to realize that I would not be able to address standard pompous academic questions to someone named Frosty, as in: "What, precisely, did Nietzsche mean when he said, now that God is dead, man is left to confront the abyss, *Frosty?*" I have as a teacher used last names ever since. When I recounted this to a young man working in the office of a literary agent, he replied that he would have loved being called by his last name by a teacher, but it had not happened once in his four years at Princeton. Learning about this, Christian Gauss, I dare say, would have been ticked to more than the min.

Part of the problem is that naming has itself become comic. I recently read an article about the former basketball player Rick Barry and learned that one of his children is named Canyon Shane Barry. The splendid outfielder Andre Dawson has a daughter named Diamond Nicole Dawson. This naming of children after geological phenomena could get out of hand. If Canyon, why not Ravine? If Diamond, why not Zircon? If geological names, why not culinary ones? How easy it is to imagine a girl named Marinade, a boy called Au Jus. In Nora Ephron's novel *Heartburn,* one of the characters is said to have gone out with the first Jewish Kimberly. I have heard about a girl named Page Goldstein. I am sure that there must by now be Jewish girls named Kelly. Poor children, victims of their parents' rather sad yearning for distinctiveness and elegance, they shall have to drag these pretentious names around all their days.

Like Billy Wilder, who said, "I have always had more fear of pretentiousness than of failure," I fear pretentiousness in myself and mock it, to myself, in others. It doesn't exactly tick me off, even to the min; I suppose it gives me the droops. Mention of the droops — a neologism of my own devising — reminds me that more language is needed to register these gradations and calibrations of negative feeling. Only the other day I learned a new word in this line, *chuffed,* which apparently means to be irritated, disgruntled, more than a little displeased. I suppose it falls betwixt ticked to the min and ticked to the max; after the latter comes furious, outraged, enraged, inflamed, and completely out-of-control, full-hemorrhage-ahead apoplectic.

"*Du calme. Du calme,*" the examining physician in Brussels tells Marlow in *Heart of Darkness,* his best advice for surviving in the tropics. Not such bad advice for urban living, either. I go along thinking that my own temper is fairly well under control, then — ping! — out of the box it pops. It seems under better control when I am on foot than when I am behind the wheel of my car. Seated in my car, I tend to forget that I am a smallish man and, consequently, incapable of impressive physical violence.

The other day, taking a shortcut, I drove down an alley near my apartment and was stopped by a parked car with an older — older than I — man in it who had one of those red faces that suggests high blood pressure and possibly ulcers. When I asked him if he would please move his car just slightly to allow me to pass, he told me that he wasn't about to move his car, that I could forget about it, and that I could back my car nearly a full city block out of the alley. It turned out that I was able to squeeze through, barely, but while doing so — ping! — I heard myself calling this man a disagreeable old fornicator. Fortunately for me, he wasn't ready for a fight. A fine spectacle the two of us would have made there in the alley, struggling on the ground to some sort of ignominious draw. I see torn trousers, broken glasses, possibly a chipped tooth or two, lawyers to follow. *Du calme. Du calme.*

I have never thought of myself as having a strong temper, but, as Conrad also says (in *Lord Jim*), "No man quite understands his own artful dodges from the grim shadow of self-knowledge." I go whole fiscal quarters without losing my temper, though now that I write it out, *losing* strikes me as almost precisely the wrong word. What happens is that my temper *finds* me. It usually finds me when I am frustrated or when I think someone has acted unreasonably — unreasonably, that is, to me. Then, there he is, my temper, crude fellow, blatant and coarse, full of profanity, hyperbole, rarely witty, certain to say the wrong thing, always going too far.

Once it was thought that it was good mental hygiene to tell people off regularly. Get it off your chest, don't keep it all locked up inside — repression is the enemy. I have known men who worked together who could tell each other off brutally — gloves off, no holds barred, to mix a boxing and a wrestling metaphor — then go off to lunch together laughing. Not me. I can neither tell anyone off nor bear to be told off (and I never have been, except in print on various occasions, where the humiliation may be greater but at least the embarrassment is less).

I suppose there are advantages to having a hot temper. People tread carefully around you. The hot-tempered and the deeply neurotic, I have discovered, often tend to get their own way. Disputing with them, most people feel, usually just isn't worth it. My temper has never done me any good in this line. The preferred position to be in, I should think, is to have people say about you, "He's very nice, but don't cross him." I fear that people can more accurately say about me, "He's not all that nice, but, not to worry, you can cross him all you like."

Temper comes out of the word *temperament*, and when I consider the old division of temperament into four types — sanguine, choleric, phlegmatic, and melancholic — I conclude that the second and fourth, in a combination favoring the fourth, apply to me. No one, at any rate, has accused me of being either sanguine or phlegmatic. Melancholy seems to me a sensible mood with which to regard the world. Was it F. Scott Fitzgerald who said that depression is the natural state of an intelligent man in middle age? If so, he was right to say it, not least because, dying at the age of forty-four, he himself never got beyond early middle age.

Fitzgerald had his own list of things that ticked him to the min — and well beyond. In "The Crack-Up," an essay of 1936, he listed the things he could and couldn't stand. "I couldn't stand the sight of Celts, English, Politicians, Strangers, Virginians, Negroes (light or dark), Hunting People, or retail clerks, and middlemen in general, all writers . . . and all the classes as classes and most of them as members of their class." On the cheerier side: "I liked doctors and girl children up to the age of about thirteen and well-brought-up boy children about eight years old on. . . . I forgot to add that I liked old men. . . . I liked Katharine Hepburn's face on the screen, no matter what was said about her pretentiousness, and Miriam Hopkins' face, and old friends if I only saw them once a year and could remember their ghosts."

Fitzgerald claimed to be describing a crack-up, his own, but, though I have a much nuttier list of antipathies, I am still claiming mental health. For example, I find I don't like the new abbreviations for states, and I refuse to write IN or OR or ME or MI or IL or IA. Never friendly toward zip codes to begin with, I really dislike the four numbers that now come after zip codes in many addresses. (These additional four numbers must have a name, but I'd rather not learn it.) I also dislike lengthy addresses generally, and I will put off writing a letter to anyone who has an address that runs to more than five lines (unless, as in England, one of the lines is the name of the house). My antipathies are not strictly separable from my snobberies, but I can live with that.

Clearly, I much prefer my snobberies to other people's. Clothes or luggage with designer labels or the designer's name writ large on them tick me lightly to the min. When I see Ralph Lauren's minuscule polo player on a man's shirt, or M. Louis Vuitton's intertwined monogram on a woman's handbag, or the small Hermès insignia on a necktie, I tend to think rather less of its wearer or carrier. They are willing to pay too much money for a little false prestige, and so, not to put too fine a word on it, they are chumps. They lose status in my eyes.

I am not ignorant of the lure of brand names, for as a boy tennis player I wore only Fred Perry shorts, René Lacoste shirts, Jack Purcell shoes, and I am not altogether above them now, but a little understatement is called for. Instead, overstatement grows, and designers' names — Gucci, Yves Saint-Laurent, DKNY, the all too effable Calvin Klein — dominate the front of sweatshirts, T-shirts, and underwear. Can it be long before some savvy surgeon gets to one of these designers and begins a line of designer surgery? I imagine that little man with his polo mallet aloft just above a fresh appendix scar, or perhaps an Armani quintuple bypass with the most careful double stitching and a slight break just above the aorta.

I remain half tickled, half ticked by too cutely named shops and firms. I not long ago saw an advertisement for Net to You, an operation that sets up one's computer and teaches one how to negotiate the Internet. Surely there will soon be competition from a firm called Charlotte's Place, which teaches one how to negotiate the World Wide Web. On the North Shore in Chicago, there is a glove and (I assume) women's accessory shop that calls itself Glove Me Tender. I have always wanted to buy the commercial space next door to it and open a men's scarf store and call it Kick Me in the Ascot. Perhaps it is best that I do not have unlimited funds.

Do other people get mildly worked up by such things? I rather hope that they do, but I have no way of knowing. Perhaps researchers at Pennsylvania State University have done a study on being ticked to the min. If they have, it will of course be contradicted by a study on the same subject done by researchers at Stanford University. "Studies," so called, ought by now to tick us all to the min — no, more than that, they ought to leave most of us soundly chuffed, especially studies on foods that cause cancer and heart disease. These have been bounding back and forth for years, keeping us all nicely nervous about nearly everything we take into our bodies, including the air.

We have all been receiving a good beating on this front, being told what we cannot eat now, what we shouldn't have been eating years ago, what we probably shan't be allowed to eat in the future. I am glad to have been born in a gastronomically prelapsarian time, for I was able to spend a few decades eating exactly as I wished, before so many snakes (in the form of these blasted studies) were let loose in Eden. I find myself bugged, sometimes more than mildly, at not being able to eat, in decent quantity and with a clear conscience, things that I crave. Ticked again, naturally.

In the realm of ticked to the min, I mustn't neglect all the strong evidence of our going to hell in a handbasket, which, as you may have noticed, we really are. Take, for instance, the phrase "You're welcome." People are now in the world, I believe, who are entirely ignorant of this expression — and of the concept behind it. As a big thank-you man out of the Midwest, I find myself handing out lots of thank-yous for services rendered — to supermarket baggers, store clerks, garage attendants —

and getting nothing back in return. Not infrequently I have an exchange at a drugstore or bakery where the clerk deliberately, it seems, chooses not to look at me, as if to ensure that no human contact is being made. Will there be more and more of this in the world in the years ahead? "If this is really so," as the Liverpool magistrate said upon learning that oral sex was widely practiced in England, "I'm glad I do not have long to live."

The inability to get the small but necessary things right, though becoming commonplace, nonetheless does not lose its power to tick to the min. The sad lapses in grammar, especially on the part of people who are paid for their putative skill at language — writers, journalists, clergymen, psychologists — are part of it. So is the vast number of typographical errors, not least those that show up in my own books and articles. I have a reader who, in a monotone voice, occasionally telephones to report that he has found another typographical error in one of my books. I believe he thinks he is doing me a good turn — maybe he is naïve enough to think that publishers, in new editions, take care to correct such errors. ("My rare books," said the English minor writer Reggie Turner, "are the second editions.") Meanwhile, his calls are the equivalent of being told that, at the prom forty years ago, you may not have noticed but you had ketchup on your shirt, and that, oh yes, at your wedding, you had this odd bit of spinach between your front teeth. With a downcast heart, I thank this fellow for pointing out these typos. But before I hang up the phone, I find myself wanting to say, "Write if you find work."

Ralph Waldo Emerson ticks me to the min, and sometimes just a little beyond. With the exception of his book *English Traits* and portions of his journals, I find I cannot read the old boy. I find Emerson a great gasbag and a highly contradictious one: if he has said something with which you disagree in one place, he is sure to have said the reverse someplace else. With his abiding humorlessness, his oracular prose, his galloping garrulity, he has given the essay a bad name, making it seem no more than a sermon with drool added. What must Europeans who read him think of America! What must American schoolchildren who read him think of literature! He was the original talk-show host, with no guests other than himself.

Perhaps it is Emerson's opinionatedness that gets to me. His confidence about matters in the flux of controversy is preposterous. He is the father of all American pundits. Punditry no longer works for me. I recently read the introduction to a book of essays by a woman pundit, who went to great lengths to assure her readers that she continued to regard herself as solidly liberal, though she was against certain kinds of left-wing nonsense. As the sentences spun by — "I think . . ." "I never said . . ." "I never intended . . ." — I found myself saying, "Madame, why do you suppose anybody gives a rat's rump? How do you come to think that your opinion is so very important? We have a deep problem here, and, if you want my opinion (since you have no hesitation about giving me yours), I'd say it stems from too much love in the home. Less confidence, more shyness is needed."

I, too, have a great many opinions, and I now have to ask if they add up to a point of view. All these items that I claim tick me to the min would once have been called pet peeves. I wonder if they aren't called "pet" because people who have them quite enjoy stroking them. One comes to depend on them. After a time, they give comfort, though there's always the danger that one becomes the sum of one's crotchets.

Growing up in Chicago, I remember men who used to love to start the day with Colonel Robert McCormick's *Chicago Tribune,* whose strongly isolationist, right-wing views would get them so worked up that it raised their blood pressure and provided them with body warmth in the winter months. My father was among them. So strong was his detestation of the old *Tribune* that, one day during a snow storm, when he had a flat tire and the driver of a *Trib* delivery truck pulled up, got out, and asked if he could help, my father, normally a mild and uncontentious man, told him to get the hell back into his truck, he didn't need his help. That, I believe, provides a swell example both of being ticked to the max and, as my father telling the story used to point out, of the irrationality of passionate anger.

Do my own peeves perform the function of getting my circulation going for me? Why is it that I find it difficult to imagine life without them? Everywhere I turn, I find these peeves awaiting me. I watch a movie in which one character, putatively a writer, claims that he and his lady friend "love one another" — "each other," I mutter. I get a letter from a business acquaintance written on the bottom of my own letter to him, and I think, "Ah, the CCNY school of business-letter writing." The first person I knew who wrote on the bottom of letters was the late Irving Howe; then I discovered that others who went to CCNY in the 1930s did so as well. Something mildly slovenly about it, I have always thought, something that suggests that your letter isn't worth saving, or that your correspondent is too busy to get out a clean sheet of stationery, or that you are not really worthy of clean stationery. In any case, receiving such a letter does, ever so slightly, tend to tick.

But, then, you might say, what, for me, doesn't? From the presence on my television screen of the last eight presidents of the United States to the gradual disappearance of the hyphen in such words as *antiestablishment,* not much, I have to report. How to account for this low-grade yet wide-ranging irritability?

Ought I to double my dosage of wine with dinner? Am I a candidate for Prozac or some other pill that will put a finer sheen upon life for me? The fear, of course, is that I shall turn into a crank, if I am not one already.

Delacroix at the age of fifty-five writes in his journal of having recently read Joseph Addison on old age and being in complete agreement with "his placing tranquility in the first rank among the advantages which age gives us over youth." He then most tranquilly discourses on the lessening ambition that men in mature life ought to feel, asking, "Is there anything more ridiculous than agitating oneself at the age when everything invites us or forces us to repose?" He goes on to posit that even "the man of merit whom circumstances have not favored should still, in the situation where his declining years are passed, enjoy the calm which that situation brings with it." How sensible, how thoughtful, how philosophical! How contradictory, however, that in the journal entry preceding this one, Delacroix is on the attack against the mediocrity of his own time. "No one imagines to what degrees mediocrity abounds: Lefuel, Baltard, a thousand examples press in on one, of men having heavy commissions in the arts, in the government, in the armies, in everything. Those are the people who everywhere block the machinery set in motion by men of talent." Delacroix, there can't be much doubt about it, is ticked.

Is being ticked, mildly or madly, the natural state of human beings, since, shall we say, the permanent age of transition that began with departure from the Garden of Eden? It seems to be my natural state. Being steadily and readily ticked, I sometimes begin to feel, is rather like having tics: it may not be elegant, but it does give one something to do.

Yet how much I would prefer serenity to this regular low-level agitation that I seem to visit upon myself. *Serene* — what a beautiful word! How I aspire to the condition it describes! How pleasing it would be to exist above all this fiddle of popular culture and manners! How much finer to be like Santayana in Rome — polite, cool, and informal, passionate only in my vocation, well above the usual jumble of ordinary irritations! Or even to be like the late Joseph Brodsky, of whose belief in hierarchy Czeslaw Milosz recently wrote: *"hierarchy* means respect for that which is elevated and unconcern, rather than scorn, for that which is base." Yes, that is it exactly — "unconcern, rather than scorn, for that which is base." Unticked, beyond ticking, tick-free.

Arguably . . . but here we come directly up against the problem. That word *arguably* — such a weak word, a word for people who like to sit on the fence (and may they come away with many small and painful splinters), content to say that something can be argued rather than getting down in the trenches and arguing it one way or the other. Why would anyone wish to use such a word unless he is fearful of taking a position? What semantic cowardice! What wimpishness! I'm ticked, as you can plainly see, ticked once again — nicely, happily, inevitably ticked — ticked to the min and, I suppose I may as well face it, ticked for life.

Trivial Pursuits

I F   I   H A D   A press agent, I would ask him to call a press conference at which I would announce my retirement as a sports fan. "Today, I consider myself the luckiest man on the face of the earth," said Lou Gehrig when he announced his retirement from baseball. My opening line would run only a little differently: "Today, I consider myself the stupidest man on the face of the earth." I would then go on to explain that for more than half a century I have watched boys and men and a lesser number of women throw, chase, and hit various balls in various parks in various cities and countries, that doing so has not made me one whit smarter about the world or my own life, and that if I had it to do all over again I would spend the time learning to play the harpsichord.

Why this heavy note of regret? Why this confession of a misspent youth and middle age? Because I feel foolish for having spent so much time on what now seems an empty enterprise: sports — and I mean just about all sports. The only game that I continue to admire, the game of golf, I have never even played and rarely watch. For the rest, I have just been part of the crowd of suckers, of whom surely more than one is born every minute. And I would like to get out now, before I wind up dying in front of a televised ball game, the last words I hear those of some multi-millionaire athlete, in a flurry of "you know"s claiming that he always tries to give 110 percent.

Dying in front of a television set during a game reminds me of what I now think of as a minor literary embarrassment. Roughly twenty years ago I published an essay titled "Obsessed with Sport" in *Harper's Magazine*. It may be the essay of mine that has been reprinted more than any other; it appears chiefly in high school and college readers, for the reason, I suppose, that the subject of sports has some intrinsic interest for young male students. I shall get to what I said in the essay presently, but I regret to have to report that at the essay's end I wrote about an older neighbor who quietly expired while listening to a ball game. The final sentence in that essay reads: "I cannot imagine a better way." Now, twenty years later, I can think of lots of better ways.

My chief point in "Obsessed with Sport" was that sports, at least sports down on the field, are free of fraudulence and fakery. Athletes, I argued, either come through or they don't; in their world, performance is all and public relations nothing. "Much has been done in recent years in the attempt to ruin sports — the ruthlessness of owners, the greed of players, the general exploitation of fans," I wrote. "But even all this cannot destroy it." I was wrong. They have destroyed it. I continue to watch an enormous amount of sports, mostly on television, but increasingly I have begun to get up from a game the way I often do from a movie, saying to myself, "Well, that was clearly a bloody waste of time."

Sports have crossed a line of a kind that a once charming neurotic might cross into harmful psychosis. It's neither amusing nor refreshing anymore. Has it always been this bad, and have I allowed myself not to notice? "Fifty years in the business," says Zero Mostel in *The Producers* in a line I have always loved, "and I'm still wearing a cardboard belt." Fifty years of watching sports, I say to myself, and I only now discover how mean and dreary it all is.

"Serious sport," wrote Orwell, in a brief essay called "The Sporting Spirit," "has nothing to do with fair play. It is bound up with hatred, jealousy, boastfulness, and disregard of all rules." Orwell felt that the rise of sports since the end of the nineteenth century was tied in with nationalism — "that is, with the lunatic modern habit of identifying oneself with large power units and seeing everything in terms of competitive prestige." Orwell was, of course, especially good at making things seem as grim as possible. "One of the most horrible sights in the world is a fight between white and coloured boxers before a mixed audience," he wrote. He believed that sports do little more than mimic warfare, and he noted: "If you wanted to add to the vast fund of ill will existing in the world at this moment, you could hardly do it better than by a series of football matches between Jews and Arabs, Germans and Czechs, Indians and British, Russians and Poles, and Italians and Jugoslavs."

Ten, even five years ago, I would have attempted to dispute Orwell on every one of his points. Today I don't feel all that confident in challenging him on any one of them. One of the things that made sports seem worthwhile was the notion of sportsmanship, and this, it strikes me, is all but dead. Except in the game of golf, the spirit of fair play — of doing the right thing, of putting aside the question of winning or losing in order to play the game as it is meant to be played — has now disappeared.

First, fans gave up on sportsmanship. Nearly every crowd for a sports event — from boxing to tennis, from football to baseball — is now a key element in deciding the contest itself. The ugliest sports crowds are probably those for boxing who clearly want to see blood ("In hell," the sportswriter Thomas Boswell has written, "boxing would be the national pastime"). But fans seated under the baskets at professional and college basketball games are today given balloons and placards to distract visiting-team players shooting free throws. Large football crowds maintain a level of screaming that doesn't allow visiting teams to hear their quarterbacks' signals. The crowd at a sporting event is often called the twelfth, or tenth, or sixth man, and a damned unpleasant man he mostly turns out to be.

Whether the crowds are following the athletes or the athletes the crowds in this unsportsmanlike conduct remains an open question. Athletes and, even more, their coaches have come to specialize in strategies that years ago would have been considered little more than cheating. I'm thinking here of such things as running out the clock in football games, basketball coaches screaming at referees in order to gain an edge on close calls, tennis players disputing every decision that goes against them as a form of terrorizing linesmen.

When I was a boy tennis player, playing without an umpire or linesmen, we boys called our own games. One of the working principles, or so I was taught, was for me to give all close calls on my side of the court to my opponent, and for my opponent to give all close calls on his side of the court to me. A crucial moment in the decline of sportsmanship came with the rise to the top stratum of tennis of Jimmy Connors and John McEnroe. Before these players, there was nothing contradictory about being fiercely competitive and at the same time absolutely honorable. After them, the nature of competition itself changed: because one was competitive, it was understood, one didn't wish to lose any edge at all. One was permitted to complain about every close call and to behave badly, to use profanity with officials and to act like a perfect creep on the court. I regularly found myself rooting for Connors's and McEnroe's opponents, and to this day, now that they have become rather revered senior players, I find myself still rooting against them. Not that I enjoyed sports chiefly as a branch of ethics, but I did feel that — perhaps naïvely, I now begin to think — it contributed to discipline of the sort that could lead to good character. I am not sure why I felt that, since, come to think of it, the list of gentlemen athletes is extremely small. The great golfer Bobby Jones is indubitably on it, a man who not only may have been the best ever to play the game but was also successful in other areas of his life: Jones finished the four-year engineering course at Georgia Tech in three years, passed the Georgia bar halfway through his second year at Emory University School of Law, wrote (very well) every word of his own books. ("I was misquoted," said Charles Barkley, of the Phoenix Suns, when someone mentioned something from his autobiography.) From all accounts, Walter Johnson also qualifies; a friend tells me that Johnson was scrupulously careful about pitching inside to opponents lest he injure them with one of his blistering fastballs. Rod Carew seems to me a gent, as did Arthur Ashe. I have the impression that the same can be said of Al Rosen, third baseman of the Cleveland Indians, Mike Schmidt, third baseman of the Philadelphia Phillies, and Andre Dawson. Julius Erving, the elegant Dr. J., qualifies, as does Cal Ripken, Jr., who seems a nice man in the mold of Stan Musial. Bob Gibson, the great St. Louis Cards' pitcher, may not have been a gent, but he has always seemed to me an entirely serious person. I'm not sure any football players, amateur or professional, qualify.

If sports has not produced a long roster of gentlemen, it has produced a good number of characters, oddballs, nuts. Casey Stengel, he whose syntax was surpassed only by his semantics —

on his seventieth birthday he said, "Most people my age are dead at the present time" — easily makes the cut here. So does Whitey Bimstein, the fight trainer, who, when training a fighter in the Catskills, was asked what he thought about the country and answered, "It's a pretty nice place." Lawrence Peter Berra, who could float a full famous-quotations volume on his own, clearly makes it: "In baseball," Yogi once pithily said, "you don't know nothing." The light heavyweight Archie Moore, who fought nearly into old age, earns a starting position on the interesting-character team. This list could be greatly expanded.

Why are there today so few athletes who seem worth meeting for a cup of coffee? Where once there were a fair number of gents or amusing characters among athletes, today there are a great number of what can only be called sad cases: guys with drug and booze problems, women athletes with serious eating disorders — let us not even speak of paternity suits. "Drug-taking and dealing, alcoholism, drunk driving, spousal abuse, manslaughter, tax evasion — the sports page reads like a police blotter," writes Bill Brashler, a Chicago journalist. "Culminating, of course, with O.J."

Any even moderately successful athlete today is of course a multi-millionaire. Instead of causing them to hide under the bedsheets at night, trembling and thanking God for this lovely piece of good luck, the money seems only to have made athletes unpleasantly arrogant. So many contemporary athletes are clearly in business only for themselves. Oddly, some of the biggest moneymakers, not only in salaries but in endorsements, have been some of the most unpleasant human beings: the football players Brian Bosworth and Deion Sanders, the tennis players Andre Agassi and Jimmy Connors, the baseball players Barry Bonds and Jack McDowell, the basketball players Derrick Coleman and Christian Laettner.

In pointing out the unattractiveness of contemporary athletes — and let us not forget the equally odious supporting cast of team owners and agents — I am scarcely making an original point. The sportswriter Mike Lupica, in *Esquire*, gives out what he now calls the "Annual Deion Awards" (after Deion Sanders; they were formerly called the Andres, after Andre Agassi), and he never seems pressed for endless examples of egregious behavior, from taking drugs to selling out fans to impressive greed. Much of this is owing to the huge quantity of money that is thrown at them. Even on those occasions when people in sports forgo more money for what seems to be loyalty, there is something slightly dubious about it. Rick Pitino, then the basketball coach at Kentucky, and Gary Barnett, the football coach at Northwestern, decided not to take more lucrative jobs in order to remain with their schools, teams, and fans. Yet, one cannot help noting, these guys have not exactly chosen to join the Salvation Army. Both men, after endorsements, will probably make more than a $1 million a year anyway, and Pitino has since fled to the NBA. Northwestern coughed up $400,000 in salary for Barnett, which must be more than the head of the medical school or the president of the university makes. I remember the days, in the early 1960s, when the University of Arkansas paid its winning football coach, Frank Broyles, $25,000, which forced the university to raise the salary of the president to $26,000, for appearance' sake.

Today even appearance is gone. So has the guise of modesty on the part of athletes. "Once modesty was the norm," Thomas Boswell has remarked. Even if some athletes were terrible creeps in private, they felt the need to come off as honorably self-effacing in public. This is less and less true today. The bow is part of the performance, yet the spectacle of the touchdown dance, the shattered backboard, the showoff home-run trot round the bases — all this is something new and dreary in sports. Boswell thinks the change came about in the 1960s — Muhammad Ali and Joe Namath were central figures in the breakdown of modesty — and was reinforced by the worship of money that came out in the open in the 1980s. "They don't pay nobody to be humble," Deion Sanders says, and he may, regrettably, be correct about this.

But even when athletes don't act badly, they seem to me to have become strangely self-absorbed and immensely uninteresting. One of the criticisms of NBC's coverage of the 1996 Olympics was too great a concentration on the personal lives of the athletes. What I found most striking was how little in the way of personal lives they had. Almost every man and woman jack among them was a fanatic, an obsessive, a deep-dish dullard and drip who, apart from his or her ability to run or swim or jump, was of very little human interest. Such mad concentration on bodies isn't what sports ought to be about. In the lives of these athletes, things have gotten badly out of proportion. Even the heroics of the Olympic gymnast Kerri Strug, who achieved an impressive vault with a badly sprained ankle, made her seem somehow quite as sad as gallant. Whatever the payoff — cash, glory, personal satisfaction — all the training, pain, contorting of body and personality don't seem really worth it.

Perspective on sports has pretty clearly gone more than a little askew. Red Smith, the best American sportswriter, once wrote: "I tried not to exaggerate the glory of athletes. I'd rather if I could preserve a sense of proportion, to write about them as excellent ballplayers, first-rate players." Yet Smith worried that he had nonetheless "contributed to false values — as Stanley Woodward said, 'Godding up those ballplayers. . . .' These are just little games that little boys can play, and it isn't important to the future of civilization whether the Athletics or the Browns win. If you accept it as entertainment, then that's what spectator sports are meant to be."

During a recent summer in Amsterdam, taking a breather in my hotel room after a long afternoon with seventeenth-century Dutch painting, fighting alongside my detested fellow pilgrims for a closer look at various Rembrandt self-portraits, I turned on a BBC television broadcast of a golf tournament in England to hear an announcer say about an English golfer that he was "usually the most wonderful of chippers," and I thought what a nice thing to be, the most wonderful of chippers. This same announcer said of another figure from English golf who had just died, "He made many a beautiful persimmon-headed club for me. He'll be sorely missed." I have left instructions that I be shot in both kneecaps if ever I even mention buying a set of golf clubs, but I found all this talk enchanting in its right perspective, its proper proportion. In another BBC broadcast, this one of a women's doubles championship, an announcer remarked: "The audience applauds in appreciation of some lovely skills on display." Just so, just right — and just about impossible nowadays in American sports.

John Dos Passos, who was himself myopic and poor at games, once observed that the average American is not a failed artist but a failed athlete. I fear that it is true of me. Not long ago I gave a half-hour talk in Los Angeles that went unusually well. I was playing at the top of my not-all-that-powerful game. Diction, rhythm, timing, everything seemed to be in excellent order. The crowd responded to each of my small witticisms and seemed to grasp my larger points; I could feel them absolutely on my side, enjoying themselves as I was soon enough enjoying myself — the perfect ham, elegantly sliced and handsomely served. Afterward, coffee was provided. Thirty or so people must have come up to tell me how splendid they thought my talk, which I clutched, twelve pages in a manila folder, to my chest, rather as I might a tennis racquet.

It occurred to me that I wished it was a tennis racquet. And I felt about this sweet praise the brief but elevating adulation I had always hoped to win from sports when I was a boy but never quite did. I wanted to be a brilliant athlete and never was, but for less than half an hour I was a brilliant talker — and so I was able to win through intellectual talent what had been denied me by physical talent. Small though my triumph was — perhaps there were two hundred people in the audience — it felt very good, yet I needed the analogy with sports to make the pleasure fully comprehensible to myself. Something very strange about all this.

I have friends who compete in triathlons, others who play in senior men's tennis tournaments, and still others who play golf for sums of money that would cause me to change my shirt every few holes. But I am myself fresh — and I suspect permanently — out of personal sports fantasies. I picture myself on no dream teams, even in my dreams. I don't imagine ever playing any game in an earnestly competitive way again. Competition has almost no interest for me, and the only sport it can be said that I participate in is a constant wrestling match with the English language, from which, most days, I settle for a draw.

And yet, in ways I don't quite understand, I remain hooked on sports. I note from my journal of a few years ago that I went to the Cubs-Phillies game at Wrigley Field, took a not-quite-four-hour break — a break for bread between circuses — then watched the Chicago Bulls play the Seattle Supersonics in a playoff game. Both teams won. Sammy Sosa, the Cubs right fielder, hit three home runs, Michael Jordan scored twenty-eight points in a game the Bulls won by a restful seventeen points. I guess it was a fine day.

I read somewhere that a man who has watched sixteen straight quarters of professional or college football can be declared legally brain-dead, so that his living will ought to go into effect. Been there, as we currently say, done that: I have watched four bowl games on New Year's Day, and maybe more than four if you count a fair amount of channel surfing. My brain might have been a bit mushy at the conclusion of the day, my bottom put to the test, but I was otherwise unimpaired.

My life is measured less by nature's seasons than it is by the sports seasons. And the sports calendar, along with being fuller than the regular calendar, is more seamless as one sports season slides into another. This past year the NBA season ended in early June as the U.S. Open in golf ended, so that one could turn to baseball, only to be distracted for a few weeks by Wimbledon, then by the Olympics, then by the opening of the pro football pre-season, the U.S. Open in tennis, and then turn back to follow baseball as it rolled into playoffs and the World Series, at which time the NBA season had begun again. A good thing I have no interest in hockey, or the year would have to be extended by another two months.

I don't know if there is a twelve-step recovery program for withdrawal from sports spectatorship, but if there is, I should be interested in joining it. The athletes, in their guise as human beings, are helping my withdrawal a good bit, and so are the games themselves. I find myself, for example, watching less and less professional football. So brutish have professional football players become — we are now well into the age of the three-hundred-pound-plus lineman — that it is rather difficult in any way to imagine oneself one of them. When I was a boy of ten or eleven, I used to imagine myself a fleet-footed, splendidly elusive halfback for the Chicago Bears exquisitely loping through the broken field of tacklers from the Washington Redskins or New York Giants. If I were ten or eleven today, I don't think I could quite bring off such an imaginative feat.

Today I should not be shocked if, on the sidelines, one of the Chicago players removed his helmet to reveal he was not an uppercase but a lowercase, real bear. Maybe this is the tack that professional football will take in the future: no more human beings, but actual bears pitted against actual rams, or actual lions against actual Bengal tigers. This would doubtless infuriate the animal-rights people and cause the National Football League to be accused by a certain kind of academic of speciesism, but it would have the compensation of making contract negotiations easier. How it would affect the free-agency rule I do not pretend to know.

If I am now watching a good deal less pro football, regaining my autumn and winter Sundays, I am also easing off on watching tennis. Along with the enjoyment in the game I had as a young player, what really captivated me about tennis was its intrinsic elegance. The white clothes, the simple geometry of the court, the handsome wooden racquets, the sweet terse chatter exchanged by players — "take two," "too good," "ad out" — all of it delighted me. Almost all of it has now changed. The Davis Cup, once a highlight of the tennis year, seems to have lost its meaning and is being played out perfunctorily each year, like a dull marriage. Although the players of today may be better than those I admired when young — Pete Sampras might have swept Pancho Gonzales; Andre Agassi, Rod Laver (though I doubt it) — the game gives nowhere near the pleasure it once did, at least not to this spectator. Watching Monica Seles play Arantxa Sanchez Vicario, two players who grunt with every stroke, I feel that I am inside a hernia testing center. Watching the finalists at Wimbledon or at the U.S. Open, I find that one of my biggest problems is figuring out whom to pull for; and often I am unable to make a decision before the match is concluded. I hope soon to cut out all televised figure skating and gymnastics competitions. Tonya Harding's 1994 attack on the knee of her rival Nancy Kerrigan before the U.S. championship seemed an almost logical extension of the intense competition, with its great pool of money awaiting the ultimate winner, that is bred by the sport. But Nancy Kerrigan's own nearly blind mother's protestations about her daughter's being cheated out of an Olympic gold medal a year or so later, when she finished second to Oksana Baiul, was not itself exactly a thing of beauty either. The pressure on the kids from every quarter — parents, coaches, sponsors — seems too great; it seems, in fact, inhuman. And the sport itself, which seems to come down to whether one can make a series of six or seven triple jumps of various kinds without misstep, in the end isn't all that interesting.

Scarcely anything remains to be said about the allied sport of gymnastics, especially women's gymnastics, which has come to seem almost a division of S & M, with the coaches in the role of sadists and the poor emaciated girls in that of masochists. "I can't bear to watch any more of that sad dwarf throwing," a friend of mine remarked apropos of a recent Olympic gymnastics competition. The sport is just too cruel, allowing no tolerance for the least imprecision. The tales of the training that these kids go through come uncomfortably close to child abuse. Apart from the sheer physical horrors of their training, girl gymnasts are put to listening to Norman Vincent Peale tapes and reading sports inspiration books about thinking tough. I don't believe this is quite what Plato had in mind when he advocated gymnastics as an essential part of the training of future philosopher kings.

Whenever I hear about the many hours of practice, the sessions in the weight rooms, the playing through pain, and the rest of the regimen of obsession and torture that contemporary athletes put themselves through, I become more and more convinced that the only kind of athlete to be is a natural athlete, someone to whom sports comes naturally and remains easy, someone gifted by the gods. I grew up around a few such athletes, and now more than ever they are my ideal.

At the age of thirteen, I worked shagging balls and occasionally demonstrating strokes for a tennis pro named Paul Bennett, Sr. At the clay courts where he taught, a boy of seventeen named Al Kuhn was far and away the best player around. So good was he, in fact, that one year he was — if memory serves — ranked second in the country for boys eighteen and under; first ranked was a kid named Barry McKay, who went on to play for the University of Michigan and had a reasonably successful professional career. But what impressed me about Al Kuhn was that he seemed never to practice. Sometimes he would show up at the courts at eight in the morning, smudges of lipstick on his face supplying the evidence that he was just returning from a date. He would proceed to play a dazzling, nearly flawless set and then return home, either to sleep off his long night out or to arrange for a date for the next night. I don't know what became of Al Kuhn, but I hope that he is a very rich man living in some pleasant clime and that his avoidance of hard work has paid off handsomely.

The other great natural athlete I grew up with was Ronny Rubinstein, a boy two years younger than I who, by the time he was twelve years old, was already being touted for his talent at our local gym. Rube became an all-city basketball player in Chicago and subsequently started at guard for Louisville, which then and now had one of the country's great quasi-semi-professional college basketball programs. Rube later became one of the top racquetball players in the United States, and today he wins local seniors tennis tournaments. I suspect that he does it without training too rigorously, and, though I haven't seen him for a good while, I imagine he isn't in particularly great shape. If you can't win easily, why bother?

To return to my retreat from sports, I watched scarcely any college basketball last year, and then, when the time came for the NCAA tournament — "the Big Dance," as the television hype calls it — I watched it only sporadically and with disengaged interest. The Monday night of the final game, I went, with no hesitation, to a concert. The problem with college basketball, to my mind, is that it is becoming almost impossible to imagine it as anything less than a training ground, a minor league, for the National Basketball Association. And this has come to seem all the more so when kids drop out after their junior or sophomore or now sometimes freshman year to enter the NBA draft. What's more, they are probably correct to take the money and run. It's not as if their college degrees, almost inevitably in hopelessly soft subjects, are worth much anyhow. The coaches themselves seem as far as possible from amateur. The tantrums of Indiana University's Bobby Knight no longer amuse, and the earnestness of Georgetown's John Thompson or Duke's Mike Krzyzewski no longer persuades. These coaches are all just guys out there hustling a living — and, with shoe contracts and other endorsements, a jolly lucrative one.

I was close to achieving a similar freedom from college football, but in recent years Northwestern University, where I teach, fielded not only winning but very attractive teams. The year the

Wildcats went to the Rose Bowl, they beat the dreaded Notre Dame early in the season, which got my attention. After blowing a game to their weakest opponent, Miami of Ohio, they, as we clichémeisters have it, never looked back. This was a team that didn't stage little stag parties in the end zone after scoring a touchdown; its players didn't do the obscene sack dance after mauling a quarterback. Its blocking and tackling seemed clean and crisp. Whenever any of its players was interviewed, he seemed both modest and well spoken. Although the Wildcats lost in the Rose Bowl, they acquitted themselves honorably against the University of Southern California, another of the standard football factories.

And yet, somehow, I do not wish them to do it again. I can wait — in my grave, surely — another forty-eight years for Northwestern to return to yet another Rose Bowl. Even though the school apparently did everything very much on the up-and-up — Rick Telander, a seasoned and therefore sufficiently jaded sportswriter, has called the Northwestern coach, Gary Barnett, "incredibly moral and ethical" — there is something about sports in our age that makes even this magical season, at least to me, mildly depressing. For one thing, the coach imbued his players with heavy dosages of positive thinking. A place-kicker on the team, a young man then seeking a master's degree in journalism, said that if Coach Barnett told him that he could go through a wall, he would believe it. I myself don't think he should believe it. For another, in the aftermath of the victorious season, both admission applications and alumni contributions to the school greatly increased. Owing to football, a spirit of boosterism prevails. Sales of hats, T-shirts, sweatshirts are way up. People seem to have, you should pardon the expression, Wildcat fever. I have a touch of it myself, though in me it comes with an ample serving of dubiety. Still, I fear I am now hooked into another season. Go . . . so to speak . . . Wildcats.

I am also trapped in another season or two of watching the Chicago Bulls, at least until Michael Jordan retires. Michael Jordan is, in my lifetime, the athlete of athletes. In his understanding, execution, and dominance of the game of basketball, he comes close to being a genius. And unlike such geniuses as Edison, Einstein, and Picasso, he is beautiful to watch in action. He does a number of tricks with gravity that no one has hitherto thought possible. My cynic's radar pings a bit at the stories of Michael Jordan's personal goodness, yet Michael, as everyone now calls him, doesn't too often descend in his speech beneath the banal, which, these days for an athlete, is notable.

Much as I enjoy watching Michael Jordan do on a basketball court what, as a kid player, it never occurred to me to dream of doing, I look forward to his retirement so that I will no longer have to concern myself with the fortunes of his team. This is the insidious way sports entrap you: you follow a player, which commits you to his team. You begin to acquire scraps of utterly useless information about teammates, managers, owners, trainers, agents, lawyers. Next thing you know, you — I, actually — are listening to a sports call-in show on the car radio, where the pressing question of the day is, "Would you date Dennis Rodman?"

While I believe I shall be able to walk away from professional basketball easily enough after Michael, not watching baseball games is a more complicated matter. I ceased playing baseball, or what we used to call hardball, after grade school, and I was not all that good at it to begin with, so I find it odd that this game means more to me than any other. "Professional football and basketball are spectacles," George Will has written, "baseball is a habit." Baseball denotes the arrival of spring. I like the sound of a game humming away on the car radio. It can be an excellent soporific and one I sometimes use to assist a Saturday afternoon nap. Radio broadcasts of night games from the West Coast are the surest cure I know for insomnia. Geometrical and simple though the game appears, it is a game about which, after all these years, I continue to learn new things. People complain about the dullness of baseball, but I side here with Red Smith, who once described it as "only dull to dull minds."

When Ken Burns's documentary on baseball was shown on our local PBS channel, I received a call from one of the station's producers asking if I would agree to come down to talk briefly about my happiest baseball memories. "Sorry," I answered, "but I haven't any." This is chiefly owing to my being, through the accidents of geography and birth, a Chicago Cubs fan. Everyone has heard all the Cubs jokes, which mostly have to do with long suffering. People theorize at great length about why the Cubs' record has been so dismal: the team hasn't appeared in a World Series in more than half a century. And now some mad physiologist has concluded that defeat in sports results, both in athletes and fans, in lower testosterone levels. A journalist in Chicago named Richard Babcock, noting this, remarked that, if it were so, Cubs fans would long ago have become extinct.

So, of course, would all Cubs, except that they are frequently traded or, when free-agency time rolls around, they sell off their services to a higher and more winning bidder. We have reached the extraordinary condition in sports in which fans are more loyal to their teams than players. Most of the latter do not live in the city from which they haul away their obscenely large salaries. Fewer and fewer have any genuine interest in baseball history and traditions. Fans seem to be of no interest to them. Owners, for their part, could perhaps care less about fans, but it is difficult to see how. There was much talk about fans' being put off by the 1994 baseball strike, but I wasn't. I didn't need a strike to remind me of how selfish both players and owners have become. Yet I cannot quite bear the notion of giving up this game. I go out to Wrigley Field six or seven times a year and enjoy the entire ritual. I leave home roughly an hour before the game to get a free parking space — which tells you, with some precision, how I rate my own hourly worth. I buy a three-dollar bag of peanuts outside the park from the same good-natured man; he looks to be about my age, and we usually chat for five minutes or so. Through the courtesy of a friend, I have good seats eight rows off the field, on the first-base side near the visiting team's on-deck circle. I generally go to the game with someone, but I have also gone alone and been perfectly content. The greenness of the park lulls me; the people around me seem splendidly normal, neither corporation men nor women with the least pretense to belonging to the *chicoisie*. I much prefer it when the Cubs win, but even when they don't, it still feels like it has been a good outing.

I only feel this way about Wrigley Field. I no longer care about going to Wimbledon, or the Rose Bowl, or a Super Bowl, or a big heavyweight fight, or the Kentucky Derby, or a World Series game (unless, fat chance, the hapless Cubs happen to be in it). I wish vaguely only to *have gone* to such events — not actually to go. I have sat in a $325 front-row seat at a Chicago Bulls game and been a little disappointed that at this price one didn't get to keep the chair; it was amusing to have done this once, but I do not long to do it again.

First one gives up one's athletic fantasies, then one gives up one's fantasies even as a fan. I believe that this leaves, in the matter of sports, only reality. And reality here seems vulgarly to insist that, since I am no longer a child, perhaps it is time to put away childish things — and, sadder, that, past a certain age, being a fan is perilously close to being a chump.

A sports-free, like a smoke-free, environment ought to be my goal, but I fear I have too great an investment, in time and in habit, in all these games to hope to achieve it. No, I probably haven't the character to cease watching sports entirely. I am a hopeless old addict, never to be completely cured, who can only pass along this advice — with thanks to the verse scheme of Philip Larkin — to the generations not yet born:

> Games are the trivial invention of man.
> Better to pull a book or CD from the shelf.
> Leave off watching when you can,
> And never play any games yourself.

What's in It for the Talent?

O F THE VARIOUS kinds of snob I undoubtedly am, it is as a talent snob that I wish above all to be known and, I hope, remembered. People who have real ability, who can do dashingly what most people cannot do at all, have my number. The kinds of talent I am able to appreciate are not merely varied but appallingly varied. I love Vermeer and Blossom Dearie, Sugar Ray Robinson and Maurice Ravel, and with very little strain I could come up with much wilder juxtapositions. Talent — the real, the vital, the magical thing — turns me soft and atwitter. I sometimes lapse into thinking that talent is all that matters in the world, even though I know that there are many things — decency, loyalty, courage, good-heartedness — that matter much more. But then, of course, the overvaluing of talent is what makes me a talent snob in the first place.

Talent is a not a word that the dictionaries have served very well. Its origin seems to be in the ancient unit in which precious metals were measured. In most definitions, natural endowments are mentioned; so, too, special aptitudes; and sometimes — getting closer to the nub of the matter — the word *gift* comes into play. The fourteenth edition of the *Encyclopaedia Britannica,* which devotes an article to genius, says of talent only that it "refers to a native aptitude for some special kind of work [and] implies the relatively quick and easy acquisition of a particular skill." Valéry, who said so many striking things, also said that we really need a word to cover the stretch that lies between talent and genius. Much as I like the ring of that, I find it a touch confusing because, though the one term is usually defined with reference to the other — with genius always given the higher place — neither has ever been properly locked up semantically.

My natural inclination is to prefer talent to genius. Genius is, as the English say, a bit of a muchness, or as we Americans say, too much. Geniuses have generally been more than a little sloppy. Aristotle claimed that "there is no great genius without a mixture of madness," and there is a good deal to it. Think of Picasso with his Communism, woman chasing, multiple small stupidities; Einstein with his political naïveté, silly hair, many minor cruelties; Shaw with his wish to reform English spelling, his utter vanity, his vegetarianism (imagine what the SOB would have been like had he eaten meat). Genius is so all-embracing, so all-round, yet I find I rarely wish to embrace it, let alone walk all the way round it.

I may have acquired this mild antipathy to genius from Max Beerbohm, who seems never to have met a genius he didn't dislike. (His distaste for George Bernard Shaw was considerable.) He wrote a brilliant little essay, "A Clergyman," that comes to the defense of an unknown cleric bullied, in the pages of Boswell's biography, by Dr. Johnson. When Max met W. B. Yeats, he felt that "the pleasure of meeting Yeats was not for me an unmixed one. I felt always rather uncomfortable, as though I had submitted myself to a mesmerist who somehow didn't mesmerise me." Yeats, in time, became his genius — that is, someone slightly other than himself. "His dignity and charm were as they had always been," writes Max. "But I found it less easy to draw caricatures of him. He seemed to have become subtly less like himself." The genius, I gather, had taken over, leaving the man behind.

Even Goethe, that universal genius of all geniuses, is not exempt from these Beerbohmian criticisms. In his essay "Quia Imperfectum," Max notes that Goethe has often been described as "the perfect man" and was "a personage on the great scale, in the grand manner, gloriously balanced, rounded" — "from no angle, as he went his long way, could it be plausibly hinted that he wasn't sublime." One waits, after such a buildup from the always measured Max, for the blade to fall, and now it does: "But a man whose career was glorious without intermission, decade after decade, does sorely try our patience."

Max goes on to show, through describing a minor incident in which Goethe was trapped into having his portrait painted by a failed German artist named Tischbein, the great genius's vanity, naïveté, conceit. "Deep thinking and high imagining [such as geniuses go in for] blunt that trivial instinct by which you and I size people up," Max writes, and that, before he is done, ain't the half of it. The essay is ostensibly about Tischbein's failure to complete his portrait of Goethe. Max speculates that Tischbein may have abandoned him to court the beautiful future wife of the English ambassador to Naples. But "a likelier explanation is merely that Goethe . . . irked him." By the essay's end, Goethe comes out rather resembling that part of the horse that jumps the fence last.

The only modern genius whom I admire is Winston Churchill, and I wonder if this isn't so because, along with being a political genius, he was also an immensely talented man: an excellent writer, a brilliant talker, a not-half-bad painter. Churchill got so many things done, in different lines and fields. I also prefer my geniuses to die young, à la Mozart, Schubert, and

Keats, and not stick around to grow as egomaniacal as Wagner, as grotesque as Ezra Pound, as mean as Robert Frost, or as bombastic as Frank Lloyd Wright. I have met three or four men of astonishing erudition and a few brilliant scientists of the first rank, but I've never met a true genius. A genius is someone who changes one's very conception of the possible, whose originality is such as to take him outside the traveled paths, there to create or explore things the world would probably not have come upon without him, or at least not as quickly. "What, indeed, is genius," asked Walter de la Mare, writing about Joseph Conrad, "but a power of receptiveness so individual that its revelation in the form of art is the revelation of a new universe."

A real distinction ought to be made between scientific and literary genius. The scientific geniuses, from Newton on, form a chain of sorts, one link building on the one before it; while literary genius — Dickens, Tolstoy, Joyce, Proust — is a one-shot deal, coming out of nowhere and often not leading to anything beyond itself. But perhaps you can sense me swimming out of my depth here, so I had better head back to shore.

I, who for most of my youth worried about my lack of talent, even now show a certain effrontery in talking about genius. Although I grew up Jewish and middle class — in an atmosphere where people, stereotypically, worship cultural talent of all sorts — only two kinds of talent were really appreciated in my neighborhood: athletic talent among the young and the ability to earn a good living among our parents. (All those Jewish boys, and not a violin in sight — what a waste!) General intelligence, taste, and good manners seemed to count for little. In any case, I, as a boy, hadn't any of these talents or qualities in proportions significant enough to matter.

Apart from paddle and racquet games and gin rummy, I did

have a small, most incipient talent for mimicry and for using words. The two were connected. Witty responses frequently occurred to me; an amused sense of the grotesque and of the comedy of pretension fortified me as I looked out at the world. My imitative powers allowed me to mimic the speech of friends and celebrities with some accuracy. Certain words fascinated me — *malodorous, reiterate, reprobate* — and, when used in proper rhythm, they positively excited me. This excitement was evidence of an innate interest in writing, though I had no way of knowing it then, for I knew no writers and hadn't even remotely considered the possibility of making my living as a writer.

In fact, I knew almost no grammar and even less punctuation. But my imitative powers, once I went off to the University of Illinois, allowed me to write passable, if less than Gibbonian, compositions. I should probably have been asked to write no compositions at all had I studied business, as most of my friends did. And I would indubitably have studied — "majored in" — business but for my complete certainty that I would have failed accounting. I saw those drab textbooks, I looked upon those accounting worksheets, and I knew straightaway that I hadn't a chance — one semester of accounting and I would be a goner.

The first time in my life that I ever heard the words *liberal arts* was in connection with my fleeing the study of business. Studying the liberal arts was, I discovered, an alternative to studying business. (There was engineering, but, with my mathematical powers, it was out of the question.) The liberal arts have meant a great many things to a great many people, but to me they meant an escape from accounting. Like most of the fateful decisions in my life, the decision to study the arts came about all but by accident.

The liberal arts curriculum at the University of Chicago required a sustained immersion in reading and a fair amount of writing. For the better part of my undergraduate education, I wrote defensively — that is, in fear of making some rudimentary mistake. I was never so foolhardy as to attempt a sentence with a semicolon in it. As for the dash — the insignia of the ironist and long since my favorite punctuation mark — it hadn't, as far as I knew, been invented.

Sometime around my last year at Chicago, things began to click into place. I began to read the intellectual magazines, which were refreshing after an unrelieved diet of great books. I began to read more attentively, always with an eye out for what I could steal for my own writing; I began to realize, too, that my writing had greater fluency when it imitated my speech. If I could be faintly clever in conversation, then why not in writing? Yes, why the hell not?

Friends tell me that letters I wrote in my early twenties read very much like my writing of today. I had, apparently, a characteristic note, a voice, a — could it actually be? — style. For the first time in my life I began to wonder whether I might have the magical thing itself, talent, or at least a touch of it. "This is what we mean by talent — by having something fresh to contribute," wrote Henry James about the Goncourt brothers. Did I have something fresh to contribute? I couldn't have answered that question.

What I did have was an almost preposterously ardent desire to be a writer. Please understand, I was in pursuit of neither truth nor beauty. What I wanted was print, my words in print, my name in print. The day that I learned, sometime in my twenty-second year, that I had an article accepted by a magazine was among the happiest of my life, up there with weddings and the birth of children. Edith Wharton, when she first learned of the acceptance of her poems by a magazine, ran up and down the stairs of her house to work off her excitement. I, less exuberantly, carried my letter of acceptance folded in my shirt pocket, and every chance I got I ducked away from my job and into the bathroom to re-read it.

Whence does such desire derive? Why does it visit only certain people? The answers to these questions have become no clearer to me over the years. They are, moreover, questions that pose themselves to me with some insistence because for more than two decades I've taught a fairly large contingent of would-be writers. Many of these kids have demonstrated talent well beyond what mine was at their age. Some among them have written things that seem to me close to being publishable; and a few have gone on to publish reviews or essays or longish newspaper pieces; three or four have drifted into jobs in journalism. But in all the time that I've been teaching, none has established him- or herself as a full-time, full-blown writer, despite immensely impressive youthful talent. None has yet proven that he or she has "something fresh to contribute."

My own belief is that the element of desire has not been sufficiently strong in them. I have had to conclude that they have not wanted it badly enough. By *it* I mean the desire for mastery through sustained practice of the craft of writing. Part of the problem may be that they enjoy life — its everyday pleasures, diversions, and attachments — too much. "Only a monomaniac gets anything done," said Einstein, to which one might add that only monomania will suffice to bring talent to fruition. The need for relentless work comes up again and again among the great achievers in art. "Inspiration is merely the reward for working hard every day," wrote Ravel, who also told the young composer Manuel Rosenthal: "You must work very hard, because someone who is gifted has to work harder than someone who is not." Henry James averred: "I have sweated blood to give an amusing surface to my style." James, not yet thirty years old, also wrote to Charles Eliot Norton: "I have in my own fashion learned the lesson that life is effort, unremittingly repeated, and . . . I feel somehow as if real pity were for those who had been beguiled into the perilous delusion that it isn't."

In his notebooks, Gerald Brenan writes: "In the old Provençal or Limousin language talent (*talens, talans, talanz*) meant desire, longing, inclination. In Dante *talento* means lust. The change in the meaning of the word suggests that it is the strong desire that creates the ability to do so." The other side of the lust for using one's talent is the disappointment, self-loathing, actual depression that visits when one is not using one's talent. I first realized that I was really a writer when I became almost physically ill after letting too long a time lapse without doing any writing.

Something close to a full literature exists on the subject of the destruction of talent. Legions have been accused of abusing, misusing, or selling out their talent. Others have almost specialized in wasting their talent. Harold Acton wrote: "I have made mistakes and wasted my talents, but I looked upon my failures as stepping stones toward the more beautiful and the most beautiful." F. Scott Fitzgerald always worried about whether he wrecked his talent by writing for money, first turning out slick-magazine stories, then taking himself off to Hollywood, where he was a great bust. When I was young, merely to be employed by Henry Luce on any of his Time-Life magazines was to have been thought of — and to have been allowed the dramatic self-importance of thinking of oneself — as having sold out one's talent. Edmund Wilson claimed that Luce and Hollywood were the two great destroyers of talent in his day.

Even someone who seemed so effortlessly talented as W. H. Auden worried a good bit about misusing his talent. "He was almost in awe of his own gifts," Auden's friend Thekla Clark has written, and "constantly afraid of not using them properly." She recounts Auden telling her that, during his political years, raising money for refugees in the Spanish civil war by boisterous speechifying, he "felt just covered with dirt afterwards." He worried about being proud, about not doing his best even in quite trivial matters. For Auden, not in dreams but in talent began responsibility.

Perhaps the most renowned talent waster of the current century was Cyril Connolly, who all but cultivated failure the way other Englishmen cultivated dahlias. Connolly discovered enemies of promise everywhere and may in fact have invented a few on his own. Of Connolly, Edmund Wilson, a man who did get the most out of his talent, wrote:

> Cyril Connolly
> Behaves rather fonnily:
> Whether folks are at peace or fighting,
> He complains that it keeps him from writing.

I say that Wilson got the most out of his talent — he was an indefatigable worker — but his was not quite the talent he wanted. Clearly, being the most pervasive and in some ways the most influential critic of his generation was not good enough for Wilson. He also wished to write fiction; but he couldn't make his characters come alive. Dawn Powell once devastatingly wrote of Wilson that "what he does not understand is all life that is not in print."

To know one's own strengths — and limitations — is another lesson that the talented are at some point forced to learn. It may well be that through understanding his limitations a person defines his talent. Max Beerbohm, with his perfect perspective on himself, wrote to a man who first proposed to write a biography of him: "My gifts are small. I've used them very well and discreetly, never straining them; and the result is that I've made a charming little reputation."

Somerset Maugham, who was very smart about all things having to do with literary production, had a keen sense of his own talent and its limitations. "Genius," he wrote to his friend the painter Gerald Kelly, "is a combination of talent and character, but character to a certain extent — I do not know how much, but I believe enormously — can be acquired." Maugham's view of his own artistic resources was that he had more character than brains and more brains than talent. He felt he could not acquire an ornate or interesting vocabulary, and he had no real powers of metaphor-making. "I knew that I should never write as well as I could wish, but I thought with pains I could arrive at writing as well as my natural defects allowed. On taking thought it seemed to me that I must aim at lucidity, simplicity and euphony."

Maugham's acknowledgment of his having no talent for making metaphors is corroborated by Aristotle's belief, set out in the *Rhetoric*, that the making of metaphors is apparently a natural gift and one that cannot be learned. Which brings me to the question of natural and developed talent. "There are two kinds of talent," Pearl Bailey said, "man-made talent and God-given talent. With man-made talent you have to work very hard. With God-given talent, you just touch it up once in a while." Interesting if true, but is it?

Most God-given talent, with the exception of musical and mathematical talent, seems to be physical: the talent for singing, for dancing, for running and throwing and other athletic feats. These, of course, need more than the occasional touching up that Miss Bailey suggests, but one of the nice things about them is that they tend to show up early. If one decides on a career in music or athletics, one can generally make that decision based on reasonable evidence and hence predict a reasonable probability of success. As a teacher of would-be writers, I envy teachers of music, who can know early the quality of the talent with which they are dealing and thus avoid leading on students who are certain to experience heartbreak. In writing, especially given the number of impressive late-starting careers — Joseph Conrad's being only the most magnificent — talent has a way of showing up in one's thirties and even beyond. The problem, of course, occurs when, like Godot, it doesn't show up at all. Lucky, in my view, are the parents whose children have no interest in becoming artists.

That is a sentiment to which Noël Coward's mother would never have subscribed. Violet Coward was a stage mother, but of a decent sort; besides, her son didn't require much in the way of pushing. I tend to think of Noël Coward as talent personified. He spoke of himself as having a "talent to amuse" and would never, no matter how great his success, have been so deceived as to think himself a genius. He was something of a connoisseur of talent. He thought, for example, that intelligent actors were "seldom as good as the unintelligent ones. Acting is an instinct. A gift that is often given to people who are very silly as people. But as they come on to the stage, up goes the temperature."

Coward's most recent biographer, Philip Hoare, claims that, "for a man with a notoriously low threshold of boredom, [Coward's talent] was a necessarily rapid talent." He was a terrifically fast worker, writing some of his most successful plays in less than a week. He was also determined to stay in the spotlight, which didn't hurt either. According to Katharine Hepburn, he had "no patience with weakness. He just thought it was stupid." Cecil Beaton, who was no admirer of Coward, noted of his skill as a performer that "nothing is left to chance; [it was created] by tremendous wit and polish." Noël Coward's estimate of his own talent strikes me as dead-on right: "My good fortune was to have a bright, acquisitive, but not, *not,* an intellectual mind, and to have been impelled by circumstances to get out and earn my living and help with the installments on the house."

I don't mean to sound like a University of Chicago economist, but perhaps no better forcing house for talent exists than the marketplace. Does anyone really want to buy what you, with your talent, produce? A daunting question, especially when one is young. Economic pressure pretty clearly works both ways: it can stimulate or eliminate talent, especially incipient talent. I sometimes think that if I had had the good fortune when young to have been given the equivalent of a MacArthur Foundation five-year grant, I would still be living in France, putting the finishing touches, in my early sixties, on a first volume of technically perfect, quite vapid poems. I have a friend whose husband was one of sixteen cousins who had each been given a trust fund that brought, in the early 1980s, an annual income of roughly $60,000; only one of the sixteen finished college, the rest lapsed into drugs, alcoholism, purposeless travel, and other forms of ne'er-do-wellism.

Cyril Connolly, in *Enemies of Promise,* speaks of the discouragement that marriage and family life can bring to a young writer. I seem to remember his noting that few things can dishearten a young writer more than a "perambulator in the hall." Ravel thought artists shouldn't marry at all and that, because they existed in a dream state, doing so was an act of cruelty to the people they married. Yet the free, the single life can also have its baleful influences. In art, there are no rules, except the rule that there are no rules.

I was a married man responsible for four children when I was twenty-six. I don't recommend this as the best environment for testing one's talent, but it worked well to test mine. I couldn't, of course, make enough money through my writing to support this chaotic household — I, in fact, worked at various editing and social-work jobs — but this responsibility did teach me how to make use of time; and it taught me how much I wanted to write, which was as much as anything in the world. "It took me fifteen years to discover that I had no talent for writing," noted Robert Benchley, "but I couldn't give it up because by that time I was too famous." My own situation was that it took me fifteen years to discover that I had damn well better have a talent for writing, since I really couldn't give it up — by that time I knew that I was good for nothing else.

Things shouldn't be made too easy for talent — and they usually aren't. Most of the talented people I know who have gotten the best out of their talent are tough men and women, not at all the sensitive types that artists are supposed to be. A hostile environment only encourages them. They do, at least for a while, better work when they feel unappreciated. Too much appreciation often only depresses the talented. It encourages self-doubt. ("A best-seller," wrote Logan Pearsall Smith, "is the gilded tomb of a mediocre talent.") It removes the element of challenge and of fear. Fear — specifically fear of failure — is necessary. André Previn, no genius but a very talented musician, not long ago told an interviewer that he had engaged himself in a heavy conducting schedule because he worried about growing complacent; having to perform often as a conductor, with its challenge of public humiliation, sent enough fear through him to make life artistically exciting.

Solid generalizations about talent are not easily made. Why, for instance, does it show up in clusters, as it does in some endeavors — for example, among the writers of musical comedy between the 1920s and the 1950s — and then quite disappear?

The twenties seems the richest American decade for talent across the arts. But how account for the great Russian writers — novelists chiefly — of the second half of the nineteenth century, or the English Romantic poets of that century's first half? Then there was the astonishing seventeenth century in Dutch art, followed, as Huizinga put it, by "the general collapse of Dutch culture in the eighteenth century." A generation of astonishingly talented physicists, or biologists, or mathematicians will arise, then generations will pass in which the talent of the leading figures in each of these sciences seems so much less.

Some kinds of talent — in mathematics, in music, in athletics — are apparently reasonably predictable across generations within families. Other talents show up once and never reappear. Some skip a generation. Sometimes a generation will be skipped with two powerful talents operating in quite different fields on either side of it. The son of Moses Mendelssohn (the philosopher), who was also the father of Felix Mendelssohn (the composer), is supposed, poor fellow, to have exclaimed: "When I was young I was the son of the great Mendelssohn; now that I am older, I am the father of the great Mendelssohn." No talent, apparently, for Mr. Inbetween.

One mustn't forget, too, the slightly odious category of the too obviously talented. Talent shouldn't be allowed to lapse into pure showing off. It should never say, except with an understated and discreet charm, Look at me! "The legend of my modesty grew and grew, [and] I became extraordinarily unspoiled by my great success," said Noël Coward in 1936. "As a matter of fact, I still am." Most of the too obviously talented come, of course, from show business — Sammy Davis, Jr., Anthony Newley, Barbra Streisand, perhaps Liza Minnelli. Danny

Kaye came close to falling into this category but narrowly averted it. Robin Williams falls into it. In literature, John Updike tends from time to time to lapse into it and becomes, like these others, a star bore. Even when they are frightfully good, the inability of such people to disguise their deep satisfaction with their own performance allows one easily to fight off the seduction of their magic and instead mutter to oneself, in the words of Queen Victoria: "We are not amused."

New York is clearly Talent Central in this country and, except at odd periods, always has been. In the past the talented felt they had to test themselves in New York: "If I can make it there," as the song has it, "I'll make it anywhere." One definition of talent — Stanislavsky's, actually — holds that it is "nothing but a prolonged period of attention and a shortened period of mental assimilation." The latter, which accounts for the quickness of New Yorkers, so many of whom are people from elsewhere who have brought their talents to market in New York, may contribute to the city's essential rudeness, which derives from its even more essential impatience. Everyone picks things up so quickly, and no pity goes to those slow people unable to keep the ball in play. What makes all the great world cities — London, Paris, New York — exciting is the unusually high proportion of talented people living in them.

Yet to live exclusively among the talented is not my idea of the good life. The talented can be charming, but there is a firm kernel of selfishness at the core — perhaps it *is* their core — of most people with talent. Certainly they tend to be rivalrous among themselves and often a bit contemptuous of people unlike themselves. "Every writer and artist wonders what in the world people of other professions can find to live for," Gerald Brenan once remarked. One can, if pressed, think perhaps of a few things: love, children, life itself outside the exercise of one's little talent. But these things are not likely to occur at first to the talented person, who has his mind on other things — or on one main thing, really, his talent.

It takes one, they say, to know one. And speaking as one, I do believe I know whereof I speak. Once I decided — with a minuscule portion of the world concurring — that I was a modestly talented fellow ("Don't be so humble," Golda Meir once said, "you're not that great"), I began to feel rather justified in my own selfish need to exercise that talent, and I have remained so. One of my greatest fears is that I shall not get the best out of myself, and so I find myself putting my work first against the claims of family, friends — just about everything else — and slightly resenting having to leave my desk for anything outside my work. It doesn't take much to imagine what an utter swine I'd be if I were a genius.

In the case of my own small talent, I came to recognize it chiefly because people told me I was talented. Whereas once I asked magazines to publish my work, magazines, with pleasing insistence, began to ask me. Praise, for which I have, I fear, an appalling appetite — the one appetite that hasn't seemed to diminish as I grow older — helped, too, though my pleasure in praise became qualified and somewhat refined. I liked praise above all from those men and women whose own talents I admire. (I should have liked it even more from the great figures of the past, though I know this presents certain technical difficulties.) Suddenly, I found myself in (mild) demand. Would I agree to write a movie? Might I agree to a three-day professorship in Texas? Would I give a lecture in London? A woman in Seattle, a perfect stranger, wrote to say that she would pay my airplane ticket and other expenses if I would agree to appear at a birthday dinner for her husband, who is among my most devoted readers — her plan was for me to be his surprise birthday present.

This is all very nice. It puts a touch of excitement into the trip down to the mailbox. But does it finally convince me, finally reassure me of the quality of such talent as I might have? Of course it doesn't. So many others — names on request — even less talented than I garner even more of the world's little rewards, which has served to divest so many of the sequins from the glittering prizes.

Although there may sometimes seem to be a basic injustice in the way talent is distributed in the world, this injustice is mitigated somewhat by the fact that those with talent — except when they are working with it — aren't made very happy by it. People who have the gift for moneymaking often seem to acquire little direct pleasure from the piling up of money. People with musical gifts, I have noticed, are often hounded into unhappiness by their perfectionism. Athletes must be haunted by the day, never far off, when their talent will be spent and no longer of value. "Blessed are those without talent," Emerson noted in his *Journal,* and the remark, when one thinks a bit about it, isn't quite as paradoxical as at first it might seem, little as I like to acknowledge the wisdom of the Concord gasbag.

In a limited sense, I suppose, we do live in something resembling a talentocracy. Once it is decided that a person has talent of a sort that is admired, gates open to him, hands reach out to light his cigar, dinners are offered. Talent can confer social freedom of a sort. I was born into the philistine middle class, and most of my circle of friends today belong to what the English call "the chattering classes," but I feel that, in a pleasing way, my small talent has sprung me from the class system or at least away from any anxiety about social class. My talent is to unfurl slightly oblique observations in sentences that, if properly spun, sometimes yield a small surprise. I operate at the level of the sentence. I live less in the world than in my head. I long for a wisdom I know I shall never attain. I am a writer lucky beyond all luck to have found not only his forms but his perfect audience. The number of this audience is small — ten or twenty thousand maybe — but select, and of them a respectable proportion, at one time or another, have written to me. ("My correspondence," I have been heard to yell, in my best Butterfly McQueen voice, "is killing me.") I have the readers I deserve, and — *mirabile dictu* — they turn out to be people a lot like me. Nothing I write is over their heads or beyond their imaginations. ("It appears that my stuff has been over their heads," wrote Henry James apropos of the excuse given him for having been fired as the Paris correspondent of the *New York Tribune*. "Imagine their stature!") Although many of my readers write very well, the chief difference between us is that I have put in more time learning how to shape my sentences than they, and I have turned out graphomaniacal.

Mine is a talent that has nothing to do with originality. Mine is instead a talent for a certain quality of literary intimacy. I am sometimes able to say what other people think but have not yet formulated for themselves. And when I am able to say it correctly, with lucidity and wit, I can, for my limited audience, give pleasure, amusement, and — if I'm really cooking — a touch of solace.

What is in all this for me? What's in it, as the crassest of agents might say, for the talent? Work is for me the antidote, not for any of the world's ills, but for all of my own. Work keeps the black dog from the door, the blue funk on the other side of the window. When working well, my life falls into place; I needn't search for life's meaning but seem temporarily to have found it; I am, in a world not notably arranged for sustained felicity, as close to happiness as I am likely to get. That's what's in it for the talent — the sweet delight in exercising one's gifts — and that is everything.

The Pleasures of Reading

FIVE OR SIX years ago, I was informed by my literary agent that two of my books were to be recorded by a firm called Books on Tape. Although the advance was not such as to earn me an honorable discharge from the financial wars, this was nonetheless pleasing news. Five or six months later, two smallish boxes arrived with the actual tapes. Ah, thought I, now here is a scrumptious little snack for the ego. I shall play these tapes in my car as I drive around Chicago, or on the Indiana Tollway, or up the Pacific Coast Highway. How soothing, how delicious the prospect, driving along and listening to that most amusing of people, oneself, or at least one's own thoughts. Wasn't it Philip Larkin who said that sex was altogether too good to share with anyone else? Listening to oneself on tape seemed the literary equivalent of Larkin's sentiment. Onan, I'm phonin', dear boy, to say you don't know the half of it. Or so I had supposed.

When I slipped my first tape into the tape player in my car, waiting for the lush cascade of words — my words, every last darling one among them — I was aquiver with anticipation. Cutting now directly to the chase, allow me to tell you that I didn't end up wrapped round a telephone pole, a silly grin of ecstasy on my face. No, I never made it through the first tape — I never made it, in fact, through even the first five minutes of the first tape. As it turned out, the man assigned to record my books had an odd, slightly twerpy accent; his rhythms were not mine; and listening to him rattle on, rolling obliviously over my careful punctuation — all this was more than I felt I could take.

I have since had four other of my books recorded on Books on Tape. The most recent of these has been a book of short stories, which contains ten or twelve Yiddish words that the (I assume under-employed) actor hired by Books on Tape, in his conscientiousness, actually called to get official pronunciations of — such words as *mishagoss, narrishkeit, mishpacha*. But I found I could not listen to these tapes, either. I didn't even open the boxes in which they arrived. What is going on here? I know lots of intelligent people who listen to books on tape with intellectual profit and simple amusement. Why can't I?

Before getting round to an answer, let me go on to a further confession: I cannot read detective or spy fiction. Deep down I really don't care all that much about who done it. It is not my immitigable highbrowism, for my highbrowism turns out to be pretty easily mitigated. I don't in the least mind watching detective or spy stories in the movies or on television. Some of the best Hollywood movies — *Double Indemnity, The Maltese Falcon, Farewell My Lovely, The Day of the Jackal* — have been detective and spy stories, with the rest probably westerns; and while I wouldn't think to read a Tom Clancy novel, at my regular evening post as couch potato I find I am able to watch VCR versions of his movies and feel no pain whatsoever. I just can't bear to read the stuff.

The problem for me is that reading is I won't say a sacred but nevertheless a pretty serious act. A very sensual act it is, too. I take account of the look, feel, even smell of a book. I like, or feel uncomfortable with, its heft in my hand. In reading, pace means a great deal, and one of the good things about a book, as opposed to a tape, is that you can read it at your own pace: flying on by, stopping, re-reading, even nodding, nodding more frequently, till — *ka-boom* — the book drops from your hand.

I read, for the most part, very slowly. The mere notion of speed-reading is repugnant to me. ("Read *Anna Karenina* last night," an old joke about speed-reading has it. "A book set in Russia, isn't it?") The better the book, the more slowly I tend to read it. The older I get, also the more slowly I read — not so much because my mental faculties begin to break down, which I'm sure they do, but because I am no longer so confident, as when younger I was, that I have a respectable chance of returning to re-read the book in my hand. Besides, the notion of speed-reading is doubly repugnant for speeding up a pleasure. If speed-reading were really to catch on, can speed-eating be far behind? Let us not speak of other pleasurable activities.

Benjamin Cheever, a great devotee of listening to books on tape, has recounted that he not only listens to books on a tape player in his car but walks around the house wearing a Walkman "so that I can listen to a book while I run, rinse the dishes, make coffee, or shave." I myself rarely leave the house without a book, and I have been known to read a few paragraphs in the elevator in our building, or possibly finish a page or two while in line at the bank, and even catch a quick paragraph in my car at a longish stoplight. But whenever, or wherever, I read, I need a pencil nearby to make my inevitable sideline of something I consider important, or plan to return to, or need to look up. I sometimes copy out things from books I am reading in a commonplace book I keep. I cannot depart from a book until I have a distinct sense of my place, and usually prefer not to cease reading until I arrive at the beginning of the first full paragraph on the left-hand page. You may think me very anal, but I need to observe all these little idiosyncrasies. ("Anality!" a character in an English novel exclaims when accused of it. "Anality — my ass!")

Being a writer also makes me a slower reader. Anyone — and I exclude only Ludwig Wittgenstein from this proposition — who reads a sentence has to make the following little check on it: 1. Is it clear? 2. Is it (grammatically, semantically, logically) correct? 3. Is it interesting? 4. Is it true? 5. Is it (charming bonus) beautiful? And then, if he or she is a writer, three further questions arise: 1. How was it made? 2. Could it be improved? and 3. What, for my own writing, can I steal from it? I have never met a good writer who wasn't also a penetrating reader; and every good writer, with varying degrees of consciousness and subtlety, is also, in an indirect way, a plagiarist.

Shocking to report, now past sixty, I still do not know all the words in the English language. The other morning I was reading Owen Chadwick's fine book *Britain and the Vatican during the Second World War* and came upon Chadwick's description of Myron Taylor, President Roosevelt's personal envoy to Pope Pius XII, as "rhadamanthine." It bugs me not to know a word. I am content not to know the meaning of the universe, or why God sent sin or suffering into the world, but not to know what a word means is beyond my tolerance. I trust you will think me on this matter altogether too rhadamanthine, which is to say, severe, or strict, coming from the judge Rhadamanthus in Hades in Greek mythology. But there it is, a tic, and I am stuck with it.

I am also stuck, though at last becoming slowly unstuck, with the notion of finishing any book I begin and of reading every blasted word of it. I was pleased, some years ago, to discover that Justice Holmes, a wonderfully penetrating reader of excellent taste, suffered the same affliction until the age of seventy-five. Behind this was Holmes's worry that, at the gates of heaven, Saint Peter would quiz him about his reading, and he didn't want to be caught saying he had read a book that he hadn't really finished. I read this in one of the collections of Justice Holmes's letters, of all of which, take my word on it, I have read every word.

I have at long last arrived at the age of skimming, which I still don't do with an altogether clear conscience. But why, I now tell myself, should I suffer painful *longueurs* in novels, too lengthy plot summaries in biographies of novelists, long quotations from third-rate sources. I may be beautiful, as the blues song has it, but I'm goin' to die someday, and, I now say to myself, how 'bout some better readin', before I pass away.

Gertrude Stein said that the happiest moment of her life was that moment in which she realized that she wouldn't be able to read all the books in the world. I suppose what made it happy for her was that it took off a fair amount of pressure. I have finally come to the realization that I shan't be able to read even all the good books in the world, and, far from making me happy, it leaves me, a naturally acquisitive fellow, a little sad. It does make rather more pressing, once one grants a world of limited possibilities, the question of which books one ought to read and which exclude.

The late Alexander Gershenkron, an economic historian at Harvard, once took up the matter of how much one can read in a lifetime, and with depressing statistical consequences. Gershenkron was then near seventy, and he estimated that, in his adult life, which he felt began at the age of twenty, he read roughly two books (outside of his professional reading) a week. This meant that, over fifty years of reading, one will have read only five thousand or so books. A piddling sum when one realizes that something like sixty-odd thousand books are published annually in the United States alone.

Given this daunting logistical problem, Gershenkron, in an essay in *The American Scholar,* remarked that it is a shame to have read too many of the wrong books, and so set out to discover criteria for establishing which are the right — or best — books. He arrived at three criteria: 1. a book should be intrinsically interesting; 2. a book should be re-readable; and 3. a book should be memorable. These criteria are thoughtful, impeccable, and, as by now you may have noticed, utterly useless. How, after all, can one know if a book is interesting until one has read well into it, or re-readable until one has read it through a second time, or memorable until long after one has finished reading it? One can't.

Advice about books has always been plentiful. The more practical the better I like it. The *Wall Street Journal* columnist Irving Kristol used to tell students at the NYU Business School never to show up for a job interview carrying a novel, which seems to me very sound advice, unless you happen to be interviewing for the job of literary critic or novelist. The late Arnaldo Momigliano, the great historian of the ancient world, once told me, in his strong Piedmontese accent, "You know, the cheapest way to acquire a book remains to buy it." I puzzled over that for an hour or two, before figuring out that what Arnaldo meant was that if you bought a book, rather than have it given or lent to you, at least you weren't under any obligation to read the damn thing.

Perhaps in America, where cultural confidence has always been a bit shaky, advice about what one ought to read has also been especially plentiful. As early as 1771, a man named Robert Skipwith, who was to be Mrs. Jefferson's brother-in-law, asked the then twenty-eight-year-old Thomas Jefferson to draw up a list of books "suited to the capacity of a common reader who understands but little of the classicks and who has not leisure for any intricate or tedious study. Let them [these books] be improving and amusing." Jefferson obliged with a list of 148 books, mostly in the classics but with a few intensely practical works, among them a book on horse-hoeing husbandry and Nourse's *Compendium of Physic and Surgery.*

The flow of such advice since has never ceased. There was Harvard's once famous five-foot shelf of classics and, later, Encylopaedia Britannica's *Great Books of the Western World.* In the early 1980s, a book was published titled *The List of Books: A Library of Over 3,000 Works.* By the time it was published, of course, the list was dated, being filled with books of that day on politics and popular culture: instructing one on the importance of the novels of Kurt Vonnegut, the Vietnam history of Frances FitzGerald, Frantz Fanon's *The Wretched of the Earth,* and other books that one now turns away from at the asking price of 25 cents at garage sales.

No one, I fear, can offer much useful advice on what you ought to read, apart from making the important distinction between serious and unserious books. I once suggested in an essay that certain books were age specific — that is, that certain books ought or ought not to be read before or beyond certain ages: no Thomas Wolfe after eighteen; no F. Scott Fitzgerald beyond thirty, no Chekhov before thirty; no Proust before forty; no James Joyce beyond fifty — that sort of thing. Perhaps the best and only worthwhile distinction is that made by a character in an R. K. Narayan novel who divided his personal library into good books and bad. In mystical fact, books have a mysterious, unpatterned way of appearing when one needs them. Or so at least they have in my life.

I grew up in an almost entirely unbookish home. Although

neither of my parents was an immigrant, and both were well spoken, I don't remember there being an English dictionary in our apartment. Magazines and newspapers were around in plenty. Only two books were kept, these in many copies, and both were stored in the basement. These were books written by my grandfather, in Yiddish and Hebrew, published in Montreal, where he lived, and subsidized in good part by my father. Whenever someone visited us who read Hebrew or Yiddish, I was instructed to run down to the basement to supply him or her with one of my grandfather's seemingly never diminishing stock of books.

I mention all this even though it does a bit of damage to one of the more pleasing stereotypes about Jews — that they are all bookish, artistic, sensitive, intellectual, born with something I can only call a culture gene. I grew up in a mostly Jewish neighborhood in which this gene seems never to have shown up. None of my boyhood friends was a reader, and neither was I. None of us played the piano, and certainly not the violin, that Jewish instrument *par excellence*. What we played were American sports, and what we yearned to be was wise in the ways of the modern city. The sons of moderately successful businessmen, we were adolescent gamblers and artful dodgers who hoped to grow into savvy men over whose eyes no one could pull the wool (make that cashmere).

Lonely children, or at least lonely boys, read books, and I was never lonely. When a boy I read a book or two — *Hans Brinker and the Silver Skates, Black Beauty* — but for the most part my reading consisted of comic books and a publication still in circulation called *Sport Magazine*. When it came time to give book reports, I cheated by giving them from Classic Comics. When we were in, I believe, the fifth grade, a woman from the Chicago Public Library visited our school and, in a treacly accent, told us, "Boys and girls, *boooks* are your friends. They will take you to unknown shores and reveal to you hitherto hidden treasures. Yes, boys and girls, *boooks* truly are your friends, so you must never bend their backs or write in their margins or dog-ear their pages." This most impressive little talk put me off serious book reading for at least another full five years.

I have since come not only to agree with the library lady, to whom I owe an apology, but to go a step further with Marcel Proust, who in his essay "On Reading" claims, with some justification, that books, at least as company, are really superior to friends. One need engage in no small talk with a book, as Proust noted, no greetings in the hall, no expressions of gratitude, or excuses for delayed meetings. With books, unlike with friends, no sense of obligation exists. We are with them only because we absolutely wish to be with them. Nor do we have to laugh, politely, at their attempts at wit. As Proust says, "No more deference: we laugh at what Molière says only to the degree that we find him funny; when he bores us, we are not afraid to appear bored, and when we decidedly have had enough of being with him, we put him back in his place as bluntly as if he had neither genius nor fame."

We may even, in extreme conditions, and contra the library lady, break the back and dog-ear the hell out of a book, which we certainly cannot do to friends. Besides, as you cannot with a friend, you can deal with a book at the pace you prefer: maundering, skimming, or plowing straight through. You can argue with a book, or even curse it, and not have to worry about being put down by a superior mind. (An Evanston used-book seller once told me that he was much amused with a book that came into his shop that contained, in the margin of one of its pages, the remark "C'mon, Ortega!")

The first book that really, that deeply, engaged my interest arrived when I was thirteen. It had a thick red cover, trimmed in black, and was titled *All-American*. It was written by a man named John R. Tunis, and was, as I had hoped it would be, about football — high school football. It was illustrated by a man named Hans Walleen, had a protagonist named Meyer Goldman, a Jewish halfback (anti-Semitism was part of the story), and was so immensely readable that I lapped up its 250 fairly large-print pages in a single day. As we should say nowadays, it blew me away.

How to recover what Marcel Proust calls the original psychological act of reading? I am not sure I can do it justice. I remember being swept up in John R. Tunis's story. I remember pulling for characters — wanting them to win through. I remember wanting to rush to the end of the story, to make sure it ended in a victory for goodness, fairness, and decency (not to worry, it did). At the same time that I wanted to know how things worked out, I didn't really want the book to end and so to be ejected from this swell world that John R. Tunis had created.

All-American did something that not many other things I had thus far encountered in life were able to do — it took me out of myself and put me into a larger world. Not all that much larger, now that I come to think about it, but larger enough to stir my imagination. Even the details of reading the book return to me, nearly fifty years later. I read part of it in our living room, and finished it, supine, propped up on my bed, on top of the spread, leaning on my right elbow.

I can remember the conditions surrounding the reading of lots of books that had a strong effect on me as a boy. I remember sitting up all night, in the bed next to which my father slept in the Brown Hotel in Des Moines, Iowa, where at sixteen I had gone with him on business, to finish Willard Motley's *Knock on Any Door;* I remember sitting, legs crossed, reading John Dos

Passos's *U.S.A.* in a park called Indian Boundary on the North Side of Chicago. I remember reading *The Catcher in the Rye* on a train headed for Champaign, Illinois. Oddly, I don't remember the conditions under which I read *The Grapes of Wrath,* another key book for me in my youth. All of these books I read with no sense of their quality or place in the general hierarchy of critical importance, for these things, pleasant to report, had not yet any meaning for me; these books excited me because they seemed to take hold of life, and consequently they took hold of me.

Proust, that brilliant anatomist of passion, recalled everything about his own reading experience, about which he reports both in *Remembrance of Things Past* and in "On Reading." Characteristically, he laments the passing of the intense pleasure that his boyish reading gave him. Reporting on his emotions upon the completion of a book, he writes:

> Then, what? This book, it was nothing but that? Those beings [its characters] to whom one had given more of one's attention and tenderness than to people in real life, not always daring to admit how much one loved them, even when our parents found us reading and appeared to smile at our emotions, so that we closed the book with affected indifference or feigned ennui; those people, for whom one had panted and sobbed, one would never see again, one would no longer know anything about them.

"How do you manage to know so many things, Monsieur France?" Proust is supposed to have asked Anatole France, to which the older writer is said to have replied: "It's quite simple, my dear Marcel. When I was your age, I wasn't good-looking and popular like you. So instead of going into society I stayed at home and did nothing but read." Later in life, given a choice, would Marcel have preferred going to a party or staying home with a book? It would depend, I suppose he might have answered, on who was giving the party and whether certain duchesses would be there. And of course much later in life, he preferred to stay home to write a book that has kept many of us at home reading it for weeks on end.

I ought to have known that I was in danger of being seriously hooked on books and the pleasures of reading when, one sunny summer afternoon in my fourteenth year, I stayed home to read another John R. Tunis novel, this one about baseball. When I could as easily have been outside playing the game, I preferred at that moment to continue reading about it. A bookworm, clearly, was in the making.

Still, the hook took a while to sink in. I read scarcely at all in high school, and then mainly books about the slums. *The Amboy Dukes* by Irving Schulman, a novel about a bunch of thuggish kids in Brooklyn, was a much thumbed book in my high school. In print — in actual print in those happily prudish times — it used the word *jugs* to refer to a girl's breasts. I read other books in this general line of hoods-in-the-slums books, including one actually called *The Hoods,* by a man named Harry Grey, from which, owing to the perverse games that memory chooses to play, I still recall the sentence "Cockeyed Hymie at the wheel, the big boat pulled into the night and I thrilled to the sensation of the clutch."

Although I was never a good student, the University of Chicago did teach me which were the important books. I was, though, pleased to depart that exalted setting so that I might read, alongside all those great books, a number of merely good ones, of my own choosing and to be read in my own unsystematic way. My own unsystematic way included a few key motives, among them reading to discover what life was supposed to be like and how one was supposed to live it. "Genius," wrote Henry James, "is only the art of getting your experience fast, of stealing it, as it were." I hoped to steal a lot of experience from books, and believe I may have done so. Then, too, the question implicit in reading every great writer, or so I began to sense, is, What would he or she have thought of me? Reading a serious book, it turns out, provides a way of reconsidering one's own life from the author's perspective.

I have never clocked myself here, but my guess is that rare is the day that I do not spend anywhere from four to five hours reading. Apart from ablutions and making coffee, reading is the first thing I do in the morning and generally the last thing I do at night. I once tried to go a day without reading and found it compared in difficulty of deprivation with going a day without smoking; and I speak as a former two-pack-a-day man. My children seem to recall the most repeated phrase from their growing up with me as their father being, "One moment: I'll be with you as soon as I finish this paragraph." Whenever I am abroad, in no matter how exotic the city — Athens, Istanbul, Jerusalem — at some point I yearn to stay the day in the hotel room and do nothing but read.

I am always amused to note, when the *New York Times* prints one of its Man or Woman in the News pieces, one of these men or women listing under hobbies such items as "tennis, travel, *reading.*" The notion of reading as a hobby to one for whom it is very nearly a way of life is comically absurd. With any luck at all, I shall never be the Man in the News, but if I am, I should as readily list under my hobbies, "tennis, travel, and *breathing.*" Hilton Kramer, another voracious reader, has more than once remarked of certain jobs — in government, as directors of large museums and other cultural institutions, as presidents of universities — that they are among those jobs "which never allow you to read another book." A poet, a Russian proverb has it, always cheats his boss. A really serious reader, a proverb I have invented for this occasion has it, is probably better off not being a boss.

I don't wish to make my own reading seem grim, a lonely quest for wisdom, a form of psychotherapy by other (and less expensive) means, onward ever onward, beating on, boats against the current, working in the dark, my passion my task . . . and the rest of it. On the contrary. My motives in reading are thoroughly mixed, but pure pleasure is always high among them. I read for aesthetic pleasure. If anything, with the passing of years, I have become sufficiently the aesthetic snob so that I can scarcely drag my eyes across the pages of a badly or even pedestrianly written book. I count myself one of Henry James's little band, "partakers of the same repose, who sit together in the shade of the tree, by the plash of the fountain, with the glare of the desert around us and no great vice that I know of but the habit perhaps of estimating people a little too much by what they think of a certain style." Along with the love of style, I read in the hope of laughter, exaltation, insight, enhanced consciousness, and dare I say it, *wisdom;* I read, finally, hoping to get a little smarter about the world.

Such are my hopes. But what, exactly, do I actually get out of this activity on which I spend so many hours daily? What is the point? I explain to my students that I by now have probably forgotten more than they have read — a remark made not in a spirit of braggadocio but in literal truth and true regret.

Plots do not stay all that long in my mind. I do not, as previous generations did, memorize vast stretches of poetry. What I consciously take away from many of the books I read are scenes, oddments, bits and pieces. I am somehow less interested in the final meaning of T. S. Eliot's "The Love Song of

J. Alfred Prufrock" than I am in the fact that so many of the phrases from that poem have stuck in my mind for more than forty years. From an Isaac Bashevis Singer story, I recall the earlock of a yeshiva student, flapping in the wind; I remember the little finger of Father Sergius, in Tolstoy's story of that name, twirling in the air after he has chopped it off in his struggle to hold sensuality at bay; I remember the hero of one of Henry Miller's novels — one of the *Tropics* — making love standing up in a hallway in Paris when a coin drops from his companion's purse and the Miller narrator remarks to himself, "I made a mental note to pick it up later"; in Owen Chadwick's *Britain and the Vatican during the Second World War,* I already suspect that, in the years to come, I shall recall only the diary entry of the British envoy to the Vatican, D'Arcy Osborne, who, unable to leave the Vatican while Italy was at war with England, noted: "I reached the grave conclusion during the mass that I am nothing but a pencilled marginal note in the Book of Life. I am not in the main text at all."

Reading is always at its best for me when the writer makes of it a sheath of words with which to capture the rich, unpredictable, astonishing flow of life. The metaphor of the sheath comes from Willa Cather, who in *The Song of the Lark* has her opera-singer heroine, Thea Kronborg, while standing in a stream in the pueblo country, reflect: "what was any art but an effort to make a sheath, a mould in which to imprison for a moment the shining, elusive element which is life itself — life hurrying past us and running away, too strong to stop, too sweet to lose?"

Not only am I unclear about what the main text of the Book of Life is, but I am not always sure what the main texts of actual books are. Am I, I wonder, insufficiently interested in such ideas as works of literature may be said to contain? There are those, and I am among them, who claim that, when it is going at its best, literature sails above the realm of ideas anyhow.

"He had a mind so fine no idea could violate it," said T. S. Eliot of Henry James. By that lovely rhythmic formulation I take Eliot to mean not that James was incapable of grasping or of functioning at the level of ideas, but instead that his true interest was elsewhere. James, Eliot is saying, was not interested in the knowledge contained in the various ideas or "isms" of literature, but in the truths known to the human heart and soul, the truths of sensibility — interested, that is, in what for the artist are the higher truths.

T. S. Eliot, at the age of thirty, writing to his friend Mary Hutchinson, allowed that there were two ways in which one ought to read: "1) because of particular and personal interest, which makes the thing one's own, regardless of what other people think of the book, 2) *to a certain extent,* because it is something that one 'ought to have read' — but one must be quite clear that this is *why* one is reading." Eliot goes on to say that, apropos of reading, there are two kinds of intelligence: "the intellectual and the sensitive — the first can read a great deal because it schematises and theorizes — the second not much, because it requires one to get more out of a book than can immediately be put into words." He then adds that "*I* read very little — and *have* read much less than people think — at present I only read Tudor drama, Tudor prose, and Gibbon — over and over — when I have time to read at all. Of course I don't count the countless books I have to skim for lectures, etc."

Marguerite Yourcenar said that there were three sources of knowledge in the world: that knowledge which comes from observing fellow human beings, that knowledge which comes from looking into one's heart, and that knowledge which comes from books. Is there any point in ranking the three according to importance? I suspect not. Not to observe others is to put oneself in danger in the world, not to observe oneself is to lose the permanent use of that unnamed organ responsible for reflection, not to read is to risk barbarizing oneself — leave any one of the three out and you have a less than fully equipped human being.

I am not sure Marcel Proust would agree. He had strong notions about the limitations of reading. He thought reading especially useful to the indolent mind, which cannot think in solitude but requires the lubrication of another, superior mind to set its own in thoughtful motion. My guess is that Proust thought his own a mind of this kind. I know my own is; if my thoughts are ever to catch fire, I need to rub them up against those of a finer-grained mind than my own.

Proust thought that the true point of reading was to waken us to the life of the spirit. The danger in reading, he felt, was when it tended to substitute itself for this life of the spirit — when, as he wrote, "truth no longer appears to us as an ideal we can realize only through the intimate progress of our thought and the effort of our heart, but as a material thing, deposited between the leaves of books like honey ready-made by others, and which we have only to take the trouble of reaching for on the shelves of libraries and then savouring passively in perfect repose of body and mind."

Yet this danger, of substituting books for intelligence, Proust thought, grew less as intelligence grew greater. Once we knew that we could "develop the power of our sensibility and our intelligence only within ourselves, in the depths of our spiritual life," books become, as Proust calls it, "the noblest of distractions, the most ennobling one of all, for only reading and knowledge produce the 'good manners' of the mind."

I suppose one can accept Proust's strictures on the limitation of books, with this one qualification: how does the flame of intelligence grow greater without the substantial kindling of books to ignite it? Sometimes, too, more than mere intelligence is ignited by reading.

Consider, for example, the following scene. A very nervous young black man, not long up from Mississippi, appears at the desk of a branch library in the city of Memphis, Tennessee. He has forged a note, asking the librarian to give him some of the books of H. L. Mencken, an author whose name he had come across in that morning's paper. (It is the late 1920s, and the reason the note has to be forged is that blacks are not allowed to use the Memphis public library.) After a very nervous-making exchange, the young black man, whose name happens to be Richard Wright, is given two Mencken titles: one of these is *A Book of Prefaces*. Wright, in *Black Boy*, his autobiography, provides an account of the effect of his reading H. L. Mencken for the first time:

> That night in my rented room, while letting the hot water run over my can of pork and beans in the sink, I opened *A Book of Prefaces* and began to read. I was jarred and shocked by the style, the clear, clean sweeping sentences. Why did he write like that? And how did one write like that? I pictured the man as a raging demon, slashing with his pen, consumed with hate, denouncing everything American, extolling everything European or German, laughing at the weakness of people, mocking God, authority. What was this? I stood up, trying to realize what reality lay behind the meaning of the words. . . . Yes, this man was fighting, fighting with words.

He was using words as a weapon, using them as one would use a club. Could words be weapons? Well, yes, for here they were. Then, maybe, perhaps, I could use them as a weapon? No. It frightened me. I read on and what amazed me was not what he said, but how on earth anybody had the courage to say it.

Richard Wright continues:

> I ran across many words whose meaning I did not know, and I either looked them up in a dictionary or, before I had a chance to do that, encountered the word in a context that made its meaning clear. But what strange world was this? I concluded the book with the conviction that I had somehow overlooked something terribly important in life. I had once tried to write, had once reveled in feeling, had let my crude imagination roam, but the impulse to dream had been slowly beaten out of me by experience. Now it surged up again and I hungered for books, new ways of looking and seeing. It was not a matter of believing or disbelieving what I read, but of feeling something new, of being affected by something that made the world look different.

Let me italicize Richard Wright's phrase *the impulse to dream,* which, he says, "had been beaten out of me." At times, much less brutally than in ways the young Richard Wright had to undergo, I grant you, life beats it out of all of us. And books, "that noblest distraction," can replace it, sometimes in direct, sometimes in subtle ways.

Because I was born into a family with a strong practical cast, which I cannot shake off, nor want to, I have to ask myself what does all my reading mean? What does it come to? Again I ask: What is the point of spending so much time, on my duff, a book in my hand, reading vast quantities of lovely prose and poetry, much of which I shall probably forget?

I have asked this same question of my students. For the better part of four years, I say to them, you have read a mass of poems, plays, novels — what does it all come down to? Their answers, though not unintelligent, are a bit predictable. All this reading sharpens their minds, they say; it tends to put them in touch with noble ideals; it lets them experience things that, without books, they could never experience (the eighteenth century, for example). All these answers, though a mite platitudinous, are nevertheless correct. I have the advantage over them of at least making a living off all my reading. But does all their reading come together, does it add up to something at least philosophically, if not commercially, useful? Is there, in the impatient phrase of the day, a bottom line? Here, in searching for an answer, they stumble. I'm sure I couldn't have answered it myself at twenty or twenty-one, but I should like to attempt to do so now.

A fair amount of reading, of a belletristic kind, I have come to believe, confers on one — or at least ought to confer on one — what I think of as "the literary point of view." This point of view, which is taught not by any specific book or author, or even set of authors, teaches a worldly-wise skepticism, which comes through first in a distrust of general ideas. "As soon as one creates a concept," says Ortega y Gasset, "reality leaves the room." (Right on, Ortega! I hope someone will write in the margin of this essay.) The literary point of view is distrustful of general ideas and above all of systems of ideas. It teaches, as Henry James advises, that you should "never say that you know the last word about any human heart." It teaches one to hold with Chekhov, who favored no sides or classes but wrote: "I believe in individuals, I see salvation in isolated personalities scattered here and there throughout Russia; whether they're intellectuals or peasants, they are our strength, few of them though there are."

The most complex lesson the literary point of view teaches — and it is not, to be sure, a lesson available to all, and is even difficult to keep in mind once acquired — is to allow the intellect to become subservient to the heart. What wide reading teaches is the richness, the complexity, the mystery of life. In the wider and longer view, I have come to believe, there is something deeply apolitical — something above politics — in literature, despite what feminist, Marxist, and other politicized literary critics may think. If at the end of a long life of reading the chief message you bring away is that women have had it lousy, or that capitalism stinks, or that attention must above all be paid to victims, then I'd say you just might have missed something crucial. Too bad, for there probably isn't time to go back to re-read your lifetime's allotment of five thousand or so books.

People who have read with love and respect understand that the larger message behind all books, great and good and even some not so good as they might be, is, finally, cultivate your sensibility so that you may trust your heart. The charmingly ironic point of vast reading, at least as I have come to understand it, is to distrust much of one's education. Unfortunately, the only way to know this is first to become educated, just as the only way properly to despise success is first to achieve it.

Let me return and give all but the last word to Marcel Proust, who wrote:

> Our intellect is not the most subtle, the most powerful, the most appropriate instrument for revealing the truth. It is life that, little by little, example by example, permits us to see

that what is most important to our heart, or to our mind, is learned not by reasoning, but through other agencies. Then it is that the intellect, observing their superiority, abdicates its control to them upon reasoned grounds and agrees to become their collaborator and lackey.

That seems to me impressively subtle, immensely smart, very wise. I came upon it, you will not be astonished to learn, in a book.

Will You Still Feed Me?

Ⅰ KNOW IT'S no great achievement — I realize people are doing it every day — but I am rather smugly pleased to have reached the stately age of sixty. I am pleased because, while the actuarial tables suggest I ought to have made it, nonetheless I have "the imagination for disaster," in the phrase of Henry James, who claimed to have "seen life indeed as ferocious and sinister." I am always not so secretly delighted when the worst doesn't happen. James also called death, at his final illness, "the Distinguished Thing." The Distinguished Thing has not come knocking at my door, at least not yet, though it regularly pays check-out calls on people my age and much younger: Harold Ross at fifty-nine, Whittaker Chambers at sixty, and François Truffaut at fifty-two were all required to pack their bags.

The few friends to whom I have mentioned that I am sixty seem mildly impressed. I am a little impressed by it myself. My birthdays have until now not much moved me. I have always felt my age, and I have tried to act my age, too, which, in a society that vaunts youthfulness, hasn't always been easy. I used to see my official retirement date — 2002, when I shall be sixty-five — on documents and viewed the number as more properly belonging to the realm of science fiction. I read the other day that Chicago, the city in which I live, hopes to have the Olympics in 2008, and I wonder if I shall be around to attend them.

As I clicked off the decades in my own life, I made note of what they were supposed to represent: thirty — the end of young manhood; forty — the onset of true earnestness; fifty — midlife, the halfway point (though, chronologically, not really), the age that evokes all sorts of empty symbolism. But sixty, sixty I think is fairly serious. There is nothing ambiguous about being sixty, the way there is about being in one's fifties. If one takes to chasing young women in one's sixties, for example, one is, officially, a dirty old man. At sixty it is even too late to undergo that greatest of all masculine psychological clichés, a midlife crisis. If one does so, one is not in a crisis but is merely being a damn fool.

In a Mavis Gallant story called "An Unmarried Man's Summer," the hero is told by his father, "If your life isn't exactly the way you want it to be by the time you are forty-five, not much point in continuing." He adds, "You might as well hang yourself." I suspect that the advice — apart from the hanging — is sound if the age, in accord with the longer-gevity of our own day, were set at sixty. At sixty, one probably does well not to expect wild changes, at least not greatly for the better. Probably best not even to expect a lot in the way of self-improvement. Not a good idea, I think, at this point to attempt to build the body beautiful. Be happy — immensely happy, in fact — with the body still functional.

At sixty I am now too old to die young, which is, somehow, pleasing. I am too old to expect a dramatic shift, apart from illness, in my life: too old to turn gay, or go motorcycle or Hasidic. The cards have been dealt, I have taken my draw, and I must play out the game. I happen to think I drew a pretty good hand. (A joker or two, I realize, is still to come.) Had I my first six decades to live over, there are lots of things I might have done differently. Yet I realize that had I done them differently, I might not have been able to do most of the things that I am now glad to have done. If you are satisfied with your life and its few accomplishments — and I, for the most part, am — even serious mistakes made early in life come to seem not only sensible but necessary. If you are not pleased with your life, of course, the reverse applies, and everything seems both a mistake and unnecessary.

Can you bear much more of this smugness? I'm not sure that I can. One of the nice things about *Hamlet,* it has been said, is that at least Polonius, who may himself have been around sixty, gets stabbed. To become Polonius-like, to start dispensing vast quantities of advice, is one of the temptations of growing older. When with young people, I find I already have to guard against playing the kindly old gentleman. I have sworn off all sentences that begin, "You may not remember this, but . . ." or, "When I was a kid . . ." or, "During World War II, I remember . . ." or, "In my day . . ." At sixty, one begins to feel one is entitled to such sentences — and one is, of course, wrong. Better, I think, to save them until age ninety-six or ninety-seven.

Sixty can have this strange effect on people, rather as if one is suddenly driving in a different gear. The most radical case of a sudden shift at sixty I know about belonged to W. H. Auden, an odd enough man in his own way before sixty but very odd indeed after sixty. It was as if at sixty precisely Auden was able to live as the old man he had earlier longed to be. He had carried carpet slippers around with him before, but now he began wearing them full-time and in all sorts of weather. He rarely changed his clothes. He would tell the same anecdotes over and over, often to the same people and within a brief span of time. "At my age," he averred, "I'm allowed to seem a little dotty."

After sixty, Auden emphasized all the little crankinesses that had earlier added to his charm but now chiefly irritated his friends. He became tyrannical about other people being punctual. He insisted on early bedtimes, and would leave other people's dinner parties at nine, or chase people from his own apartment at the same time. He liked to say that he had given up sex. (He hadn't.) He allowed himself mildly right-wing views, which he repeated to the point where they became set pieces. He became a monologist. He ceased to exercise. ("A *walk?* What on earth *for?*") Friends said that he had lost all spontaneity and that he longed for death. By sixty-two he seemed, in the words of one of these friends, Margaret Gardiner, "a very old man." Sixty, for W. H. Auden, was clearly a serious mistake.

If turning oneself into a mangy old coot at sixty is a grievous error, what are the other possibilities? Philip Larkin, on his sixtieth birthday, wrote that he looked "forward to the decent obscurity of autumn." With his excellent deadpan, he wrote to a friend that he thought it "a bit hard to call someone sixty just because they've been fifty-nine for a year." Yet he felt "being sixty is rather grim," adding, with just the right measure of Larkinesque rue, "I can't say I *feel* unduly old; I'm bald and deaf and with a Falstaffian paunch, but these have been with me for several, if not many, years. A chap in the *Guardian* said that the best thing about being sixty is that it isn't being seventy, and while this is true it's something that time will cure, as Pitt said when accused of being too young."

Auden said seventy was a good age to die, though he thought he would live to eighty-three; in fact, he pegged out, in 1973, at age sixty-six. Larkin, who was always conscious of passing time and of the time left to him, departed the planet at sixty-three.

"Who am I now?" Auden wrote, in a poem called "Prologue at Sixty":

> An American? No, a New Yorker,
> who opens his *Times* at the obit page,
>
> whose dream images date him already,
> awake among lasers, electric brains,
> do-it-yourself sex manuals,
> bugged phones, sophisticated
> weapon-systems and sick jokes.

I am myself a Chicagoan who also opens his *Times* at the obit page. No news more interesting than that having to do with those who have left the court. It seems, at this point, as if someone I know, or someone connected to someone I know, dies nearly every other day. I consider a fine morning one on which the *New York Times* prints obituaries about five people — four who died in their early nineties and one who died at eighty-nine. A bad morning is one on which three of the deceased are younger than I and two are just a few years older. This means that the machine gunner is out and firing indiscriminately. It would be a great help if one knew the exact date of one's own death — one's own true, so to say, deadline — though I am sure that, even with years of warning, one would still manage to be unprepared. I have always regarded the phrase "untimely death" as the poorest possible usage; hard to imagine, for oneself, a timely one.

Meanwhile, small warnings keep cropping up. I note what look like a few mottles, or age spots, on the top of my left hand. Graying of hair, rotting of teeth, loosening of flesh — all seem nicely on schedule. ("What is life," said Carlyle, "but a continual dying!") My handwriting, never very good, begins to approach the indecipherable. An eleven-year-old girl, with the utter candor of kids, one night at dinner said to me, "You don't have an upper lip." When I checked in the mirror, this turned out to be quite correct. I am getting a mortgage banker's mouth: two thin lines with teeth in between. Standing before the mirror, I practice the sentences "You should have thought of that earlier. I'm sorry, but we are going to have to foreclose on the farm."

In the press, I see photographs of people — chunky men with ringed pates of white hair, women in what appears to me an advanced state of decrepitude — and, *sacrebleu!,* they turn out to be four years younger than I. People even much younger hold jobs I assumed would always be held by people much older than I. Our poet laureate was the student of a contemporary of mine; the current secretary of state once worked for my wife.

I see photographs in the press of people a year or two older than I, and I tell myself that surely I don't look anywhere near as old as that. Yet when I last went to the movies, I gave the young woman selling tickets a twenty, and, as I counted my change, I noted that she had charged me the senior-citizen rate. I put down a book on the counter at my Korean dry cleaner's, and the owner asked me if the photograph on the back is of me. It is, in fact, a photograph of Isaiah Berlin, who was already in his eighties.

I am thought to have a good memory. What I have, in fact, is a writer's memory. For mysterious (and extraordinarily lucky) reasons, I seem to be able to call up all sorts of odd facts and memories required by things I happen to be writing. But when not writing prose, I have become quite as forgetful as other people my age. Names drop away, titles of books and movies frequently aren't there when I need them, bits of information get lost: the other day, for example, I could not recall the word *spleen;* a few days earlier, I mislocated the name *Borsalino,* the

Italian hatter. I seem especially bad at keeping past time straight. Events that I recall as being five or six years past turn out to be eight or as many as ten years past. I remember scarcely anything of trivial movies that I have seen as recently as three or four years ago. It is rather charming, really, allowing me to come to these ephemeral entertainments as if afresh.

Please do not get me wrong. The ongoing struggle, as the Communists used to say, keeps on going. A significant decision about growing older, it seems to me, has to do with whether or not one wishes to keep roughly abreast of new technologies, computers chief among them. I think that, had I been ten years older, I might have taken a pass on the computer age, contenting myself with using the computer only for its word processing. But I decided to take an interest. I haven't my own Web site, but I am, in a limited way, a World Wide Webster, partial, like nearly everyone else who uses it, to E-mail and unable to read anything of any length on the Internet. I am even a disappointed and now lapsed subscriber to *Wired*, a magazine that suggests the promise of computer technology's bringing about a new sensibility. After reading *Wired* for more than a year, I have decided to stay with my old one.

Hanging in there, I continue to read young novelists and short story writers: Allegra Goodman, Nicholson Baker, Mark Leyner, Julie Hecht, David Foster Wallace. I read these writers partly because much of my education has been through fiction, partly because I still love the novel and short story above all other literary forms, and partly because I hope they will tell me things I do not know about the way we live now. I find I do learn some of these things, though I am not sure I am getting a healthy return on my investment. But, then, I may have reached the age when nothing seems quite new and everything begins to remind me of everything else. I may be coming to a time when only amusing children and acts of inexplicable goodness are capable of astonishing me.

A certain distaste for change has begun to set in, even — perhaps especially — in minor matters. I find I do not wish to contemplate the notion that there is now a football team called the St. Louis Rams. The Rams have been in Los Angeles for as long as I can remember, and they ought to have had the decency to stay there — at least for my lifetime. When a house or building is razed along one of my habitual routes of travel, I feel a touch of loss, as I would after losing a back tooth that I hadn't hitherto been conscious of. A good deal of what passes for elegant food in modish restaurants seems to me overly ambitious, and I long for plain good food. Not all my positions and emotions are rearguard. I find, with the help of Pierre Boulez, that I am coming to enjoy modern musical composition, though I appreciate it less on CD or on the radio. But I am most content when in familiar surroundings and among old friends.

I pick up a literary quarterly to discover that there is an interview with Alice Fulton by Alec Marsh. I don't know who Alec Marsh is. I don't know who Alice Fulton is either, or why she is worthy of being interviewed. Turns out she's a poet, has written a book with the amusing title *Sensual Math,* and seems to be interested in the issue of "the poet's relationship to our electronically mediated world." I used to know the names of all the poets. Also those of all published short story writers, novelists, critics, reviewers, key publishing editors. I knew the mastheads of all the magazines, including those in exceedingly small print in *Time* and *Newsweek.* No longer.

My interests seem more limited generally. Am I, subconsciously, delimiting them? The list of things I no longer know about — and, perhaps more significant, no longer care to know about — grows. I know the names of fewer and fewer movie stars, United States senators, major league pitchers. I am not all that interested in politics — either its nuts and bolts or its larger structures. I can on occasion be shocked, but I am less and less surprised. I recently read an entire book on prostate cancer.

Just as my interests seem more limited, so have my fantasies become more sparse and attenuated. I am no longer able to dream my way into complex sexual intrigues with beautiful women with lush foreign accents. Staring at striking young women is an activity I now consider to be at a scale of seriousness three levels below that of window-shopping. I have no power fantasies whatsoever: I don't wish to be CEO of General Motors, editor of *The New Yorker*, president of Yale, secretary of HUD. My fantasies now include picturing myself enjoying long stretches in peaceful settings, amid the people I love, with a complete absence of aggravations, small and large.

Age consciousness has begun to set in. With the exception of classical music concerts, the places I frequently find myself in — restaurants, movies, plays — are places where I am not infrequently the oldest guy in the joint. "I think I have been more than most men conscious of my age," wrote Somerset Maugham. "My youth slipped past me unnoticed, and I was always burdened with the sense that I was growing old." Maugham reports, in *A Writer's Notebook*, that he always seemed older than his contemporaries, and adds that "it is not a very pleasant thing to recognize that to the young you are no longer an equal. You belong to a different generation. For them your race is run. They can look up to you; they can admire you; but you are apart from them; and in the long run will always find the companionship of persons of their own age more grateful than yours."

I have many younger friends. I used to have many friends much older than I. But by now, I believe the balance between younger and older has shifted. I do not myself feel a great gap between us, though perhaps my younger friends feel our age difference more than I. Can it be that they want from me what I wanted, in my turn, from my older friends: regard, respect, finally admiration to set the seal on my own less-than-sure estimate of my quality? It may seem odd to require the approval of one's elders when in one's fifties, but I felt this and still feel intense pleasure when I learn that someone I admired as a young man now has a good opinion of me.

Maugham goes on to report that one of the pleasures of growing older "is that on the whole you feel no need to do what you do not like." He adds that you are less likely to care what people think of you, whereas when young one is "bound hand and foot with the shackles of public opinion." Henry James, in a letter written in his sixtieth year to his friend Grace Norton, corroborates this, affirming that he has "reached a state of final beatitude in which one cares not a fraction of a straw what any one in the world *thinks* of one." I tend to agree. I might go a bit further and say that I am pleased to have some of the enemies I do; their dislike, I feel, honors me. When one gets to sixty, one is reconciled with oneself; one is what one is. Injustice of opinion matters less and less. Only true justice hurts; and, lucky fellow, I have come this far without having to undergo it.

What makes sixty feel different from, say, fifty-seven, is that finitude sets in in a big way — finitude combined, even now, with hope. If I can make it, I say, I'd like to teach ten more years. With a little luck, I say, I can write another eight books before the lights go out. Knock wood, I say, if I can only make it to eighty, my grandchild will be twenty-seven and I will have helped see her into relatively safe harbor.

This notion of finitude, of no longer playing with a fully loaded shot clock, has been with me for some time. I note an entry in my journal for October 10, 1992: "Autumn setting in in earnest. Sweater weather. Leaves near peak of color change. How many more autumns will I see? God knows — and nobody else — and it is not clear how much He cares."

With the reign of finitude well in place, one's resignation becomes greater. No sooner does one begin to recognize how quickly time is moving — it's not the minutes, it's those damn decades — than one recognizes as well all that one won't accomplish, at least in this life. "In the next life, *perhaps*," I find myself more and more saying, trying to get the italics into my voice, whether I am referring to not being able to acquire a new foreign language, or read a multivolume work, or play the piano, or go into retailing. I now know for certain that there are many things I shall never do: own a mansion, cook elegant dishes, read musical scores. I can, as they say, live with this; in fact, I am hoping to live for a good while with it.

One is resigned, too, to the world's comedy: idiots rising to the top, fanatics dressed up as idealists, boobs confidently in control. Henry James, in a formulation on which I cannot improve, noted:

> Life *is* a battle. On this point optimists and pessimists agree. Evil is insolent and strong; beauty enchanting but rare; goodness very apt to be weak; folly very apt to be defiant; wickedness to carry the day; imbeciles to be in very great places, people of sense in small, and mankind generally, unhappy. . . . In this there is mingled pain and delight, but over the mysterious mixture there hovers a visible rule, that bids us learn to will and seek to understand.

I wish that by now, at sixty, I could say that my own understanding of life is deep. It ain't. I remember, at twenty, taking a Shakespeare course in the University of Chicago's adult education program and being struck by how in the dark about life so many of my fellow students, many of them then in their forties and fifties, seemed. I don't know that I myself am currently all that much more enlightened. I like to think I am a little less connable than I was twenty or thirty years ago. I like to think I now at least understand how things *don't* happen, which is not at all the same as understanding how they *do* happen. I have never fallen for either of the two big stories of our century — Marxism and Freudianism — but that doesn't mean that I have come up with any big story of my own. In the Hegelian triad, I am all antithesis. I am left, really, with a few self-invented folk sayings: "In for a penny, in for a pounding" is one; "You live and you yearn" is another.

One of the things I yearn for, of course, is greater understanding. I don't at all like the idea of leaving the theater without understanding the play. Shall I be able to build up enough small insights to allow the parts to begin to approximate a whole? I continue to hope to get better at my work. For some years now, I have been telling myself that, as a writer, I have not yet begun to get worse, though I could use a good quality-control guy. Will I know about it when it happens? Short of dying or simply ceasing to write (as I type out this introductory phrase, the two seem to me almost the same), is there any way that getting worse can be avoided? Short of early death, probably not.

Being sixty changes a sentient person's notion of the future. Curt Gowdy, the old sports announcer, used to say of young athletes that they had their whole future ahead of them. Where else, I wondered, would anyone's future be? But, growing older, I begin to sense that much of my future is behind me. Certainly, I think differently of the future. It is no longer all open doors and wide horizons, enticing prospects and endless possibilities.

If one has children and grandchildren, one's sense of futurity is bound up with them. I myself listen to the plans of the young — and the young tend to be full of plans — and try not to smile, remembering the old joke: "Know how to make God laugh? Tell him your plans."

If sixty changes one's sense of the future, it absolutely knocks the hell out of one's sense of progress. What, at this point, is one progressing toward? And yet life, without a sense of progress, can seem an arid thing. My dear friend Edward Shils, then in his late seventies, told me that he had to have a sense of intellectual progress if he were to continue as a teacher and a scholar. Without this sense, teaching becomes empty, scholarship barren. Edward, practicing what he preached, broadened and deepened his own knowledge of China when in his early eighties, and he began to teach courses in sinological subjects.

When younger, one tends, brimming with hope, to assume progress: that next year will be better than this; that one will continue to grow smarter; that fortune will smile on one. At sixty, it is no longer quite so easy to believe such things. Candide, after all, was a young man. Had Voltaire made him sixty, he would have been not merely a fool but an utterly hopeless idiot.

"It is *difficult* to know something," says Wittgenstein, "and to act as if you did not know it." What one knows at sixty is that time is beginning to run out. So one lessens one's expectations, limits one's possibilities, resigns oneself to the hard facts of life — and yet plays on through. Life may be a mug's game — a game, that is, one cannot finally win — but it still seems well worth playing. In an unexpected way, these limitations can make things seem even richer: one loses passion and gains detachment, gives up ambition and hopes for perspective. The comic element of life seems, in some ways, greater than ever.

229 / *Will You Still Feed Me?*

Perspective is the trick of life, and I have not come anywhere near mastering it. Such perspective as I do have applies almost exclusively to other people, not to myself. Another of the pleasing things about attaining a certain age is that one begins to make out the arc of other people's careers. One sees patterns in their lives — the intellectual of poor character who has no real work to his credit as he nears fifty; the woman, stimulated by worthlessness in men, left alone in her sixties; the academic of profoundly bad taste who has wasted more than a decade of his adult life promoting a dreadfully dopey idea. These and other lives are worthy of contemplation.

I am, I fear, a sucker for the notion, first formulated by Novalis, that character is destiny. I feel reassured when people of strong character win out and people of poor character go down the drink. Evidence of a clean cause-and-effect relation clears the intellectual sinuses. Unfortunately, too often people of good character also go down the drink — for want of energy or because of bad breaks and crucially mistaken decisions — while the shoddy, the dreary, and the miscreant flourish, as the psalmist said, like the green bay tree. Naturally, I ascribe my own little successes in life to good character, though such character as I have is owing to my wish to avoid guilt and shame and to the loss, fairly early in life, of my taste for serious delinquency.

Writing to his friend Lady Georgiana Morpeth, who was going through a patch of depression, Sydney Smith recommended, among twenty different points, that she "be as busy as you can," "live as well as you dare," and have "short views of human life — no further than dinner or tea." Sound advice, especially the part about short views. At sixty, a long view may not, after all, be that long. Living with short views, enforced short views, may be one of the most interesting things about being sixty. Like hanging, it concentrates the mind — or at any rate ought to.

Does it concentrate it, however, too much on depression? Mild depression seems to me a natural and even sensible state to be in when entering late middle age. More than half the game is over, and one's equipment is in less than dazzling condition. A reader of a short story I not long ago published wrote me a letter in which he remarked on my *Weltmüdigkeit,* or world-weariness. He went on to say: "I hope I'm not being flip or jumping to a conclusion here — I'd guess that you, like many guys in their fifties and sixties, who have to preoccupy themselves with their own mortality (I am now in my middle seventies!), are also depressed." I prefer to think I'm not. I don't think of myself as being able to sustain depression beyond a few hours. But, maybe, it comes with the territory.

At sixty, one begins to spend a fair amount of time, at least mentally, with the dead. Oddly, I think less about my own death and more about dead friends and family. I miss them and find myself often talking to them. I cannot bear to remove from my Rolodex the names of such dead friends as Erich Heller, John Wain, and Samuel Lipman. The other day at the Paulina Market butcher shop I felt the presence of the now dead friend who first took me there; my wife's uncle came strongly to mind as I passed Schulien's, a neighborhood German restaurant where he and I sometimes met before Cubs games; my mother pops up everywhere, so often, in fact, that I may spend more time thinking about her now than I did when she was alive.

If one is lucky — that is to say, long-lived — at some point one's dead friends figure to outnumber one's living friends. Slowly, but increasingly, conversation about health with contemporaries begins to dominate; it already has begun with me. The other day's mail brought a catalogue from a necktie manufacturer in Vermont. Two of his ties seemed to me pleasing, but then I thought of all the neckties I now own — perhaps sixty of them — and decided that I already have enough, in the English phrase, "to see me out." Edward Shils would not agree. In his early eighties, he sometimes stopped to buy some piece of kitchen equipment; he claimed that doing so gave him a feel for the future; even on his deathbed, he still seemed pleased to acquire a new book.

But his was a remarkable generation. Someone recently said to me that he thought of the generation now in its late seventies and eighties as "the strong generation." Something to it. They lived through the Depression, fought in World War II, came into man- and womanhood early and lived their lives as, if you will pardon the expression, grown-ups. This gave so many of them not merely substance but gravity of a kind I do not find in my own or subsequent generations. Is it natural to think of one's own generation as a bit thin? Did such people as Joseph Conrad, Willa Cather, or William Faulkner think of their own generations as thin? Seems doubtful.

The feeling has begun to set in with me that I shall never again meet people as extraordinary as people I have met who are now departing the scene. As I view this scene, I find few celebrated people whom it would thrill me to meet: no one in scholarship, no one in sports, scarcely anyone in the arts. I cannot summon the awe. A few years ago, I was invited to a lunch at the White House for the presentation of medals to artists. When I was told I could not bring along a "spouse" — one of the ugliest words in the language — I declined, saying that I would instead content myself with a sandwich at home. I felt absolutely no regrets. Is this what is meant by being jaded?

I begin to take a keener interest in old age. I now cringe at stories about people who have sent up the yellow flag of senility.

I note carefully the way younger people shun the very old, as if they were lepers. I have begun to be a connoisseur of death, thinking a fair amount about the various diseases and modes of departure. I think, too, of styles of dying. A friend recently told me about his former lawyer, who loved opera. Knowing that his death from a debilitating disease was imminent, he arranged to travel to London and, seated in a wheelchair, he watched and listened to opera at Covent Garden on the last thirty evenings of his life. I read in Primo Levi's *Periodic Table* a description of Levi's Uncle Bararicô: in his old age "he ate almost nothing, and in a general way he had no needs; he died at over ninety, with discretion and dignity." To die with discretion and dignity — that seems a fine thing.

Yet better, I realize, to live with discretion and dignity. What turning sixty, that fatidic age, has done is make me want to live more carefully in the years left to me. Observe I say "carefully," not "cautiously," though caution may enter into it, too. I wish to minimize my stupidity, maximize my intelligence. "For those who are not angry at things they should be angry at are fools," wrote Aristotle, and yet, I sense, to be angry is, somehow, to be wrong. I want to limit to amused contempt my response to life's irritations. I realize that I cannot stand in the way of regress. I wish to live with a respect for the complexity of life without unduly complicating my own life. (*"Complexe mais pas compliqué"* was one of Ravel's mottoes for his art.) Which is another way of saying that I long for the perspective that is supposed to accompany my age.

I dearly want to learn at last to live in the moment. From early adulthood, I have spent much of my time living, mentally, in the future. Ah, when I'm older, when I've achieved this or that, when things have at last fallen into place, then life will begin in great glorious earnest. The current temptation, now that the future has arrived, is to begin living in the past: to remember the good old days when I thought so much about the future. Enough already. I have to lose my yen for then, suture the future, and at long last put the pow! in now — to make each day, that is, as delight-filled as possible.

In his poem "Lullaby," W. H. Auden writes, "Let your last thinks be thanks." A good deal to that. Especially in my case, since, as has become apparent to me, I have been one of the world's lucky people: paid for doing what I like most to do, rich in friends, in good health, lucid, still laughing. I have had a very good roll of the dice.

Not that I am in any way ready to pass these dice along. Ten years ago, in Florence, in a shop outside the Church of San Lorenzo, I purchased an ascot — brilliant blue, niftily splashed with red, and flecked with gold. I have yet to wear it, thinking it too pretentious even for me, who normally doesn't at all mind a touch or two of pretension. How much longer do you suppose I have to wait to get away with wearing this ascot? My neck, already aflap with loose skin, is certainly ready. But am I? Not quite there yet, I feel. Perhaps in another decade.

Yes, at seventy, if I get there — I have just touched wood — I shall be ascotted and ready to roll. You will see me coming. You won't be able to miss me. I shall be this old dandy, Italian silk at his throat, looking a bit distracted, because he is still thinking of the future while living in the past — and wondering where all the time has gone.

Anglophilia, American Style

ANGLOPHILIA came to me almost as naturally as hemophilia to its unfortunate victims — it was, that is to say, in my blood. It began with my father, who was born a Canadian and thus into Dominion status and who had enormous admiration for the English. Along with stories from the Bible, his first readings to me were stories of King Arthur and the Knights of the Round Table and of Robin Hood. So it was from the English, or at least in an English version, that I gained my first notions of honor and integrity and social justice. From the first, my heroes had English names and spoke in English accents.

The head of my mother's family was her mother, a widow and grand matriarch, who had come to America from Leeds. Although poor, she had somehow managed to have a Cockney maid, a woman with the extraordinary name of Minny Tumbletee. Rather late in life, Minnie Tumbletee married a man named Ted White, a retired sergeant in the British army who had many tattoos and a Cockney accent two stages beyond indecipherable. I have no memories of my grandmother, who died when I was three, but Minnie Tumbletee always told me that I was her favorite grandchild and that it was my grandmother's desire, somewhere along the way thwarted, that I be named Adrian; this would, I am sure, have made me a much better street fighter than I am today.

Still, I might never have become an Anglophile had I not been born in 1937, for my first, still strong, experience of history was World War II. This was the war that, in my mind, was won by the English, "the stolid English," who, in Primo Levi's words, "had not noticed that they had lost the game." Two years old when it began and eight when it ended, I then saw World War II, as I continue to see it today, as the good war, the war without moral equivocation, whose outcome was owed to English righteousness, endurance, and courage.

For an American boy growing up in the Midwest, World War II was fought at the movies. I fought it at the side of such gallant — and elegant — officers as Major Ronald Colman, Colonel Douglas Fairbanks, Jr., Captain Noël Coward, Commander Cary Grant, and Lieu(actually Lef)tenant Errol Flynn. Even in American movies, the English officers always came off as the most suave, most intelligent, most heroic of fighters. A few months ago, I watched again the Noël Coward–David Lean film *In Which We Serve,* which, despite its obvious propagandistic intention, still moved me greatly — to something near tears, if the ghastly sentimental truth be known.

Only a good deal later did I learn how much bravery was required of English civilians to endure the relentless nightmare of the blitz. How great this sacrifice was seemed all the more impressive to me, both as an American and as a Jew. In the Midwest, isolationism was still strong in the early 1940s, and its chief organ was the *Chicago Tribune,* the paper owned by the greatly anti-British Colonel Robert McCormick. All the American isolationists of the day — including, alas, H. L. Mencken — were anti-British, all full of suspicions about the craftiness of the English, who they believed would somehow trap us in a war that was, strictly speaking, none of our damn business. The plight of the Jews was never lost on Winston Churchill. Far from it. As Martin Gilbert has recently pointed out, the inexorability of the Nazi death machine was always on Churchill's mind, and much of his strategy during the war was devoted to rescuing as many Jews as possible. Churchill, not Franklin Delano Roosevelt, was, and has remained for me, the premier hero of World War II.

The next great English influence in my life came from the best of all colonizers, English literature. In the public schools of Chicago, such literature as was studied, apart from the thin gruel of a bit of Longfellow and Washington Irving, was English literature. Christmas, as I understood it, was practically invented by Charles Dickens. Dickens, too, in *Oliver Twist* and *David Copperfield,* described the poignant conditions of poverty and of being orphaned. He also taught one to have great expectations. And, once again, heroism: "For it is a far, far better thing I do, than I have ever done; it is a far, far better rest that I go to, than I have ever known." Sydney Carton's words, written by Charles Dickens, music by Ronald Colman, spoke to a longing in every boy's heart to perform acts of unknown heroism to the great benefit of a beloved. We first learned Roman history from a fellow named Shakespeare. From him, too, we learned adolescent passion through *Romeo and Juliet.* In America, our conceptions of honor, courage, romance, and decency were all imported from England.

English culture seemed to advance in perfect synchronization with my own development. I came into my adolescence in time for the wonderful Alec Guinness movies. As my own youthful anarchic humor began to take root, there was Terry-Thomas, with that malevolent gap in his front teeth. The next stop on my personal Anglophiliac express was *Beyond the Fringe*. As an American, it was natural for me to compare these performers with our own marvelously funny comedy team of Mike Nichols and Elaine May, and it seemed to me that *Beyond the Fringe* won the day. Nichols and May were more intimate, more psychoanalytic, and thus more neurotically funny. *Beyond the Fringe* was more freewheeling and more whimsical, operating from a larger, wider, and more social base.

I was, I see now, most fortunate not to have been born into a wealthier, more social-minded family, else I might have been sent to an American prep school and thence on to an Ivy League university. The American prep schools Groton, Choate, St. Paul's, Exeter, and Andover, showing the long educational influence of Anglophilia in America, were directly modeled on Eton, Winchester, and Harrow and instilled in their charges a strong tinge of snobbery. Much of what is called WASP culture, now dying out in America, had its basis in Anglophilia.

In much the same way, Harvard, Yale, and Princeton were meant to be mini-, if not imitation, Oxbridges. Yale University is said to have no fewer than seven replicas of the chapel at King's College. Throughout their by now fairly long histories, these schools have been staffed by many a stuffed-shirt English impersonator. One thinks of Barrett Wendell in the English department at Harvard who, with his insistence that English literature was best studied only by students of English descent, gave Anglophilia a very poor name.

A friend has recently recounted his memory of himself, in his second year at Harvard, walking the Harvard Yard, saying to himself: "Well, O'Brien, it's time to make a choice. Are you going to become another of these Ivy League false Englishmen or remain your good old Irish, lower-middle-class self?" He, my friend, chose the latter, which, despite rising high in the world, he remains, immutably, immitigably, admirably, today. I'm not so sure that, at the same age, my own answer would not have been "an Ivy League false Englishman."

Fortunately, I wasn't put to the test. I went to the University of Chicago, where I studied English literature. English literature and Englishness generally weren't highly valued at the University of Chicago. Science and social science and classical and Continental philosophy were the subjects that represented high seriousness there. Only two of my teachers, both in English history, neither particularly distinguished, were Englishmen. The tone at Chicago was clearly European, if not worldwide international. The social note was not hit at all. Snobbery, which has so often accompanied American Anglophilia, was confined at Chicago to pure intellectual snobbery.

Yet this didn't stop me — and not me alone — from feeling culturally inferior. American inferiority to Europe had, of course, been going on for a long time. "It is a complex fate, being an American," Henry James famously wrote, "and one of the responsibilities it entails is fighting against a superstitious valuation of Europe." James, as is well known, felt American society insufficiently dense, American culture altogether too thin, to support his own vastly complex artistic ambitions. Yet by midtwentieth century, most Americans felt, more simply and directly, that Europeans had wider and deeper experience than they and that the ground between us would probably never be made up.

Under Nazism and then under Communism, Europeans had looked the devil in the eye. Orwell, Koestler, Silone, Malraux, Pasternak — America produced no names (none that even came close) to match these. Existentialism might have made sense in France, but in America it seemed pure pretension. Being a thoughtful American in the 1950s — a serious and productive time — was the intellectual equivalent of being a yokel, a rube, a bumpkin.

Of course, the English had felt the effects of Nazism and Communism less directly than Continental Europeans, and for good reason. Something in the English character was too stolid — too sensible is the more charitable word — to be swept away by the mad ravages of ideology. England was too fair-minded a country for organized, really vicious hatred. A Dreyfus Affair was inconceivable in England; a Benjamin Disraeli was not. England might have had Philby, Maclean, Blunt, & Co., but Communism was never really a gravely serious issue. "The country," wrote E. M. Cioran, the Romanian cynic, whether with regret or admiration is unclear, "has not produced, to my knowledge, a single anarchist."

What England had traditionally produced instead was a home, a safe harbor, for anarchists, Communists, and other international troublemakers and losers, along with such occasionally valuable men as Alexander Herzen. The rightness, the spiritual generosity and handsomeness of it, was not lost on one of the world's most impressive Anglophiles, Joseph Conrad, as he made plain in *The Secret Agent*. The genius of England, as Conrad knew, had much to do with its parochialism, a parochialism that refused to go flying off in pursuit of millennialist dreams at the expense of its integrity. This integrity derived from centuries of good humor, courage, and common sense and prepared the ground for Anglophilia.

Some Americans came to their Anglophilia by descent. Others, who could not claim England as an ancestral home, found in England what they felt was a spiritual home. As a burgeoning intellectual, I know I felt this myself. The fact is, even though I was otherwise perfectly at home in the United States, I never quite felt intellectually at home here. I did not, for one thing, feel that my country's literature spoke to me. I recognized the raw genius of its greatest books — the best stories of Hawthorne, *Moby-Dick*, *Huckleberry Finn*, *The Great Gatsby*, Dreiser's *An American Tragedy*, Willa Cather's *The Professor's House*, the stories of Ernest Hemingway, the novels of William Faulkner — but they didn't, in some fundamental way, touch me. The reason they didn't, I have come to believe, is that they all take the individual to be always and forever at odds with his society. I have never felt that; nor do I wish to feel it.

Only recently did I find my inchoate thoughts on this subject nicely formulated for me in one of Lionel Trilling's lesser-known essays, "An American View of English Literature." Early in this essay Trilling makes a striking distinction that ought to have been obvious to me long ago. He wrote:

> The difference [between English and American literature], lies in the way the two literatures regard society and the ordinary life of daily routine. As compared to American literature, British literature is defined by its tendency to take society for granted and then to go on to demonstrate its burdensome but interesting and valuable complexity. And American literature, in comparison with British, is defined by its tendency to transcend or circumvent the social fact and to concentrate upon the individual in relation to himself, to God, or to the cosmos, and, even when the individual stands in an inescapable relation to the social fact, to represent society and the ordinary life of daily routine not as things assumed and taken for granted but as problems posed, as alien and hostile to the true spiritual and moral life.

W. H. Auden puts the matter much more starkly: "American literature is one extraordinary literature of lonely people."

It is to the point that Lionel Trilling, one of the subtlest of American minds to turn to literary criticism in the twentieth century, himself felt less than at home in American literature. Would Trilling have functioned better in England? Difficult to say. When Americans become Englishmen, of course, they tend to overdo it. When the young Henry James was admitted to the Reform Club in London, he wrote home, "J'y suis, j'y suis — for ever and a day." And England, as James's biographer Leon Edel writes, "speedily opened its arms to him, as it does to anyone who is at home with the world." T. S. Eliot, perhaps the American who most thoroughly reinvented himself as an Englishman, used to wear a white rose on the anniversary of the Battle of Bosworth, in memory of Richard III, whom he apparently considered the last true English king. It was, I think, the idea — let us call it the ideal — of a coherent society that drew both James and Eliot to England and that may have driven many lesser men and women to more or less intense cases of Anglophilia.

In the 1950s, along with the notion of England as a coherent society, an additional notion was abroad that everything in English life — food and central heating excepted — was superior. English schooling, English tailoring, English shoemaking, English manners — all were thought the best the world had to offer. Some of the most impressive Americans, in fact, came awfully close to being Englishmen themselves. Justice Holmes was, according to his first biographer, Mark DeWolfe Howe, "in many respects an Englishman"; his "commitment to the English tradition . . . set him out of the central stream of American life."

The notion of English superiority extended to English speech and the use of language generally. Not a few Americans have attempted English accents, usually with comical result. In my own Anglophilia, I have never gone quite that far. I did, though, envy the use of certain English locutions and pronunciations, all the more because I knew they were not really available to me. I avoided writing the phrases "put paid to," "in the event," and "spot on." I would not allow myself to utter the English pronunciations of *tirade* (tearod) and *controversy* (contrahvarsee), which seem to me so much more mellifluous and amusing than the American ones. I have got over all this, but shall go to my grave regretting not being able either to say or write the word *whilst,* though I see I have now at least written it, and now at last the regret is nearly gone.

Of course, much could — and has — been said against England. Begin with its class system, which, I note, Stein Ringen, Professor of Sociology and Social Policy at Oxford, claims is long gone, but it has left in its wake what he calls "a class psychology: the preoccupation with class, the belief in class, and the symbols of class in manners and dress." My friend the late Edward Shils, for many years a teacher at the London School of Economics and then at Cambridge and himself a strong Anglophile, in 1955 lectured English intellectuals on being too insular and self-satisfied, too concerned with wine and gardening, too anti-American, too much taken with cultivating eccentricity. And yet, even when one has said the worst about the English, they remain a talented and endlessly interesting people, whose "greatest asset," as G. M. Trevelyan wrote in 1940, is their national character.

My own immersion in Anglophilia, I see now, came at the height of what Noel Annan has called Our Age. If it was an age, in Annan's view, that presided over the decline of England in many ways, to an American it still seemed very grand. An emblem of it, one of the earliest to fall into my hands, was the magazine *Encounter.* My memory of that magazine, whose first issues I read in the middle 1950s, is chiefly of its general elegance: of design, of typeface, of content. Issues might contain poems by W. H. Auden, an essay on Russian intellectuals by Isaiah Berlin, a story by V. S. Pritchett, H. R. Trevor-Roper on

Arnold Toynbee, Kenneth Tynan on Brecht, Nigel Dennis on Pirandello, Anthony Crosland on the future of the Labour Party, Evelyn Waugh on aristocracy, N. C. Chaudhuri on England and India, Cyril Connolly on who cared what. In its pages everything seemed lucid, witty, and blithely learned. The American Central Intelligence Agency, it was later revealed, had secretly helped finance this extraordinary magazine. One only wishes they could arrange to do it again.

A few years later I began reading the *New Statesman* and the *Spectator,* and, less regularly, the BBC's *Listener.* The *New Statesman* was closer to my leftish views of those days and seemed to me, under the editorship of a journalist of great suavity named John Freeman, the liveliest of these journals. I read it in an "air" edition, printed on thin, almost tissuey paper. I gobbled it up — all of it: the leader, reports from the Labour Party conferences in Blackpool, the "London Diary," the zany letters, the bits on English nuttiness called "This England," the book reviews, all the arts criticism, the parody competition in the back. People spoke about a tension between the front half (political) and the back half (arts and culture) of the *New Statesman,* but I found it made things all the more piquant.

In the late 1950s and early 1960s, such figures as Evelyn Waugh, Kingsley Amis, and F. R. Leavis appeared side by side in the *Spectator,* though there was much disagreement among them. The *New Statesman* could run Malcolm Muggeridge, in his pre-Christian phase, mocking everything for which its earnest political editors seemed to stand. To mark its fiftieth anniversary in 1963, the *New Statesman* commissioned a history of itself, and then the editors assigned it for review, in its anniversary issue, to Conor Cruise O'Brien, who promptly attacked the book and the *New Statesman* itself. That spoke to a wondrous kind of intellectual confidence simply unavailable in America.

The English weeklies seemed to me easily superior to the American ones, the *Nation* and the *New Republic*. (I had myself by this time begun to write for the latter.) The American weeklies seemed half the time to be preaching, the other half to be teaching — not at all my notion of a journalistic good time. The English weeklies, on the other hand, were written for equals: it was assumed that the readers were quite as sophisticated, intelligent, and cultivated as the editors. Even if — as in my case in my twenties — it wasn't quite true, it was pleasing to be covered by the generous umbrella of such an assumption.

Not only did the English weeklies provide first-class journalism and criticism, but their editors and contributors, unlike the people who wrote for intellectual magazines in the United States, seemed to go in and out of government: Ian Gilmour, the editor of the *Spectator,* and John Freeman served in Conservative and Labour governments respectively; later R. H. S. Crossman, a brilliant journalist, after serving as a minister in the Harold Wilson cabinet, returned to edit (and damn near ruin) the *New Statesman.*

Karl Miller, who served as literary editor of both the *Spectator* and the *New Statesman,* has recently described the former — and I suspect he could as easily have included the latter — as a paper "in which Establishment and Enlightenment were conjoined." The idea that an intellectual could serve in government without being thought a sellout — well, nothing of the kind was remotely possible in the United States. Chalk up another good reason for Anglophilia.

Much of this grew out of the English tradition of the amateur, which itself derived from that of the English gentleman, who could do many things well and all with the appearance of effortlessness, easy elegance, and sangfroid. Elegance and sangfroid are at the heart of the modern concept of the cool, an

English invention, I think. Nor did one have to be born a gentleman to share in it. Kenneth Tynan claimed that Noël Coward was, for the modern era, the inventor of the cool. It was Noël Coward who, at being greatly feted upon his seventieth birthday, after receiving handsome toasts from Sir Laurence Olivier and the Earl of Mountbatten, remarked: "I am awfully overcome at this moment, and as you can see, restraining it with splendid fortitude."

English cool has always seemed impressive to Americans, certainly to the Anglophiles among us. It is represented by Evelyn Waugh, stepping out of a bunker during a Nazi bombing raid in Yugoslavia, looking up at a sky raining down bombs and announcing, "Like all things German, this is vastly overdone." It is Thomas Beecham on English philistinism toward serious music: "They don't much like music, but they rather like the sound it makes." It is Maurice Richardson, agreeing to review a book on ants for the *Times Literary Supplement* and then, in the first paragraph of his review, stating that his sole qualification for writing this review is that, as a boy, he ate ants, which he and his friends called "tramp's caviar."

English insouciance seems to me also partly based on the English distrust of the theoretical and concomitant respect for the factual. Ralph Waldo Emerson, in *English Traits,* his best book, remarks that "the English shrink from a generalization." Paul Valéry, recounting a visit to London in 1896, recalls receiving an article providing an account of German commercial competition by a Mr. Williams, "presented [Valéry notes] in the English manner: with the fewest ideas possible and the most facts."

This willingness to delimit oneself to the ground of fact, to the palpable and the knowable, is at the heart of English common sense, which is another English quality greatly attractive to

Anglophiles. Owing to this strong strain of common sense, English culture was never permeated — as American culture still is — by fashionable "isms." When asked what he thought about Freudianism, Max Beerbohm replied: "They were a tense and peculiar family, the Oedipuses, were they not?" Only an Englishman would have chosen that lovely comic sentence. When asked if he still read novels, Gilbert Ryle is supposed to have replied, "Yes, all six of them — every year," referring of course to Jane Austen's works but also speaking to the confident self-sufficiency of English culture.

The allegiance to common sense implies an automatic diminution of zeal. English humor features, in a way American humor does not, the outrageously sensible. Consider the joke about the English boy whose immigrant Jewish father, a shoemaker, puts him through Oxford and then through medical school. He soon becomes a successful Harley Street physician. Wishing to do something for his father, the young doctor sends him to his own Savile Row tailor. After five fittings, the father emerges resplendent in a most elegant, vested, pin-striped, dark gray suit. When the son compliments his father on the suit, the old man breaks down, tears flooding his face. "Papa," the son asks, "are you crying because you are so touched by my gift?" "No, you idiot," says the father, "I'm crying because, in this suit, I realize for the first time what it means for us to have lost India."

So deep runs my Anglophilia that I believe I understand what the old gentleman was crying about. Do many people, I wonder, feel nostalgia for something they have never really known? I have felt this for the British Empire. I wish I had known it; I sometimes — blasphemous thought — wish it were still intact. Despite all its injustices — see here Kipling, Conrad, Maugham, Orwell, Graham Greene, and others — the British Empire remains one of history's grandest adventures. "You belong to a race that's been bossy for years," announces a character in Noël Coward's play *This Happy Breed*, "and the reason it's held on as long as it has is that nine times out of ten it's behaved decently and treated people right."

Whatever one can say against the British Empire, it was a fine forcing house for developing men of strong character, and doing so at a very early age. George Orwell was perhaps as vehement a critic as the empire had, yet there he was, at the age of nineteen, still Eric Blair, a member of the Burmese Imperial Police, with administrative responsibility for more than a quarter of a million people. Despite his powerful criticism of all that was corrupt in colonial relations, Orwell seems to have had the character required for the task, and it made a better man of him.

But, then, Orwell was among the last of a strong generation of Englishmen. It may have been the generation that saw in the age of the common man, but it was itself made up of the most uncommon men. Considering the intellectual realm alone, think of the extraordinary historians — Hugh Trevor-Roper, A. J. P. Taylor, Herbert Butterfield, Lewis Namier; the philosophers — A. J. Ayer, Isaiah Berlin, Gilbert Ryle, and J. L. Austin; the novelists — Evelyn Waugh, Anthony Powell, Barbara Pym, and Graham Greene; the critics — F. R. Leavis, William Empson, and V. S. Pritchett. Each seems quintessentially English, even those not born in England (Berlin and Namier); none seems replaceable or likely ever to be replaced.

As a good Anglophile, I feel a nostalgia, similar to that I feel for the British Empire, for Oxford and Cambridge. When I first saw both universities, I felt a hopeless yearning, a sadness at not having gone to one of them. I have read a vast amount about them in various English novels and memoirs. I feel I have been tutored by Maurice Bowra at Wadham, occupied Max Beerbohm's rooms at Merton, thought I saw Wittgenstein depart Bertrand Russell's rooms at Trinity, and, at the age of sixty, am still hopeful about being made an Apostle. I have acquired so much information about Oxford and Cambridge that I feel entitled to a degree from one or the other — a disappointing second, perhaps.

I have myself had only the most glancing contact with some of the figures of the strong generation of English intellectuals. I met, rather late in his life, John Sparrow, who was already doing what I assume were set pieces: "Mr. Epstein, I understand that Americans believe that it is self-evident that all men are created equal. It had better be self-evident. After all, you realize, there is no other evidence for it."

I did, in the United States, work for Sir William Haley, a man of the same generation, whose kindness and strength of character only increased my own Anglophilia. Sir William had been editor of the *Manchester Guardian,* editor of the London *Times,* director-general of the BBC, and editor-in-chief of the *Encyclopaedia Britannica,* where I encountered him. (I secretly thought he was attempting to compile the world's perfect editorial résumé.) I later learned that he had achieved all he had without ever going to university; his was a career that seemed to prove Emerson's notion of England as "aristocracy with the doors open."

Sir William came to *Britannica* with the reputation of a cold man who didn't mind firing lots of people; a "Robespierre with two glass eyes" was the journalistic epithet assigned him. He turned out to be a shy and very courteous man. He seemed to have read everything. When I somewhat trepidaciously gave him something I had written, he generally returned it with a laconic but perfect capping comment. I recall sending him a copy of a review I had written of a reissue of Alexander Herzen's *My Past and Thoughts,* to which he appended the single-sentence note: "You have nicely caught his jumble." He wore heavy tweed suits through steamy Chicago summers, walked great distances in grim Chicago winters. A powerful trencherman, his language was filled with food metaphors about people "dropping their plates" and "over-egging their puddings."

Sir William hadn't known it, but, in taking on his assignment at *Britannica,* he had walked into a situation where traps were everywhere laid for him by people who wanted a different, less literary, less elegant *Encyclopaedia Britannica* than he. He soon knew about this yet refused to fight below the level of intellectual argument and high principle. He was defeated, as good sense so often is in the world, but he departed with his integrity entirely intact.

There were nearly fifty years' difference in our ages, and being the kind of Englishman he was, Sir William did not go in for easy intimacy. In fact, we became close only later, after he left America, in our letters. His own letters were splendid: full of talk about his reading, reminiscences of such figures as Desmond MacCarthy, and a generous interest in my own writing. When I reported to him that I, too, had left *Britannica,* he wrote back: "I am glad you have left. They worship different gods than we." No one, I think, could indite such a sentence today and have it carry the same weight.

"They worship different gods than we." Difficult to imagine Kingsley Amis writing that. Impossible to imagine Martin Amis writing it. If one were to chart a date for the decisive change in England, perhaps it would be 1954, the publication date of *Lucky Jim.* In a way that doesn't quite apply even to the slashing comedy of Evelyn Waugh, *Lucky Jim* seemed to announce goodbye to all that more emphatically than any other single work. By "all that" I mean good-bye to empire, good-bye to the idea of

England's playing a role on the historical stage, good-bye to the ideal of the English gentleman, good-bye to any notions of English grandeur whatsoever. I don't for one moment blame all this on Kingsley Amis — to do so would be akin to blaming the fall of Paris on Proust — but only suggest that what his riotously funny novel adumbrated was that England could no longer take its own pretensions seriously. The clock had run out, the game was over.

Shortly before the publication of *Lucky Jim*, George Santayana, in a chapter of his *Dominations and Powers* titled "The Decline of the Great Powers," wrote:

> England . . . in the eighteenth and early nineteenth centuries, acted the great power with conviction; she was independent, mistress of the sea, and sure of her right to dominion. Difficulties and even defeats, such as the loss of the American Colonies, did not in the least daunt her; her vitality at home and her liberty abroad remained untouched. But gradually, though she suffered no final military defeat, the heart seemed to fail her for so vast an enterprise. It was not the colonies she had lost that maimed her, but those she had retained or annexed. Ireland, South Africa, and India became thorns in her side. The bloated industries which helped her to dominate the world made her incapable of feeding herself; they committed her to forced expansion, in order to secure markets and to secure supplies. But she could no longer be war-like with a good conscience; the virtuous thing was to bow one's way out and say: My mistake. Her kings were half-ashamed to be kings, her liberals were half-ashamed to govern, her Church was half-ashamed to be Protestant. All became a medley of sweet reasonableness, stupidity, and confusion. Being a great power was now a great burden. It was urgent to reduce responsibility, to reduce armaments, to refer everything to conferences, to support the League of

Nations, to let everyone have his own way abroad, and to let everyone have his own way at home. Had not England always been a champion of liberty? But wasn't it time now for the champion to retire? And wouldn't liberty be much freer without a champion?

Others besides Santayana — Brooks Adams, brother of Henry, among them — predicted the decline of English power. It was not, after all, a difficult prediction to make. Nations, like persons, tire. England had had, after all, a long and magnificent roll of the dice. But when the fall came, it came pretty hard.

All that was left, it sometimes seemed, was a new, rather sad sense of limitation, along with what so often accompanies a sense of limitation among the highly intelligent — pervasive irony. The new English style was heavy on irony. "Irony," Alan Bennett has written of himself and his countrymen, "is inescapable. We are conceived in irony. We float in it from the womb. It's the amniotic fluid. It's the silver sea. It's the waters at their priest-like task of washing away guilt and purpose and responsibility. Joking but not joking. Caring but not caring. Serious but not serious."

The ironic note, sometimes the plaintively ironic note, as in much of the verse of Philip Larkin, has for a long while now seemed the characteristic English note. It is not without its charms, to be sure, but it can come to seem a bit thin. Can it be that culture unaccompanied by power loses first its authority, then its assurance?

By the middle 1960s, as the historian John Lukacs has written, "Britain was . . . represented [to the world] by James Bond and the Beatles." In a recent issue of the *Times Literary Supplement*, a reviewer notes: "There is a growing controversy in Britain about a stratum of society that is experiencing very high rates of marital breakdown, that has no steady employment and depends largely on state handouts; many of its members regularly use firearms and encourage their children to do so. But it is not only the Royal Family that is causing concern." At the 1996 women's final at Wimbledon, the television camera was placed on the Archbishop of Canterbury — who, I noted, was chewing gum. A gum-chewing Archbishop of Canterbury — here, alas, may be the poignant symbol of England at the millennium.

Yet, for all this, Anglophilia remains, if not so firmly entrenched as in former days, yet still very much alive. The last monument to American intellectual Anglophilia survives in the *New York Review of Books*. Anglophilia remains fairly strong in American universities, especially in English and philosophy departments. The most suitable Englishmen here are generally left wing and at least mildly contemptuous of Americans; and a good English accent can still be worth a significant sum in annual academic salary.

What might be called *Masterpiece Theatre* culture is still very large in America — I am myself a habitué of it — at least among those who think themselves the educated classes. Anglophilia lingers in American real estate, where suburbs, developments, apartment buildings, and hotels continue to be given such names as the Buckingham, the Dorset, the Essex House, and the rest.

Yet that greatest of British ambassadors, English literature, shows signs of beginning to fade. "Georgetown University's abandoning of the requirement that English majors study at least two authors among Chaucer, Shakespeare, and Milton . . . ," the *New York Times* recently reported, "is now the norm, a new study by the National Alumni Forum finds." In the assault of multiculturalism, all of English culture can easily be portrayed as one large dead white European male.

Where does this leave your stalwart Anglophile? Rather less

Anglophiliac, I suppose, than he was thirty years ago. And yet, as the Anglophile in question, I am not in the least sorry for my admiring immersion, however distant, in English culture. English culture, with its great writers, its remarkable statesmen, its heroic traditions, allowed me to discover a wider, and in many ways more heroic, world. As nineteenth-century Englishmen and Europeans studied the Greeks in search of an older and deeper culture, so it was to England that twentieth-century Americans, in search of the same treasure, hopefully turned. And, by and large, they were not disappointed.

In England they discovered a country that would not brook tyranny, that never for long departed common sense, that rang with laughter, that made life's possibilities seem both finer and grander. Whether there will always be an England I do not know, but the contemplation of the greatness of English history, the firmness of the impress of English character, and the richness of English talent ensures that, come what may, there will always be an Anglophilia.

Taking the Bypass

I HAVE TO BE wary that I am not writing this under the weight of depression, though you, perhaps, will judge better than I. Depression, after all, is said to be one of the not inevitable but common enough post-operative effects of bypass heart surgery, which I underwent roughly six weeks ago. I have felt several post-operative effects — at the moment, I feel a burning sensation along the path of the surgical scars on my chest and on my left thigh, and this morning, after a ten-hour night's sleep, I had breakfast and read the *New York Times,* then found I had to return to bed for two more hours' sleep — but I don't think depression is among these effects. We shall see.

By now, there must be several million Americans who have come through bypass surgery — the *Harvard Heart Letter* estimates that half a million such operations are done annually — yet it is exceedingly difficult to get a clear picture of all that such surgery entails, even though hospitals do try to educate patients about what they will go through. Most people who have had a bypass take what I suppose must be considered the healthy view: they feel mildly heroic for having survived it; they block out the more hellish aspects of it; and they tend, in time, slightly to diminish its seriousness, to look at it as a piece of repair work, like a ring job or a change of fan belts on an automobile. I wish I could feel that way myself, and perhaps in a few years I shall, but at the moment I feel that something more momentous has happened, and I think it may make more sense to try to get at what it is now, rather than to wait for time to erase the sharp lines of recent memory.

As for depression, I had already gone through it — nicely mixed with terror — months ago when I was told that I might have to have the operation, officially called cardiac arterial bypass graft (CABG) and referred to by cardiologists as "cabbage." I have known a number of people who have had bypass surgery, and I have one friend who, having had a heart attack at thirty-nine, has been through it twice. Yet however common the surgery may be, it is an operation I dreaded as soon as I had first heard about it, twenty-five or so years ago. In locker rooms, I saw men with their lengthy zipperish chest scars and shuddered.

I cannot say that I devoted my life to avoiding a bypass, but I did what I thought was a fair amount to ward off the possibility. I am five feet seven, have weighed between a hundred and thirty and a hundred and thirty-five pounds for years, and generally pass for slender. For the most part, I have watched my diet — cheating on my wife, I used to joke, meant, for me, eating steak on a business trip — and I have eaten so many turkey sandwiches that I shouldn't be surprised if feathers fell into the sink when I shaved or that my diction had picked up a faint gobble. I haven't smoked cigarettes for more than twenty years. For most of my forties I played racquetball, and, after a hip injury made that no longer possible, I acquired the monstrous appliance called the NordicTrack WalkFit, on which I strode, Louis Armstrong and Jack Teagarden tapes accompanying me, for thirty minutes every other day. I have, in short, been a fairly good boy.

Perhaps this is the place to mention that I consider myself a

Jewish Scientist, the rough equivalent of a Christian Scientist, at least as far as that church's view of medicine is concerned. Doctors make me edgy. A friend of mine once asked a medical historian at what point in history physicians began to save more lives than they destroyed. "Haven't reached it yet," the historian replied. I share the opinion of Proust, whose father and brother were doctors and who himself required the aid of doctors all his days, but who wrote: "To believe in medicine would be the height of folly, if not to believe in it were not a greater folly still." So I go to doctors hesitantly, grudgingly, a bit fearfully.

Having said all this, I have to add that I like my internist, an intelligent and lucid man in my height and weight class named Harry Jaffe, perhaps the last man in America to be given the name Harry. A long time ago, I adopted the policy of calling all physicians who address me by my first name by *their* first names — see Stephen Potter on one-upmanship in physician-patient relations — and so Harry and I have been on a first-name basis for many years. Like him greatly though I do, I had been able to avoid seeing Harry for five golden years, and probably would have continued to do so but for the inconvenient fact of my sixtieth birthday, on which I promised my wife that I would have a physical. I went in for it, stripped, took an EKG, had blood drawn, let Harry feel me for frightening lumps and bumps, and answered almost all his fact-finding questions with a smug "No." He said he would call me in a week or so. When he did, he said that all seemed well, but the results of my cholesterol tests were a bit odd. My overall cholesterol number was an enviable 169, and my so-called "bad" cholesterol was all right, but my "good" cholesterol was much lower than it ought to be. No urgency about this, but Harry thought I ought to take a stress test, just to make sure that everything was O.K.

Two or three weeks later I did, carrying a pair of gym shoes
into the office of a youngish cardiologist on Central Street, in
Evanston, where I live. An agreeable nurse wired my chest and
ankles to various monitoring devices. The cardiologist, a man
with small round glasses and wearing khakis and a dark shirt
'and necktie, his receded, well-moussed hair brushed straight
back, faced his machinery as I climbed on a treadmill and began
walking briskly to nowhere. I had heard of men and women
having heart attacks during stress tests; a common figure of
speech was that, after a stress test, they had to "peel you off the
wall." Mine was a piece of cake, nicely frosted. Though the
speed of the treadmill increased to three different levels, I found
myself scarcely breathing heavily; until the third level, I was still
talking with the cardiologist, about Comiskey Park and his
being a White Sox fan. After ten minutes, he turned off the
machine and asked me to sit on an examining table. I was still
not breathing all that heavily.

"I'm sorry," he said, "but you failed the test."

"Failed it?" I said, amazed.

"Yes, certain abnormalities have shown up. Get dressed and
we'll talk about it."

The cardiologist told me that under stress my blood pressure
went down, whereas most people's went up; and he added
that after stress my EKG took a suspiciously long time to return
to its normal pattern. He said that he was going to prescribe
some nitroglycerine pills for me and that he strongly suggested
that I make an appointment — and make one soon — to take
an angiogram. I didn't like the mention of nitroglycerine — it
sounded so dire. Why not also prescribe knee and elbow pads,
so that I wouldn't scrape myself if I collapsed on the pavement
from a heart attack?

"Look," I told him, "I am so damn depressed by this news

that I am not about to make any quick decisions about angiograms or anything else."

I had heard that people sometimes had strokes from an angiogram, a procedure that probes in dangerous places, and I asked whether there were other tests. He told me that there were two: a stress-echo test, which was more sophisticated than the test I had just taken, and a thalium stress test, which was more thorough still. I signed on for a stress-echo test, which I took a week later, with another young cardiologist, this one with a lower hairline, a thick mustache, and another dark shirt and necktie. The same abnormalities showed up, but I was still hesitant about having an angiogram.

I sent the results of all the tests to my dear friend Paul McHugh, a Bostonian who was trained as a neurologist and is now the chief of psychiatry at Johns Hopkins, and he immediately showed them to the chief of cardiology there. Paul called that same day to tell me that the tests didn't necessarily mean I had arterial blockage. The chief of cardiology said that it could be five or six other things, including a viral condition. (I remembered a statistic I had heard somewhere to the effect that more than half of all heart attacks are caused by conditions not related to blockage. Cheery thought.) But the chief of cardiology also suggested that I take an angiogram. The angiogram is the definitive test; it is, as Harry Jaffe told me, "the gold standard" in these matters.

(A word about metaphors, euphemisms, dysphemisms, and other peculiar uses of language applied to the heart, itself perhaps the most metaphorized word in the English language. One of the first things one learns about cardiologists is that they divide into plain cardiologists and "invasive" ones; the latter invade the chest, and do angiograms and angioplasties. The word *bypass* is itself a metaphor, taken from the realm of freeways and toll roads, which itself borrows from that of the heart by sometimes referring to "arterial" roads. Clogged arteries are sometimes spoken of by some people in the profession as filled with "plaque" or "rust." Healthy portions of the arteries beyond the blockage are called "good targets." Having a bypass is sometimes referred to as damming and changing the flow of one's coronary bloodstream so as to get around the blockage, or dam, as if the entire thing were a river, or series of rivers. Veins, such as those taken from my left thigh, used to form the actual bypass, are "harvested." Of course, the most dramatic phrase of all is "open-heart surgery." I never refer to my own surgery as open-heart, though it was, because even now the term slightly chills me.)

I finally agreed to have an angiogram, a procedure that usually takes less than an hour and doesn't require the patient to be put under general anesthesia or even to stay in the hospital overnight. The five or six people I know who had had angiograms assured me that the procedure was painless. Strokes or other mishaps occurred, I was told, but only in one of every two thousand cases. (This didn't provide all that much comfort. Didn't they realize that I was one in a million?) I was given a cocktail of tranquilizers before the angiogram began. I also asked to hear music while it was going on: Haydn, as it turned out. Yet another cardiologist, this time an invasive one, made an incision in my right groin and a cannula probe was inserted into the femoral artery and threaded up into my heart. An injection of dye permitted a green and black x-ray film to be made, which showed the flow of blood through my coronary arteries. Such was the power of the tranquilizers I had been given that I even watched part of the film — something I would normally be too squeamish to do. The only unpleasant part of the procedure was that I had to lie on my back afterward for nearly six hours with a ten-pound sandbag on my groin to make certain that the puncture in my artery didn't bleed.

The next day, my second cardiologist called to set up an appointment. Because he sensed that I was critical-minded, he said that he wanted me to watch the angiogram all the way through. He said that my heart was quite healthy. But the film also showed three arteries with odd constrictions, which meant blockage — not the most deadly blockage but serious enough to require, in his opinion, bypass surgery. This cardiologist, I should mention, had earlier told me that he thought of himself as medically conservative, which in these matters meant that he didn't look to surgery for all solutions. But he said that he thought my angiogram required surgery.

"Let me ask you this," I said. "If this were your angiogram, would you agree to surgery?"

He hesitated just a moment, then said, with what I thought astonishing candor, "No."

"Then neither will I," I said. "I'll rely instead on your treating my condition with medications."

I left his office with prescriptions for a beta-blocker and for a cholesterol-lowering drug called Lipitor. I was also to take Vitamin E pills and a baby aspirin for fourteen days, then a double adult aspirin on the fifteenth day. For now, at any rate, I thought I had avoided the knife. Paul McHugh sympathized with my antipathy to surgery. "You don't want these guys putting their hands inside your chest, Joe," he had told me in his good Boston Irish accent. "Not a good idea." I sent my angiogram to him at Johns Hopkins.

"Joe, Paul," my friend's voice boomed on the phone. "I hate this, but I have terrible news. I showed your test to both the head of cardiology and the chief cardiological surgeon here, and they think you don't have much choice. You really do have to undergo the surgery. God, pal, I wish it were otherwise, but I knew you would want the real lowdown."

The truth was, I didn't want the real lowdown. I still wanted above all to avoid the surgery. I asked myself that not very deep philosophical question, "Why me?" (The best answer I have been able to come up with is genetics: my father had a heart attack in his late fifties, bypass surgery at seventy-nine, and now, at ninety-one, he has congestive heart failure, which, given his age, I have taken to calling "congestive heart success.") Yet I knew that it was only a matter of time before I would have to give in and agree to surgery. Paul had explained to me that in addition to the three constricted arteries, I had what is known as "silent ischemia" — cardiac ischemia being the condition in which the heart is not receiving enough blood — the "silent" meaning that I had potential heart trouble without any symptoms: no shortness of breath, no arrhythmia, no angina. This meant that I could have a major heart attack without any warning whatsoever — run to catch a plane and, bang!, gone.

I love life too much to agree to early death; there were too many half-finished stories whose completion I wished to know; I didn't want to leave the theater just yet. I would have to submit to the surgery, to go under the knife, in the brutal old cliché. Like one of those figures on the surgical table in a Rembrandt or an Eakins painting, the swamp of my slithery insides would be exposed, my darkest interior invaded. I recall telling my wife that I looked upon this surgery as tantamount to having to face a vicious bully who was going to beat the hell out of me, but it was the price of getting back into school, and since I wanted back in there was nothing for it but to take my beating.

Paul McHugh suggested that if I wanted to have the surgery done at Johns Hopkins, he could arrange it. But the complications of out-of-town surgery seemed too elaborate. Besides,

Evanston Hospital did a great deal of "cabbage," and, according to Paul's research of the matter, it had a quite good reputation. So I made an appointment with John Alexander, the chief of cardiac surgery there. He turned out to be a man five or six years younger than I, a southerner, educated and trained at Duke, a straightforward man with no noticeable vanity, apart from a penchant for bow ties. (I happen to be a bow-tie man myself, and so find this an eminently pardonable vanity.) He was roughly six feet tall, with gray hair, receded and modestly parted. Like other surgeons I have met, he has some of the bearing, the combined confidence and implied competence, of a test pilot. I noted his hands, which seemed to me neither artistically tapered nor especially strong but perfectly ordinary. How many hundreds of hearts had they held? (He told me that he did three or four bypass operations a week.) These were the hands that would handle and stitch away at my own heart.

When I met him for a pre-surgical interview, Dr. Alexander — no John, no Joe between us — played my angiogram film, which was not more enjoyable the second time around, and told me I would require a triple bypass, but that, given the healthy condition of my heart and of my good target arteries, beyond the blockages, there was every chance of a successful outcome to the operation.

As he looked over my dossier, he noted that I taught at Northwestern University and asked me what I taught.

"Literature," I said.

"My poorest subject as an undergraduate," he said.

"I hope you'll be able to block that out during the surgery," I said.

We set a date eight days later for the bypass. Before I left, I told him that I was greatly spooked by this operation.

"I find," he said, "that the more intelligent a person is, the more spooked he or she is. And you're right to be spooked. This is serious stuff, but you're going to come through all right."

I liked him.

Owing, I am sure, to insurance company policy, one no longer spends the night before surgery in the hospital, which was just as well with me. My son and daughter-in-law and their infant son had come from California to be with my wife while I was in the hospital. We went to dinner at a nearby Italian restaurant. I took a Valium and went to bed at ten-thirty and slept without nightmare until five the next morning, when I showered using a special disinfectant soap prescribed before surgery.

I reported to Evanston Hospital at six-fifteen, left my watch, wedding ring, and glasses with my wife, got into one of those wretched hospital gowns (designed, clearly, by "a pervert," as a nurse who had fitted me out in one for my angiogram had said), and prepared to let the games begin.

I don't recall if they gave me another tranquilizer before they took me down to prep me, but for some reason suppression of terror was not a problem. As a nurse attached an IV with anesthesia to my wrist, I remember wanting to tell her the only surgical joke I knew. It was about Lucius Beebe, the veteran travel writer for the *New York Herald-Tribune* and a very great snob, who was scheduled to have exploratory surgery. "Dear me," one of his lady friends is reported to have said, "I do hope the doctors have the good sense to open Lucius at room temperature."

I don't think I got the joke off, and the next thing I knew I was in intensive care, slowly coming awake. I remember being pleased that I had no breathing tube nor any scratchiness in my throat of the kind that such tubes can cause, and I felt a blurred sense of elation.

What I missed was written up by Dr. Alexander, who in the

first sentence of the second paragraph of his surgical report states, "While the electrocardiogram and arterial blood pressure were being monitored, the patient was anesthetized, positioned, prepped and draped as a sterile field." ("Like a patient, etherised upon a table," you might say.) I was connected to a heart-lung machine that kept my heart beating and sustained my breathing. An incision was made from the back of my left knee up along the front of my thigh stopping high on my groin where the vein graft was "harvested." My sternum was cracked open, or as Dr. Alexander put it, "a median sternotomy was performed," to gain entry to my heart. My left ventricle was "found to have normal characteristics." Meanwhile, "the aorta and right atrium were cannulated for arterial flow and venous return." The vein graft was connected to those arteries whose blockages were cut away. Then, "the aortic cross clamp was applied and cold blood cardio-plegia was administered." Even now I do not read this without a shudder of the spirit. "The total time of cardiopulmonary bypass was 112 minutes." I was thus on the heart-lung machine for a little less than two hours. Paul McHugh told me that danger lay in that apparatus. "Guys our age can lose neurons on it," he said, "and we don't have all that many to lose."

I do recall a nurse with a worried look hovering over me in intensive care. I don't know how much time passed — it was, in fact, nearly two o'clock the following morning — but Dr. Alexander was also standing nearby, in full surgical getup, telling me that we would have to go back into the operating room. I remember saying, "This sounds like a very bad idea to me." He replied, "I'm less worried about you than I am about your wife," whose nervousness must have been considerable when he called to inform her.

What had happened is that I had developed something called

a mediastinal clot on the right side of my heart. I remember my gurney rolling; I recall, through a flickering consciousness, lights of a tremendous yellowish intensity. "God," I thought, "I'm not going to be awake for this. Surely not?" Did I dream this? Or did consciousness peep through. I shall never know. I was reopened, the clot was cleared, and, to quote Dr. Alexander again, "a single 7-0 suture controlled this area of bleeding." Then I awoke to the pleasing sight of my wife and son standing by my bed, telling me that I looked quite well.

And the truth was I felt pretty damn fine. I felt both lucid and elated. I was by no means manic, but perhaps something closer to euphoric, full of optimism and good will. John Alexander later told me that this was not uncommon. After this surgery, he said, patients are, at first, just so pleased to be alive that their adrenaline does good things for them. "It's only on the second day," he said, "that they realize they've been hit by a truck."

It was on the third day that it really hit me. I was sitting on a chair in the bathroom of my private room — all cardiac patients at Evanston Hospital have private rooms — being sponge-bathed by a pretty and cheerful young nurse of Dutch ancestry named Laura, when I got a look at myself and the scars on my chest, closed my eyes, and sighed.

I stayed five days in the hospital. Therapy requires the patient to walk the halls as soon as possible, and this I did, with the aid of the nurses or of my wife. I lost all appetite but my recovery was apparently natural and perfectly normal. I had nothing to complain about, though this didn't stop me from doing so, especially about three devices whose connecting tubes and wires were sewn into my chest. One, a machine the size of a thick attaché case, was connected to two tubes that helped clear my lungs of blood and other fluids; another, a telemetry device connected to a heavy remote, monitored my heart on a screen at a nurses' station thirty yards away; the third, another heavy remote, was attached to a pacemaker, which was supposed to kick in if I needed it. Because of these machines, I had to sleep on my back. When I went to the bathroom, I had to pick them up and drag them in with me; each time I did so, I felt as if I were going on a trip to Detroit. Once I must have brushed my teeth too vigorously, for a nurse, noting undue activity on the telemetry machine, rushed into the bathroom, slightly panicked, to see what was wrong.

Recovery at home has been steady but slow. Those first mornings, upon waking, I felt that I had been in a horrendous street brawl the night before. I was no longer attached to machines but sometimes I felt a heaviness, as if I were wearing the medals of a Soviet field marshal but pinned not to a uniform but to the skin of my chest. I was given painkillers, a generic version of Tylenol 3, with codeine, which helped but which could not relieve all the discomfort. One realizes, after this surgery, how many things one needs the muscles of one's chest for: most lifting, blowing one's nose, and defecating, to name only three. Twice I sneezed rather violently and thought I had blown my chest open and would have to pick my heart up off the floor. My wife did a vast amount for me in the first weeks, from putting on my tight white anti-embolism socks to helping me in and out of bed to standing outside the shower lest I grow faint and need help. One night I was so weak she had to squeeze the toothpaste onto my brush.

The psychological effects, I suppose, are more enduring. People who have had surgery tell me that in time one comes to cherish one's scars, perhaps as decorations of the battles one has survived. Mine, when I view them in the mirror, still surprise and slightly scare me, though less so with the passage of time. As I look at my torn-up body — my chest, which resembles a poor imitation of Frankenstein's monster, my left leg, which looks like the unfinished lunch of a Doberman pinscher — I realize again that bypass surgery is a brutal piece of work, even though I hope one day to be able to say that I owe to it many added years of life. I suspect that it will before long be replaced by something keener and cleaner, less devastating, perhaps something to do with a laser. Future, ahistorical generations may someday ask, "Bypass surgery — wasn't that something done during the McCarthy era?"

In the long view, I know I have to count myself lucky. In Harry Jaffe I had an excellent internist who called for a stress test when another physician might have done nothing more than encourage a change in diet. In John Alexander I had a talented surgeon who was willing to return to the job at two in the morning to get it right. In Paul McHugh I had a man of great spirit and good humor with a real genius for friendship, and one who has stayed on the case and continued to call me every week to check on my well-being. My recovery has gone without anything like a serious hitch. I now drive, I go to concerts, I eat in restaurants. As everyone says, I should, in time, be as good as new, though I myself wonder.

I feel an abiding vulnerability I hadn't felt before. The surgery has left me with what I can only call heart consciousness. I turn over in bed at night and hear my heart, and feel less in control of my destiny. Rationality, of which I have always considered myself a devotee, has its distinct limits, and one of them is over the fate of my body: it will check out when it is ready, not, as I should prefer, when I am. All this was true enough, of course, before my bypass surgery; but now, after surgery, it seems — more than merely true — ineluctably true.

A few weeks before my operation, I happened to read the Dutch writer Harry Mulisch's excellent novel *The Assault*. Mulisch's protagonist is an anesthesiologist who had "the more or less mystical notion that the narcotics [of anesthesia] did not make the patient insensitive to pain so much as unable to express that pain, and that although drugs erased the memory of pain, the patient was nevertheless changed by it." Mystical though the notion may be, I cannot help but feel that there may be something to it. This surgery has been a major event in my otherwise fairly quiet life, one that has changed me, decidedly, decisively, definitively. How, precisely, I cannot yet say. All I can say is that, in more ways than one, my heart has been touched and I am not, and shall never again be, quite the same person.

Grow Up, Why Dontcha?

EARLY IN *A Dragon Apparent*, Norman Lewis tells about his travels in Indochina and his encounter with the religion of Cao-Daïsm, in which, as he writes, "the best years of one's life are its concluding decades." In Cao-Daïsm "the dejection that encroaching age stamps so often in the Western face — the melancholy sense of having outlived one's usefulness — [is] replaced . . . with a complacency of spirit and a prestige that increases automatically with the years." The older one gets in this religion, at least if one wishes to rise in its hierarchy, the greater the number of abstentions one is asked to make. But, as an elderly adherent explains to Norman Lewis, the older one is, the better one is able to abstain from the pleasures of the flesh, and besides, as Lewis concludes, "the turn of the screw was put on gently, so that by the time you had to give things up for the Kingdom of God, you were pretty well ready to give them up anyway. It was all so humane."

It also sounds so true to human development, if not to human nature — and very un-American, if not un-Western. In America, we cling to our pleasures, feeling chagrin as each diminishes in intensity, falls away, or disappears altogether. The name of the longed-for but never-discovered secret of life is youth, perpetual youth. Through diet, exercise, cosmetic surgery, or all combined, we ardently seek it. The means may differ but the end is always the same: how to stay young, how to avoid growing old. Everyone has felt the lure of remaining young. I know I have.

Impossible of achievement, the quest is inevitably frustrated; for youth, though it can sometimes be prolonged a bit, cannot really be maintained much beyond its normal span. Trying to do so is a game that can't be won. Not that this stops vast numbers of people from playing, as witness the crowds at gyms and jogging tracks. "Fitness is about sex and immortality," Wilfred Sheed has written. "By toning up the system, you can prolong youth, just about finesse middle age, and then, when the time comes, go straight into senility." Or, I suppose, be in near perfect shape just in time for death.

One would have thought that everyone had figured this out by now. But the emphasis on youthfulness and the terror of old age in American culture, if anything, seem to have grown greater. Not long ago I came across the expression "the leprosy of old age," an all too vivid phrase that just now reflects much ghastly truth. No one wishes to succumb to old age any earlier than is absolutely required, though those of us fortunate enough to achieve our eighties will finally have to do so.

In the meanwhile, the relentless pursuit of youthfulness combined with the fear of old age has done great damage to an early ideal of mine — the ideal of the grown-up. To set aside childish things, to ascend to grown-upness, to arrive at adulthood — this, from my earliest years, was my aspiration, the name of my desire. I could not grow up fast enough. And then, lo, when I had finally done so, the notion of being grown-up, or at any rate of acting the grown-up, seemed to have disappeared, shot down from the deck of the good ship *Zeitgeist*.

Among my strongest early memories are a number of incidents in which I found myself struggling, with genuine though hopeless determination, against being treated as a child. Since I was in fact a child, in certain instances a very young child, I wonder if, as they say in both the therapist's office and the quilt maker's studio, a pattern doesn't begin to emerge.

The first memory is a series of connected incidents in which I am being put to bed well before I am prepared to depart the scene. In one room is not so much terrifying as damnably boring darkness; in the other, amusing radio shows, adults, conversation, pleasing company. The reasonableness of this arrangement, in which I must go to bed earlier than everyone else simply because I am the youngest and the smallest, never came near to being persuasive to me. Unlike the Proust kid, I didn't yearn for my mother. I wanted, instead, more action.

Mine was the last generation of males in this country that had to earn its long pants, or at least had to wait until a certain age to wear them. Between short and long pants came those dopey coverings called knickers. Knickers stopped and bagged at the knee and were worn with long, usually thick socks that never stayed up. Jeans were not then an alternative: dungarees were something farmers wore and Levi Strauss & Company had not yet turned its marketing attentions east or even midwest. Knickers, then, were all a boy could wear until at some official agreed-upon time — age nine? ten? — he was allowed a pair of long pants, generally to be worn on special occasions.

When I was six years old, my father told me that he was going to take me with him to his tailor to have a suit made for me. I thought, with great delight, that I had beaten the clock. Young as I was, going up in the elevator to the tailor's in his building on Wabash Avenue in the Loop, I sensed that I was taking part in something like a genuine *rite de passage*.

The masculine atmosphere of the tailor's shop reinforced the feeling: lots of cigar smoke, thick bolts of richly textured cloth set out on high tables, much business talk. My father let me choose my own material; and, as I recall, I did not disgrace myself. Now I am standing before a three-way mirror, and one of the tailors, a man with a strong foreign accent, is draping material over me, his mouth full of pins, which doesn't stop him from talking with my father. I inquire whether it would be possible to have the suit made with two pairs of trousers. "What do you mean 'trousers'?" says the tailor. "We're talking here about a suit with short pants." Short pants! I was heart-broken beyond tears. If I then knew the words to vent my true feelings, the air in the shop would have turned blue with profanity.

Yet another dusty resentment: when I was eight and a half, I was sent to a summer camp for boys in Eagle River, Wisconsin, where I did acquire the requisite profanity and the knowledge that my taste for roughing it was limited to tolerating relatively slow room service. My parents were planning a trip to visit me midway through the summer. Was there anything that I might need that they could bring me? they asked. There was one thing, I suggested, a hunting knife. No objection was voiced.

I awaited the knife with rather greater anticipation than I did my parents. When they arrived, they gave me the knife, an instrument roughly two inches long made by a firm named Swank; it had an outside of simulated mother of pearl and could be attached to one's key chain. Not exactly what I had in mind. When I explained what I had wanted — a hunting knife with a blade five or six inches long and a bone handle, which fit into a leather holster — my mother smiled and, cupping my cheek gently in her manicured hand, said, "You must be crazy. Your father and I would never buy a little boy a knife like that." Another disappointment.

I hope you won't think I have been storing these little incidents up as a form of grievance collecting. Not so. In each case, my parents were, of course, perfectly correct in acting as they did. But what is striking to me today about their behavior is its contrast with the wide latitude they gave me in so many other ways. Apart from these and a few other similar incidents, my parents didn't seem all that eager to keep me childish. They talked about business and gossiped about friends and relatives in front of me. I even recall overhearing them and their friends telling slightly off-color jokes. ("Rectum, hell," went the punch line to one about a man who falls off the roof of a three-story building on his duff, "it damned near killed him.")

My parents didn't have any special talk or language for children that I can remember. There was no cuddly talk for my younger brother, even when he was an infant. And I don't recall their ever being condescending in their conversation with me. Neither my brother nor I was given a vast amount of attention, let alone that special limelightish attention reserved for children these days. ("Quiet, everyone, Joey's going to recite a poem now.") My sense of my own place in the household was that of an abbreviated adult, with fewer privileges (and earlier hours) and lesser responsibilities.

My father, who was born at the end of 1907, was a man particularly marked by the Depression. It hit just as he came on stage at age twenty-one. Today, at the age of ninety-one, he still seems to me marked by it and is, vaguely, awaiting its return. Many of his principles derive from his Depression experience: don't overspend, always put something by for a rainy day, expect the worst. I vividly remember his inspecting the poor job I had done in mowing our small lawn in Chicago. He pointed out the many flaws in the job, shook his head sadly, and, turning to look me in the eye, index finger waggling, announced, "You know, in the next Depression, you're the kind of guy they fire first." I was, I believe, eleven.

Between the ages of sixteen and nineteen, during the summers, I began to work with my father. I drove him to call on customers in nearby midwestern states, and I carried his sample cases and helped him fill orders. We spent vast amounts of time alone together — on the road, as the old phrase had it — and what, one might wonder, did we talk about? Chiefly, my recollection is, I listened to my father's homilies about business. He told me, at sixteen, how important it was to keep a low overhead. He told me that a businessman really makes his money not in selling but in buying — if he buys right, all good things follow. He once told me that business is done on three different levels in America. At the highest, products are supported by national advertising and public relations; at the next level, customers and clients are wined and dined, taken to the theater, fixed up with women, bribed in various ways; and then there was the third, his level. "What happens there, Dad?" I asked. "Very simple," he said. "At my level, you cut prices."

I never consciously sought my parents' approval. Friends, not parents, were the audience to which I played. It's closer to the truth to say that I wished only to avoid my parents' disapproval, which I was able to do most of the time, so that I might go my own way. Only one of the fathers of the boys I grew up with took an active, participatory interest in his son's life by regularly coming to our athletic games, and for his interest a Latinist among us gave the poor guy the name Omnipresent. He quickly became a figure of ridicule. In those days it appeared unseemly for a serious man to find so much time for his children. Since that time — the early 1950s — most American fathers have become, out of desire or fear of guilt, Omnipresents of one kind or another.

The model of how I wished to live didn't come from my parents. This for me came from a combination of the movies and the flashier elements of the culture. My parents lived quietly, taking their social life from a small number of friends and relatives. They were conservative people really, content, never living beyond their means or longing for anything they couldn't have, though in truth they didn't want all that much. I had in mind for myself a vague but still appealing notion of sophistication. And this set in fairly early.

Adulthood got under way in earnest at the age of fifteen, when it was possible to get a driver's license in Chicago. A Chicago driver's license was the open sesame that revealed new worlds for a boy to explore, and my friends and I did so, with great exuberance, including as many of its dark corners as we could discover. We sought out many light ones, too: good inexpensive restaurants, ballparks, places to meet girls. Having the use of a car, usually one of our parents' cars, was the first powerful evidence of the freedom that being a grown-up carried with it. It seemed pretty swell then — and it still does now.

Not that I rushed toward adulthood the way some of my contemporaries did. In my high school there were a small number of boys and girls with nothing boyish or girlish about them. The boys dressed differently: no Levi's, no washpants, no loafers, but slacks and serious shoes; stockings and makeup for the girls. The boys often had their own cars. The girls had a physical maturity about them and frequently were going with fellows three or four years out of high school; they themselves were waiting for the end of high school to marry, which they often did. They were both merely biding their time in high school.

My own position in high school was that of genial screw-off; I was a half-decent athlete and an all but nonexistent student —

whether I would go on to college was a bit unclear right up until the end. In those days, 1954, not every middle-class kid automatically went off to college. Since I had shown neither interest nor aptitude for study — I finished just above the lowest quarter of my graduating class — my father, one day in my last year of high school, said to me: "If you want to go to college, I shall be glad to pay for it. But my own sense is that you would make a terrific salesman, and maybe college, in your case, would be just a waste of time." I didn't think long about it. At eighteen, much as I wanted to be out in the world, I decided that I also wanted a few more carefree years, so I enrolled myself at the University of Illinois at Champaign-Urbana, which in those days had to take all state residents, no matter how poor their high school record.

College did, in fact, what I wanted it to do: it allowed me to put off adulthood for another four years. I was able to try out various roles, among them fraternity boy, bohemian, little-magazine literatus, and deep thinker. But when it was done, it was done. I could not have lasted four more years as a graduate student.

I was lucky, I think, that the draft was still intact. The draft gave young men another two years to think about what they wanted to do with their lives. It also introduced them to a wider America than they may have hitherto known, locked as most Americans are behind their own ethnic and social-class walls. And, for me, another thing that the draft did was make me hungry for civilian — which is to say, adult — life.

Philip Larkin must have shared some of these sentiments. "It was that verse about becoming again as a little child that caused the first sharp waning of my Christian sympathies," he wrote. "If the Kingdom of Heaven could be entered only by those fulfilling such a condition I knew I should be unhappy there."

Larkin wrote this in a review of a volume of the Opies' extensive study of children and their folklore. "It was not the prospect of being deprived of money, keys, wallet, letters, books, long-playing records, drinks, the opposite sex, and other solaces of adulthood that upset me," Larkin continued, "but having to put up indefinitely with the company of other children, their noise, their nastiness, their boasting, their back-answers, their cruelty, their silliness."

I don't share Larkin's contempt for children — "the little scum," as Hesketh Pearson once called them — reserving mine for people of adult age who prefer to carry themselves as children. Recently I was reading along in a most interesting book, *The Anatomy of Disgust* by William Ian Miller, full of admiration for its author's erudition and literary power, when he, to illustrate a point about the contempt not infrequently found among members of different social classes, related an encounter between himself and a stonemason he had hired to do some work on his house in Ann Arbor. When Miller "rode up on [his] bicycle, backpack on [his] back" to say hello, he sensed the mason's contempt for him. "He a teacher?" the man asked Miller's wife. Miller remarks that the man straightaway saw him as "a feminized male," from which perception his contempt flowed.

I have to add, though a sometime university teacher myself, as soon as Miller rode up on that bike wearing that backpack, I, too, felt an involuntary touch of contempt for him. It is the backpack, not the bike, that did it. I assume that Miller, a full professor at the University of Michigan Law School, must be no younger than in his forties, perhaps older. Yet here he is boppin' around in what is essentially the garb of a student. In doing so, he seeks, I take it, a kind of agelessness — an agelessness, for all I know, he may very well feel. Somehow, however earnest he may be about his status as husband, father, teacher, he still wants to seem youthful. Had he returned home in suit or jacket and tie, my guess is that the mason would not have seemed in the least contemptuous of him. I know I wouldn't have. I don't even require a jacket and tie. But I cannot bear that backpack on anyone over thirty.

One of the divisions of the contemporary world is between those who are prepared to dress (roughly) their age and those who see clothes as a means to fight off age. At my university, there are now tenured professors teaching in deliberately un-laced gym shoes. I know of associate deans who never wear neckties. Others — balding, paunchy, droopy-lidded — have not had a fabric other than denim touch their hindquarters for decades. They, poor dears, believe they are staying young.

Clothes have played a large part in bringing about the drift away from grown-up to youth culture. In part, dress in Amer-ica — and not America alone — has changed owing to an in-crease in informality across the board in contemporary life. As a boy, I have no memory of my father or any of his friends owning any casual clothes. They wore suits everywhere, even sitting around on a Sunday afternoon; they never left the house without a serious hat. Men now dress, much of the time, like boys, in jeans, polo shirts, gym shoes, the ubiquitous baseball cap. Meanwhile, little girls dress like grown women, in short shorts, bikinis, platform shoes — sexy is the theme. The result is to erase the line between the youthful and the mature, though it doesn't really work. Instead it gives a tone of formlessness to the society that adopts it.

Why should I care about any of this? Is it my business if people wish to appear younger than their true age? If seeming youthful is pleasing to them, why not wish these people God-speed, however hopeless their endeavor? I really ought to be more tolerant. But, alas, I cannot.

The United States, if not the Western world, has been on a great youth binge for at least thirty or forty years now. My guess is that the adulation of youth, as an American phenomenon, began with the election to the presidency of John F. Kennedy. Suddenly, "to be young was very heaven!" At forty-three, Kennedy was the youngest man ever elected president. He was the first president not to wear a hat. He had an athletic build, a beautiful wife, and lots of hair. (We would subsequently learn that he had Addison's disease, a bad back, and other painful injuries to what was essentially an old man's body.) The unspoken part of Kennedy-inspired youth worship was a reduction in admiration for anyone older. To be beyond, say, fifty was, not much question about it, to be a little out of it. "As we grow older," wrote Gerald Murphy, "we must guard against a feeling of lowered consequence."

The student uprisings later in the decade of the sixties set the lock — a sort of triple clamp — on this. To be young then was not only desirable, it was required as a bona fides of one's integrity and honor. No one over thirty was to be trusted — this was one of the shibboleths of the day — for it was assumed that anyone beyond that age had already made too many compromises, was already too greatly swept up by something called the system, was too much implicated in the way things were. Perhaps at no other time in history was being young felt to be more desirable.

Teaching college students in the 1970s and 1980s, I sensed among many of them what I used to think of as sixties envy. And, of course, in our own day one still sees what are essentially sixties characters, now in their fifties, walking the streets, tie-dyed, long-haired, sadly sandaled, neither grateful nor dead, waiting for a magic bus to the past.

The cult of youthfulness may be the principal legacy of the

1960s. And this cult — more like a national craze — allows a very wide berth for youthfulness. Today one would not think to say that no one over thirty is to be trusted; that sentiment has been replaced by the notion that no one under forty needs to get serious. One of the curious qualities I have noticed about recent generations is the absence of any indecent hurry to get started in life.

Consider two successful television shows, *Seinfeld* and *Friends,* where one encounters precisely the kind of perpetual adolescent I have been attempting to describe. Played for laughs, the indecisiveness of the characters in both shows results in a richly comic selfishness, with no one having anything like a center to his or her life and with the notion of adulthood existing in the dim distance, an unreachable utopia. On one of the *Seinfeld* episodes the hopelessly selfish character George Costanza is about to enter into an affair with a married woman. "An affair!" he exclaims. "It's like stockings and martinis and William Holden. It's so adult!" Poor Georgie.

To turn to another George: in *Angel in the Whirlwind,* his history of the American Revolutionary War, Benson Bobrick remarks that "by the time he was sixteen, George [Washington] appeared in every respect an adult." Marcus Cunliffe, in his book on Washington, reinforces the point, saying of Washington that he lived at Ferry Farm with his mother, "leaving childhood behind and entering the short period of youth that in colonial times so often merged with adult life."

William Osler, the great physician, widened the point by asserting "the comparative uselessness of men above forty years of age." Osler added: "Take the sum of human achievement in action, in science, in art, in literature — subtract the work of men above forty, and, while we would miss great treasures, even priceless treasures, we would practically be where we are today."

In 1932 there was a best-seller titled *Life Begins at Forty* by Walter B. Pitkin. I never read it, but I take it that its message was that one needn't feel old at age forty, that many opportunities still existed at that hoary age — occupational, financial, romantic — and that life was scarcely over. It was, friends, just beginning.

Today that title seems quaint. Many people, far from feeling old at forty, haven't really begun their lives at all. Before forty, there is graduate school, general fooling around, possibly professional school, maybe a change in one's career choice, a late marriage, having a child at thirty-eight or thereabouts. This is how, I believe, lots of people nowadays view things. And, of course, some people wait to begin their lives till fifty or beyond — wait, in some cases perhaps, for the next life.

Oddly, this phenomenon seems most often to strike the especially bright. Because they are so bright, the world seems a sea of possibilities to them. The phrase "the despair of possibility" is Kierkegaard's. The brilliantly gloomy Dane knew that one can as easily drown in the sea of possibility as in the swamp of necessity. In *The Sickness unto Death,* he wrote:

> Nor is it merely due to lack of strength when the soul goes astray in possibility — at least this is not to be understood as people commonly understand it. What really is lacking is the power to obey, to submit to the necessary in oneself, to what may be called one's limit. Therefore the misfortune does not consist in the fact that such a self did not amount to anything in the world; no, the misfortune is that the man did not become aware of himself, aware that the self he is, is a perfectly defined something, and so is the necessary. On the contrary,

he lost himself, owing to the fact that this self was seen fantastically reflected in the possible.

So it seems with people who wish endlessly to be young, to avoid responsibility, to avoid committing themselves to anything definite, lest other doors close on them. These people remain in a perpetual state of development. As with some movies that never get made, their lives, like the movie scripts, reside in what the kids on the coast call "development hell." And hell it must be, always waiting for life to begin, thinking in the grammatical tense known as the future permanent.

Some people are in jobs where not to seem young can work to their detriment. Not long ago I wrote a screenplay for a decent and likable producer who one morning, over the phone, told me it was his birthday. When I congratulated him, he said that it wasn't altogether a celebratory occasion. He was now forty-one, and forty-one was, for Hollywood, a bit long in the tooth — unless, of course, one had a few large commercial or artistic triumphs to one's credit, which he, till now, didn't have. In Hollywood, apparently, life can be over at forty.

The point seems to be confirmed in movies of the past few decades. The number of roles for grown-ups in the movies has been very small — minuscule, even. Looking at the male side only, the actors of the 1940s and 1950s had a maturity that is absent from the actors of today. Roles were written that called for a certain grown-upness that no longer exists among us. Take Clark Gable, Gary Cooper, Humphrey Bogart, Gregory Peck, Ray Milland, Walter Pidgeon — grown-ups all. Or consider Spencer Tracy: even when young, he didn't seem young. These were men who could wear suits, not look laughable in hats. There were even parts for older gents: Lionel Barrymore, Adolphe Menjou, Walter Huston, Claude Rains. Male movie stars of our own day — Robert Redford, Al Pacino, Tom Cruise, Harrison Ford, Tom Hanks — are all, in their movie personas, essentially boys, never to be thought of as beyond their late thirties. (Redford is, in fact, sixty.) To be beyond one's late thirties, in the world projected by Hollywood, is to become a quite different persona, one, at least on the screen, strictly non grata. Some people cannot help but think of themselves as young. W. H. Auden claimed that he always thought himself the youngest person in the room; no doubt this was part of his heritage of extreme precocity. Yet Auden also said, to Robert Craft, that "obviously it is normal to think of oneself as younger than one is, but fatal to want to be younger." In *The Man Without Qualities,* Robert Musil speaks of "those practicing the profession of being the next generation." I fear this is the fate that has befallen so many people who came of age in the 1960s, who also thought of themselves as the wave of the future.

One sees them everywhere. The journalist David Frum recognized one in Austin Hall, at Harvard, when he returned to his tenth-year law school reunion: "And there in front of the class was a teacher I recognized. In his blue jeans, Eddie Bauer shirt, and hiking boots, he was hanging on to the appurtenances of youth as desperately as ever. But not even the most adamantly anti-ageist student could fail to notice that he had irrevocably passed his 50th birthday." Malraux somewhere says that "there are no grown-ups," but he may not have known the half of it.

Who was it who said that most women early choose to regard themselves, for the remainder of their days, as either eighteen or eighty? A pity if true, for there are so many interesting ages in betwixt. I myself have a bias in favor of middle-aged beauty in women as beauty at its most elegant. It's a mistake, in any case, to lock oneself into a set age too early in life. Hemingway, poor man, seems to have done that; everyone may have called him Papa, but he was finally an absurdly childish fellow. And his imitators, of course, seem even more absurd. And yet, as the disc jockeys once had it, the beat goes on. When the *New York Times* book critic Michiko Kakutani wrote a column titled "Adolescence Lives!" a man named John Frederick wrote in to add that so-called grown-ups "ape the pattern of their young. Traipsing after fads, they are preoccupied with keeping up." Mr. Frederick added the suggestion that "the symbol of our regression is the baseball cap," now worn "even in eating-places, in defiance of once-understood standards of courtesy, which adults used to set."

How many young men today are even aware that wearing a hat indoors is thought bad form? One assumes that the number is impressively small. What is lost by the absence of this knowledge? Some might argue nothing whatsoever, but I would not be among them. Not wearing a hat indoors, a man's tipping or taking off his hat as a sign of respect for a woman — these and other little touches are useful in several ways, including the aesthetic. A friend, attempting to demonstrate the difference between writing for the screen and writing for the page, once cited a scene in a movie in which a man and woman get into an elevator. There is a coldness between them. The man is wearing a hat. The elevator stops, and an attractive woman gets on. The man immediately takes off his hat. A lot is said by this gesture. But it won't be understood if people don't know that men are supposed to take off their hats indoors, especially in the company of women.

A preachy tone seems to have crept into this essay, which causes me to ask if I think of myself as grown-up. I find the answer a little less than obvious. "I always longed to be grown-up," said Max Beerbohm, recounting the early years of his life, and so, as I hope I have made plain, have I. But did Beerbohm really achieve fully fleshed adulthood? Despite his white hair and calculated effort to seem a man of another age, he spent much of his time drawing caricatures of friends and prominent people, and he doctored the copies of books written by friends so that they read crazily. I would say that, though the child in him never quite died — and a good thing for his art, too — Beerbohm was finally, in fact early, grown-up because in himself he created an extraordinary human character, handsomely burnished, of a kind that the world had not seen before and hasn't since.

Do I qualify as grown-up? Despite my having had charge of children as long as forty years ago, having more gray than brown hair, showing all the seams and scars of aging and a few for extra credit, I retain my doubts. Permit me to give an example from roughly a decade ago of the kind that stirs such doubts. Parental Guidance is invoked here. Mine is a story with blue material and one that illustrates the apothegm that a dirty mind never sleeps.

I had been asked to write a brief essay for *Gentlemen's Quarterly*, which is not for gentlemen and comes out monthly, which makes its entire name a lie. My subject was the way male academics dress. The essay went down well enough with *GQ*'s editors, but I was asked if I would mind posing for a photograph of myself in full classroom regalia to run along with the essay. I agreed. A photographer was assigned; a date set; I chose the scene of the crime, which is to say, the classroom in which the photograph would be taken.

Half an hour before the photographer and his crew showed up (he brought along a man to carry his various cameras, tripods, lights, and the rest, and a man who was officially known as a "stylist," who would set up the photograph and make sure I was less rumpled than usual), I slipped into the room in which I was to be photographed and made a slight alteration. What I did was write out a certain quotation from Baudelaire on the board in front of which I was to be posed. The quotation read: *"Plus un homme cultive les arts, moins il bande."* (Rough translation: The more a man immerses himself in the arts, the poorer his sex life.) Ever the exacting scholar, I wrote Baudelaire's name under the quotation and took a powder.

I am perhaps too pleased to report that neither the photographer nor the stylist thought to erase the Baudelaire quotation. And so it appeared, wonderfully legible, in the background behind my rather sour face in the same issue of *Gentlemen's Quarterly* as my slight, fifteen-hundred-word essay. I was ready to overlook the possibility that I looked like a poster boy for Baudelaire's aphorism. I felt as if I had pulled off a successful bank job instead of merely an oblique, perfectly impractical joke. Was this the conduct of a grown-up?

I don't think that becoming a grown-up means losing your sense of playfulness. What it does mean, I believe, is the willingness to make choices, take chances, commit yourself to one way of life over another. "If I want to be any kind of grown-up," the still-youthful novelist David Foster Wallace writes in an amusing essay on taking a luxury cruise, "I have to make choices and regret foreclosures and try to live with them." One of those foreclosures is on your own personality, which shouldn't be forever changing but should be carved out of your experience, polished like a sculpture or any other work of art. The way toward being grown-up is to be yourself. Since you have but one life to live, why not live it as an adult?

My Friend Edward

"DO YOU KNOW any intelligent people in this city?" Saul Bellow asked me one night in 1973, not long after I had met him. Before I could reply, he said, answering his own question, "I know three: Harold Rosenberg, David Grene, and Edward Shils."

All three men, along with Bellow himself, were then members of the Committee on Social Thought at the University of Chicago. Harold Rosenberg, then also the art critic for *The New Yorker,* invented the useful phrase "a herd of independent minds." David Grene, who has a reputation for being a spirited teacher, is the translator of Herodotus and the great Athenian playwrights. I didn't know much about Edward Shils — although I had read his essays in *Encounter* — except that he was a social scientist, and, when I was an undergraduate at the University of Chicago, he was known for being a very formidable figure, distinctly not a man to fool with. I only subsequently learned that he had had the decisive hand in designing what for me were the best courses I had taken at that school, the courses in the College called Social Science II and History. I was, then, already in debt to Edward Shils without knowing it. Over the following years, from 1973 until his death on January 23, 1995, this debt would grow beyond reckoning.

Perhaps because his prose was chaste, even severe, I pictured Edward Shils as tall, slender, a bit gaunt. I couldn't have been more wrong. When Saul Bellow showed up at my apartment with Edward one night, I discovered a man of five foot eight, portly (though with no flabbiness or anything soft about him), a paucity of rather wispy grayish hair, and the florid coloring that suggested the potential pugnacity of a former redhead. He carried, but didn't really use, a walking stick, and he wore a tweedy getup of various shades of brown with a green wool tie and a soft Irish hat. I took him, correctly, to be a man of good taste for whom personal vanity had a low priority. I watched his eyes roam across my living room, checking the books in my glassed-in bookcases, the prints on my walls, the plants on my window-sills. Clearly, he was, as Henry James says one must always try to be, a man on whom nothing was lost.

We dined at a Korean restaurant on Clark Street, and Edward interrogated me, calling me Mr. Epstein. He wanted to know what I was writing and for whom. He asked what I was teaching (I had begun to teach at Northwestern University that year). He inquired about what I happened to be reading at the moment. When I told him that I was reading Alison Lurie's novel *The War Between the Tates*, he tersely replied, "A book, I take it, about academic screwing." I wouldn't have thought to formulate it quite that way, but of course that is exactly what the book is about. He obviously hadn't read it, but somewhere along the way he had read another Alison Lurie novel, and, such was his ability to extrapolate, he didn't need to read any more of them. Later in the evening I described someone as a political scientist. "With the 'scientist' understood," he inserted, before deftly conveying a bit of pork and rice to his mouth on his chopsticks, "as in 'Christian Scientist.'"

I met Edward Shils around the time that his and Saul Bellow's friendship was under great, and complicated, strain, and for a while I found myself in the middle, friends to them both. They had been quite close — Bellow's biographer James Atlas has told me that Edward made substantial editorial suggestions that much improved *Mr. Sammler's Planet,* my own favorite among Bellow's novels. The morning after Bellow introduced us, I told him over the phone how remarkable I found Edward. Bellow replied that Edward was his "alter super-ego." Edward would have preferred the word *conscience,* for when I knew him he never took Freud all that seriously. I subsequently learned that he performed the function of conscience for a number of people — many students along with some professors — and indeed for entire institutions. It is an invaluable service, but not one that everybody finds congenial or that pays handsome dividends to the person willing to take it up.

As Saul Bellow and Edward pulled further apart, Edward and I became closer. For me, this was an immense piece of good fortune. My friendship with Edward, it didn't take me long to realize, was to be the crucial intellectual event of my life. Although by the time I had met him I was thirty-six years old — he was then sixty-three — and had already published a book and perhaps sixty or seventy articles and reviews in magazines, not long after meeting him my writing began to change; it could scarcely have been otherwise, for so, under the influence of Edward's presence, had my view of the world. He had released something in me that made life seem richer and writing about it consequently more joyous. As a writer, I began to see the world as simultaneously more complex and more amusing; to feel a fine surge in confidence; to be concerned scarcely at all about anyone's good opinion — except Edward's.

A small number of people called him Ed, but it was generally a mistake to do so. He himself did not go to first names easily, and to diminutives never. I was always Joseph to him, he Edward to me. I am not sure how I was able to break through to address him by his first name, or why he early chose to call me by mine, though I am glad that this happened. He had students, acquaintances, really quite dear friends of several decades whom he continued to call Mr. or Mrs. or Miss; they usually called him Professor Shils. It was part of his formality; and Edward's formality was a reminder that the word *formality* has its root in the word *formidable.*

Edward never went out of the house without a suit or sport coat, necktie, hat, and walking stick (the ones he carried were thick and dark, knotty and gnarled, sturdy not elegant appurtenances). He spoke with a mid-Atlantic accent — he had been teaching half the year in England, first at the London School of Economics, then at Cambridge, since just after World War II — often with a pronunciation system of his own devising. For example, a columnist in Chicago named Kupcinet, who pronounces his name exactly as it is spelled, Edward always called Kupchinesque. When I told him that the man himself pronounced it *Cup-si-net,* Edward said that it was a Hungarian name and that the columnist, ignorant fellow, simply didn't know how to pronounce his own name. Kupchinesque, in our conversation, it remained.

As someone known as his friend, I was often asked the most rudimentary questions about Edward. Is he English? people would ask. Is he Jewish? When the man who wrote Edward's obituary for the *Times* of London, a Cambridge don who I believe knew Edward longer than I, called me for information, he said: "He came from railroad money, didn't he?" Railroad money! Edward would have had a good chortle about that.

Edward's parents were Eastern European Jewish immigrants who settled first in Springfield, Massachusetts, then in Philadelphia, where Edward, the younger of two sons, grew up roaming the streets and reading his way through the public library. Edward's father was a cigar maker — Samuel Gompers, the first president of the American Federation of Labor, was earlier head of the cigar makers' union. Edward looked like his mother, who, though her schooling had been limited, was a serious reader, especially of Russian and European novels. The Judaic element in the household could not have been strong; fetching oysters home for dinner was one of Edward's delightful memories of a Philadelphia boyhood.

He spoke Yiddish, which he loved for its subtlety and philosophical and comical possibilities. He added to my own Yiddish vocabulary, bringing to it words that I now find myself using with great frequency, among them *hegdisch* (for serious mess), *tiness* (for grievance), *cacapitze* (for altogether trivial stuff). Sometimes he would speak in Yiddish aphorisms; sometimes he would insert the ornately precise — and often quite new to me — word in his conversation.

"Joseph," he said, pointing to three thuggish-looking youths standing on the opposite corner as we emerged one gray winter afternoon from Bishop's chili parlor on Chicago's light-industrial near West Side, "note those three *schlumgazim*."

"I'm afraid I need a subtitle for that word, Edward," I said.

"*Schlumgazim*," he readily replied, "are highwaymen who, after stealing your purse, out of sheer malice also slice off your testicles."

Edward honored his Jewishness without observing it. In the same way, he loved America, with all its philistinism and coarseness, and he once cited it to me, approvingly, as "the country of the second chance." He reveled in the country's ethnic variety, its inventiveness, its mad energy. He loved the sort of American who could build his own house. He admired Americans when they showed they would not be buffaloed by ideas put into play by academics or intellectuals (he was himself, in many of his writings, the world's leading observer of intellectuals, in both their strengths and foibles). He knew how vast our country is, how full of surprises: that it contains people hipped on grammar from Tyler, Texas, people who read through the Loeb Classics in Santa Rosa, California, and people in other unlikely places who demonstrate heroism, a winning bullheadedness, or radical common sense.

I bring up Edward's love of America because he did not seem particularly American — in fact, as he once told me, he had deliberately set out to make himself European. He had done this, my guess is, early in life, out of his regard for the older, denser culture of Europe. At the University of Pennsylvania, where he was an undergraduate, he majored in French literature. The German social theorists — Georg Simmel, Ferdinand Tönnies, and above all Max Weber — later imbued him with a love for Continental thought and for the German language.

Not long before he died, Edward suggested that I take six months off to live in France, where I might improve my own French accent. It seemed a strange suggestion to make to a man in his late fifties who was juggling three jobs (teaching, writing, and editing). Only later did Edward make plain that behind the suggestion was his wish for me to internationalize myself — as he had internationalized himself.

His success in this endeavor, I should say, was complete. His reading, his diet, his manner of dress, much of his thought had become thoroughly Europeanized. But he had become a European of the kind that, as T. S. Eliot said, Henry James had become: a man, that is, of European spirit who belonged to no particular European country. Edward accomplished what Henry James did not — nor did T. S. Eliot, who turned himself into an Englishman — which was to keep the American in himself altogether alive. What was especially impressive about Edward was that he commanded deep, even intimate knowledge of several national cultures without ever losing touch with his own.

In almost every country in Europe, Edward had a wide acquaintanceship and a few close friendships: Franco Venturi and Arnaldo Momigliano in Italy, Raymond Aron and others in France, innumerable scholars in Germany, practically everyone of intellectual importance in England from R. H. Tawney through Audrey Richards to H. R. Trevor-Roper. (Had he taken up permanent residence in England and become a citizen, he would, I suspect, long ago have been Sir Edward.) In the last seven or eight years of his life, Edward attended conferences at Castel Gandolfo, the summer residence of the Pope. Edward much admired Pope John Paul II for his intelligence and character, and there is reason to believe that his admiration was reciprocated, my guess is on the selfsame grounds.

Early in our friendship, and long before he began attending the conferences at Castel Gandolfo, Edward reported a dream to me that he had had the night before. In the dream he had been made a cardinal. It was quite wonderful, he said. He wore the red hat and robes of a cardinal, and he was permitted to roam the inner recesses of the Vatican, searching its archives in complete freedom. "And you know, Joseph," he said, "no one asked that I believe any of the Church's doctrine." He paused, then added, "Jacques Maritain arranged the whole thing."

Edward lived in India for an extended period between 1956

and 1957, and he visited the country every year thereafter until 1967. It was Edward who introduced me to the splendid books of Nirad C. Chaudhuri (author of *The Autobiography of an Unknown Indian* and other works) and to the novels of R. K. Narayan. Narayan mentions Edward more than once in his book about America, and, on the only occasion we met, gentle man that he is, Narayan's eyes glowed with pleasure when I told him I was a friend of Edward Shils. Owing to his curiosity and imagination, Edward was able to become not merely immensely knowledgeable about but quite at home in any culture.

Although Edward earned his living as a social scientist, he had read more literature than I, a literary man, ever expect to read. I never mentioned a writer, no matter how minor, whose work he had not read and whose measure he had not taken. He was a great reader of novels. He read Dickens over and over again. He regularly re-read Balzac. He adored Willa Cather. We once had a swell talk about who was smarter, Proust or James. Our conclusion was that James was deeper but that, in seeking out a restaurant or anything touching on practical matters, Proust would have been the more valuable man. Edward was much taken with George Eliot and thought her particularly fine on the Jewish family in *Daniel Deronda*. Shakespeare he felt was simply beyond discussion — and so we never discussed him. He taught a course on T. S. Eliot and was very respectful of his ideas about tradition, a subject to which, in his own writings, Edward was delicately attuned. Above all novelists, he admired, I believe, Joseph Conrad. He was impressed not alone with the great Pole's penetration but with his theme of fidelity. Fidelity, in the Conradian sense of duty before all else, was the ideal by which Edward himself tried to live. He owned Jacob Epstein's powerful bust of Joseph Conrad and kept it, along with a bust of Max Weber, in the living room of his Chicago apartment.

Edward's reading of the great writers of all languages was part of his grounding and his greatness as a social scientist. If Freud said he learned all he knew from poets, so perhaps ought social scientists to learn from novelists, though I suspect very few modern social scientists do. (Edward, his former student the distinguished Israeli sociologist S. N. Eisenstadt recently told me, came to social science through literature, not the other way round.) He also felt it his duty to stay *au courant* with contemporary culture, however empty and irritating he found much of it. Edward did not own a television set and never turned on his radio. (In an essay for *The American Scholar,* he once referred to the radio as "the wireless," a word I persuaded him to change.) During the years I knew him, he went only rarely to the movies, though he had gone much more when he was younger. As a boy he had been a baseball fan, and he had a complete knowledge of the sport up to the year 1930, when he lost interest.

Edward kept in touch with contemporary culture by reading the *New York Times* — whose ideological waffling never ceased either to inflame or to amuse him — and the large number of magazines that I saved for him. As I would drag a plastic supermarket bag or two filled with these magazines into his apartment, he could be depended on to say something on the order of: "Joseph, you are my dear friend, and it is always a great pleasure to see you, but when I look upon these wretched magazines you bring along, I realize that even the best of friendships has its cost." Once the catalogue of a southern university press was atop these magazines. "Oh, good," he said, "filled, I am sure, with announcements of biographies of Shoeless Jim Hopkins and other great southern politicians."

I was regularly astonished at how much Edward was able to get out of the magazines I brought him. Some magazines he read just to keep himself abreast, as he said, of what the dogs were up to. He enjoyed my referring to the *Chronicle of Higher Education,* a dreary journal that reports on university life, as *Pravda,* by which I meant that, like the Russian paper under the Communists, everything, to hear the *Chronicle* tell it, was going just splendidly. Edward was too sensible to read much of what I brought him all the way through. But by efficient skimming, gleaning, reading first and last paragraphs, he always caught the chief point and quickly penetrated the smoke of intellectual obfuscation to find the deep illogic or hollow complaint at the heart of the writer's composition.

As a scholar and social philosopher, Edward taught Hegel and Hobbes, Tocqueville and Weber, and he wrote papers on nationalism and civil society, on the primordial and the traditional. But as an intellectual he was interested in the popularization of ideas. Although he didn't write often for the intellectual magazines, except for *The American Scholar* and in earlier years for *Encounter,* he liked to keep a hand in. He always knew who the passing figures were, and he was able astutely to gauge their quality. Of Camille Paglia, for example, he commented, "She is more intelligent than her beliefs." Not long after I first met Edward, he called Christopher Lasch "a good graduate student whose unconcentrated anger would never allow him to become much more than that." By way of placing someone at his own university, he said, "I fear he believes Richard Rorty is a deep thinker." I once heard him upbraid his son for taking a course at Northwestern University in which one of the books on the syllabus was David Halberstam's *The Best and the Brightest.* "That," said Edward, "is a book one reads in an airport." Hannah Arendt, Susan Sontag, the Frankfurt School, the New York intellectuals, Michel Foucault — in the matter of contemporary intellectuals and academic savants, Edward knew whom *not* to get excited about.

He could be deadly in his deflationary remarks. I enjoyed these stiletto thrusts greatly, not only because they were done with great economy and insight — of a troublemaking don at Cambridge, he once said to me that his specialty was inserting bullets in other men's guns — but because they had superior perspective behind them. The three large intellectual influences on his own life were the economist Frank Knight and the sociologist Robert Park, both of whom he encountered as a young man at the University of Chicago, and Max Weber, against whose work, I believe, Edward measured his own writing. Good though he knew it was, he nonetheless found, by this measure, his own writing wanting.

Among contemporary writers and scholars, Edward much admired V. S. Naipaul, Arnaldo Momigliano, Philip Larkin, Peter Brown, Owen Chadwick, Franco Venturi, Barbara Pym, E. H. Gombrich, and Elie Kedourie. He greatly respected Aleksandr Solzhenitsyn, Sidney Hook, and Hilton Kramer for their tenacity in doing battle with liars. He was death on intellectual fraudulence. But he attacked it less through his writings, which are not notable for personal attack, than in conversation. About a famous, still-living American sociologist who in his style and manner made pretense to being upper class, Edward once remarked to me: "I'll say this about X. At least he never takes undue advantage of being Jewish." He one day told me that a New York intellectual had announced to him that, in Israeli politics, he was of the war party. "Yes," said Edward, with a nod and the peculiar set he could give to his jaw. "Israel will go to war and he'll go to the party."

Edward not only spoke his mind but could be very confrontational. At a dinner party, I once introduced him to the English journalist Henry Fairlie. "Mr. Fairlie, good to meet you," Edward said. "You wrote some brilliant things in the 1950s. [It was then, I should explain, the late 1970s.] Now, I understand you have become a socialist. Please explain yourself." Fairlie said that what had brought about his conversion was hearing Michael Harrington lecture in Chicago. "Michael Harrington in Chicago," said Edward, without smile or pause, "surely a case of worst comes to worst." Fairlie, pretty well lubricated by alcohol, went off, feeling no pain.

Edward could also be immensely courteous, holding back his true opinions, when he was fond of people in whose company he found himself. But in other surroundings he would say precisely what he thought. Since he held no received opinions whatsoever, this could often be dangerous. Someone at a party might express admiration for a particular novelist, which might cause Edward to ask that person — a married man or woman — if he or she then approved of adultery, since the novelist in question clearly did. Many of the so-called icons of our day never came close to finding a place in his pantheon. He believed I. F. Stone's Stalinism shouldn't have been so quickly forgotten. He didn't consider Isaiah Berlin great, but merely charming, a man who often wanted courage because he was intellectually hostage to certain Oxford dons. The only contemporary American social scientists he spoke about with respect were James Q. Wilson and Edward Banfield, who he thought had retained the fundamental common sense that contemporary social science seemed able to extrude from most of its adherents. Such outspokenness made him many enemies, for his witty darts not only hit but often got back to their targets.

Edward founded, and for more than twenty-five years edited, the magazine *Minerva*, a review devoted to science, higher education, and policy. (He was also, along with his friend Leo Szilard, one of the presiding spirits of the *Bulletin of the Atomic Scientists*.) To say Edward edited *Minerva* is, however, to indulge in euphemism. He really wrote most of it, often under the names of living contributors, for his own high standards forced him into heavily editing if not actually rewriting the manuscripts he had accepted for publication.

I have seen some of his letters to *Minerva* contributors. One — which I do not have before me — was to a young left-wing woman in Canada, to whom Edward wrote that he was much impressed with the research in the article she had sent him. Then he added (I am paraphrasing from memory): "It is only the opinions expressed in the article that I despise. If you would agree to remove these opinions, I shall be pleased to publish your article. If you feel the article still in need of opinions, I shall of course be only too glad to supply my own." He told another contributor that he would agree to publish his article if he would remove its barbarous academic jargon. The man wrote back to say that he wouldn't at all mind removing the jargon, which was, he supposed, really a matter of taste. This caused Edward to shoot back a note saying, "Yes, it is only a matter of taste — good versus bad taste." "I take the leather whip to my contributors," he once said to me, "but it doesn't seem to matter. They have steel bottoms."

I appear to be Boswelling my friend Edward, but perhaps this is not inappropriate, because he often seemed to me very Johnsonian. Edward himself loved Samuel Johnson. He admired Johnson's gravity, a word that Edward himself frequently used to explain his regard for certain writers. Marguerite Yourcenar was one such writer. Theodore Dreiser was another. In Edward's view, Dreiser was a much greater writer than E. M. Forster, whom Edward knew when both were fellows at King's College, because his writing had greater gravity.

An engraving of John Opie's portrait of Johnson faced Edward's desk in his apartment in Chicago. Edward shared with

Johnson that unteachable intellectual quality known as authority, a quality that in both men derived from their moral centeredness. Both knew where they stood, and the mere fact of their standing where they did made the ground beneath them firm. Like Johnson, Edward came into his authority young. In his book *The Torment of Secrecy*, written when he was in his middle forties, availing himself of this authority, he could persuade by the power of undeniable assertion.

Edward's apartment, on the ninth floor of a neo-Tudor skyscraper on Stony Island Avenue, had none of the squalor of Johnson's various abodes. Across from Jackson Park, in sight of the Museum of Science and Industry, with a spectacular view of Lake Michigan, it was roughly five blocks from his office in the Social Sciences Building at the University of Chicago. Its floors were covered with Oriental carpets, about which he knew a good deal; its walls, just about all of them, were lined with books, about which he knew everything. Eight-foot-high bookcases extending along the length of both sides of the front hall were the first things that struck one on entering this apartment. The living room was similarly lined with bookcases. The books were organized by subject matter: political philosophy in the hall; religion, European and ancient history in the living room. Reference works — the *OED*, the *Britannica* (eleventh edition), the *Dictionary of National Biography*, and various specialized dictionaries — were in a bookcase opposite his desk and in a revolving bookcase alongside the desk. The dining room table was generally at least half covered with manuscripts, correspondence, and bills, which he tended to pay with a rhythm all his own.

Another hallway, this one leading to his bedroom, held books on India and things Asian. His bedroom was the place for literature. Here one found handsome sets of the great writers:

Hazlitt, his beloved Dickens, Balzac, many French writers in Pleiade editions, all the Russians. By his bedside were the Christian mystics and wisdom writers. Social science was in the guest bedroom; a second desk and office (once meant to be a maid's room) contained books on higher education. Closets harbored back issues of *Horizon* and other journals. The kitchen and two of the three bathrooms were the only rooms devoid of bookcases, though the bathroom in which he bathed always had eight or ten books and a few magazines at the back ledge of the tub for him to read while soaking.

All the furniture was carefully chosen for its subdued elegance and feeling for tradition. In the living room, along with the Jacob Epstein bust of Conrad and the bust of Max Weber, was a self-portrait by Epstein; the few feet of wall space in this room not covered by bookcases were dominated by Piranesi prints. The coat closet in the hall contained two red fezzes, one for Edward and the other for his son, Adam, obtained in Egypt when Adam was a child of seven or eight. Another closet farther down the hall was set up as a wine cellar of sorts, with bottles of champagne, Jack Daniel's, and various quite good wines; cigar boxes were on an enclosed shelf atop still more books.

The kitchen was set up for a serious cook, which Edward was. A vast quantity of spices, teas, superior knives, and other elaborate kitchen technology lined the walls; a worktable stood in the center of the room. Edward was a gourmand, someone who not only likes delicacies but plenty of them. Apart from books, Edward's other extravagance was for what Wallace Stevens, in a letter, called "fancy groceries." Unlike Stevens, Edward could fabricate elegant dishes as well as devour them.

I always thought of his cooking — a mélange of splendid Central European dishes — as Edwardo-Hapsburg. It was immensely rich and flavorful, with no bow in the direction of odious healthy eating; the word *cholesterol* never passed his lips. He made marvelous soups (minestrone, thick bean and barley, dark lentil with sausage), he often began meals with smoked salmon, and he provided fine main courses, notable among them an aubergine (never, by Edward, called eggplant) dish known as "the Imam swoons": whether he swooned at the wonderful taste or at the expense of the ingredients, Edward once explained, was not clear. Meals generally ended with refreshing fresh fruit salads. Until near the very end, he never permitted help from guests, either in the kitchen or in the matter of cleaning up.

The conversation at these meals was quite as rich as the food. Subjects I recall included the work of the KGB in England, the fate of books among the beetles and in the steamy climate of India, the great bookstores of Philadelphia in the early decades of this century, mad old Trotskyists, and great scholars and their eccentricities. At table, talking about the splendors of the old British postal system, he once told about a letter from India addressed "Edward Shils, Sociologist, England" that was actually delivered to him. The last large meal in company I had at Edward's was prepared not by him but by his friend and neighbor in Cambridge, Thomas Moffett, who had retired as a butler at Peterhouse, where Edward was an honorary fellow, and who had come to Chicago to care for Edward in his illness. Everyone at that dinner told a story about crème brûlée, which was our dessert. All I could contribute was that a sympathetic reviewer of one of my books compared my prose to crème brûlée, saying it was very rich stuff, but you don't want to take too much of it in one sitting.

On the matter of food, as on that of books and friendship, Edward exercised very little restraint. I often took him shopping. Edward did not drive a car (nor did he type or use a computer), but he knew all the city's streets and the best places to buy the finest things. As a man who knew all the major cities of the world — he was always a great walker — he would gently mock Chicago for its crudity, but, clearly, he also loved the city. We generally began north at the Paulina Market, easily the best butcher shop in the city, an establishment that would cause a vegetarian to faint, with its more than fifteen-yard-long display cases of loins and links, steaks and chops, meats smoked and cured. It is run by a third generation of German working-class men, chiefly from the surrounding neighborhood. Many of its butchers knew Edward and called him "Professor." Professor was what he was called, too, at the N & G Produce Market, where he would pick among the vegetables and fruits, always paying his bill by check, and where he had talked the owner's son out of becoming a dental technician and into staying in the family business. We would cross the street to buy olive oil and cheese. Occasionally we would have lunch, always upstairs, at the Greek Islands on Halsted, where Edward was greeted as "Perfetcher" by the sons of the original owners, whom he also knew. Sometimes we would stop on Taylor Street for an Italian ice, which we ate in the car as we watched the passing parade of young Mexicans, Italians, and blacks. On the way back south, we would stop at Bruno's, the Lithuanian bakery, where Edward would buy the weighty and coarse-textured rye bread he favored.

Edward admired few things more than shopkeepers. He was impressed by their courage in staking everything on their small businesses. A beautiful shop, locally owned, such as the Italian ceramics shop Tutti Italia that was in my own neighborhood, set him vibrating every time we entered it together. Along with making a point of telling its young owner how elegantly everything was set out, he always bought an item or two. He once told me that he judged any city by the number of interesting blocks of shops it provided. London and Paris were the hands-down winners here.

Edward also admired working men and women. He once surprised me by telling me how large the sum was that he contributed to the staff of janitors, doormen, and receiving room clerks in his building. He had himself been pleased, many years before, at having been mistaken by another tenant in his building, an older woman, for "the city engineer." What pleased him was being taken for an honest working man of great competence, for he much valued competence wherever he came upon it. In this, as in other ways — his intellectual fearlessness as well as his physique — he resembled H. L. Mencken, who wrote: "Competence, indeed, was my chief admiration, then as now, and next to competence I put what is called being a good soldier — that is, not whining."

Edward took particular interest in Chicago's ethnic character. He enjoyed the ethnic carnival, which meant not only ethnic differences but generalizations about those differences. He was certainly not to be stopped in this mild pleasure by contemporary political correctness. (Besides, he truly judged people on their merits and so had no need to worry about being thought prejudiced.) He loved such comic ethnic distinctions as: the difference between a Hungarian and a Romanian was that both would sell you their grandmothers but the Romanian wouldn't deliver. Like Mencken again, he didn't mind calling a Krauto-American a Krauto-American. He had great regard for the Poles, Lithuanians, and other Eastern Europeans who had settled in Chicago, and he much respected the tidiness with which they kept their houses and lawns. He thought that the blacks had been sold a very sad bill of goods that allowed them to believe in their own victimhood. He was particularly hard on his own, the Jews; and on pretentious Jewish intellectuals he was hardest of all.

Edward's once great respect for intellectuals and academics had dwindled considerably after the 1960s. More and more he tended to think of academics and intellectuals as essentially quacks pushing untested ideas at no personal risk. For those true scholars — Gershom Scholem, Peter Brown, Paul Oskar Kristeller, Jacques Barzun — Edward had great regard. But for those to whom the least fraudulence adhered — names on request — he was merciless in his criticism. He frequently reverted to the Hebrew word *chachem,* meaning greatly learned wise man or woman, always used sarcastically to refer to the false wise men and women of our day. His list of the false contemporary *chachemim* would put the lights out in several major universities.

He once told me that, had he the chance of beginning life again, he might choose a career in the military. I know he much enjoyed his years during World War II, when he was seconded to the British army to interrogate captured German soldiers. I, for one, am glad he was a teacher. A life in the military might not have given him the opportunity to stock his mind as richly as he was able to stock it as a university professor. The best, though still poor, analogy I can come up with for Edward's mind is that of the magician's glass, out of which the magician takes hardy swallow after hardy swallow. When the glass is set down, *mirabile dictu,* it turns out to be still full to the brim. It seemed there was nothing Edward did not know, nothing he ever forgot: until the very last, I never knew him to stumble in his memory of a name or title of a book. Vast quantities of literature, history, philosophy, anecdotes, jokes — all were neatly filed away in his mind, which also contained a mental Rolodex that began around the year 1000 B.C. with, so far as I could determine, no names missing. I make Edward sound like a walking *vade mecum*, which, true enough, in part he was. But none of this would have been of the least interest if he hadn't had a mind capable of great powers of penetration and formulation. He amply demonstrated this on serious subjects — nationalism, civil society, tradition, collective consciousness — in his books. But his conversation glittered with his verbal gifts; his vocabulary was, for me, a continuous delight, full of surprising twists and turns. (He was endlessly curious about the etymology of phrases and idioms.) He might call a man "an ignorant zealot," not a phrase much used in our century. Scruffy neighborhood kids playing with untied gym shoes and baseball hats on backwards he might refer to as our *jeunesse dorée*. I once described an acquaintance of ours to him as rat-faced. "Yes," said Edward, "now that you mention it, he is rather rodential." *Rodential* — who else but Edward would have thought of such a word, which sounds like an insurance company for mice.

His metaphor-making powers were dazzling. Sometimes these could take on an oddly — for so urban a man — rural character, as when, in one of his books, he described congressmen as "fidgety as a hen atop a nest of woodpeckers." He used to refer to his friend Melvin Lasky, whose editing of *Encounter* he much respected and whom he frequently attempted to advise, as "a dog who knows seven languages and obeys in none." More often, his metaphors were brilliant in their ornateness. He likened the condition of his French to a set of crystal in a glass cabinet after a bombing raid on London in 1943 (which didn't stop him from reading sixteen volumes of Tocqueville's letters in fewer than three weeks).

Once, at a meeting of the editorial board of *The American Scholar*, on which Edward sat for eighteen years, Diana Trilling, one of the members, questioned the function of the board. She wondered if it wasn't, in her words, "just window dressing." "Allow me," Edward began, "to take up Mrs. Trilling's fenestral metaphor. One has a window. One acquires a shade for it. Curtains. Perhaps a cornice. Possibly venetian blinds. Drapes may be in order. I suppose all that is window dressing. Yes, we, his editorial board, are, in some sense, Mr. Epstein's window to a wider outlook on the world. But you know, just because one has a window, that doesn't mean that one wants to look out of it all the time. Mr. Epstein doesn't, after all, have to refer to us, his editorial board, ceaselessly." That, I should say, is worthy of Henry James.

The flow of wit in Edward was unsurpassed by anyone I expect ever to meet. A pretentious Czech friend once told me that, in the old days, before the advent of the Communists, his father, a high bourgeois, never shaved himself. "More likely the truth is," said Edward, when I reported this to him, "his father shaved his mother." When the University of Chicago had an embarrassing faculty member who had years before gained tenure, Edward suggested to Robert Hutchins, president of the university, that he acquire a bungalow in Gary, Indiana, and make this man dean of the University of Chicago at Gary, with no students and no responsibilities whatsoever. I called him in the midst of his preparing an elaborate dinner for an important figure at the University of Chicago, about which he commented: "I don't know why I bother. If he really cared about good food, he would surely have left his wife years ago." He once described a certain intellectual to me as "a rabid anti-Communist"; then, after a perfectly timed pause, he added, "Wait a minute — so am I."

Edward was very generous about my own attempts at wit, and he frequently improved on them. The University of Illinois at Chicago was for many years known as Circle Campus, sometimes called Circle, and I took to calling it Vicious Circle. Edward thought this quite amusing, though he turned up the joke a full notch by referring to the school as Old Vish. In company, he was always asking me to tell my jokes, and I would learn that, behind my back, he was telling a few of them himself and was giving me credit for having invented them.

Being with Edward was endlessly amusing. Once he arranged for me to be invited to a formal dinner at the University of Chicago in honor of his friend John Sparrow, then the Warden of All Souls College, Oxford. At the time, I did not own a tuxedo, and Edward's "soup and fish," as he jokingly called his dinner clothes, were in Cambridge. I told him I would acquire two tuxedos from a place that rented them. "Very well, Joseph," he said, "but something simple, you know — no rock 'n' roll, no pimpery." When I explained to the man at the tuxedo rental shop what was wanted — two simple sets of black dinner clothes, shawl collars, shirts, and cummerbunds — he said, "No problem" and then proceeded to call his downtown office and ask for "two Tony Martins." At drinks, before the dinner itself, Edward slipped up behind me and whispered in my ear, "Joseph, comforting, is it not, to know one is wearing one's own socks."

Edward was, as I noted earlier, a man on whom nothing was lost, and the subtlety of his observations seems to me often astonishing. "He is a man who often laughs but in between seldom smiles," he once said to me of Saul Bellow. He admired the economists of the University of Chicago, trained under Jacob Viner and Frank Knight; and he had spent more than half a century in the company of Milton Friedman and George Stigler and found both to be men of superior intelligence. But he felt that the Chicago economists, brilliant though they could be, were insufficiently impressed with the mysteries of life. It was these mysteries — the role of the primordial, the part tradition plays — that most stirred him, and he struggled with the questions that they posed till the very end of his own life. "Take me home, Joseph," he said to me, rather wearily one night as we were departing the Hong Minh restaurant on Twenty-second Street in Chicago's Chinatown. "I need to return to my desk to invent more stories about how society is organized."

Edward made it a point to introduce me to anyone he found interesting or charming. Many of these people I met at dinners he had prepared, and a vast number of them were Europeans: Leszek Kolakowski, Erica Reiner (the editor of the Assyrian dictionary at the Oriental Institute), the grandson of Theodor Mommsen, Hugh Lloyd-Jones, who was then the Regius Professor of Greek at Oxford. But on November 12, 1976, according to my journal, he invited me over to meet Arnaldo Momigliano. "One of the most charming men I have ever met," reads my journal entry of the next day. "Small, muffled in what seemed like many layers of clothes, peeping out at the world from behind glasses of plate-glass thickness, he proved a man of wit and of sweet humor and of great intellectual power; and along with all this, an absolute thesaurus of information. He is, as he remarked of himself, very much a Piedmontese. A lovely accent [it resembled Bela Lugosi playing Dracula], many fine gestures with his hands, a rumpled appearance, a penetrating mind — all combine in a personage at once formidable and adorable. Edward noted me gazing at him in admiration. We looked at each other, Edward and I, and smiled."

Arnaldo Momigliano was, in the truest sense, Edward's only peer. Arnaldo, who had been forced into exile by the Italian Fascists, found an intellectual home in England. He and Edward shared the international spirit in scholarship and in life. He was the only man who seemed to know as much as Edward, though Edward always advertised Arnaldo as knowing much more. Neither, in my presence, ever called the other by his first name. Edward referred to Arnaldo as Professor Momigliano, and Arnaldo, in the European manner, often referred to Edward as Shils.

Twice a year we traveled to *American Scholar* editorial board meetings as a threesome. Walking through O'Hare and La Guardia — Edward with his walking stick, Arnaldo with his crushed Borsalino hat — I always felt that we resembled the intellectual equivalent of the Marx Brothers, with me as Zeppo, far and away the dimmest of the lot. Edward looked after Arnaldo, who was less confident of his way and who had to be frisked at airport security because he wore a pacemaker. Arnaldo had various airplane tickets, newspaper clippings, and foreign letters pinned to him or sticking out of his pockets. He always carried what looked to be roughly three pounds of keys — I do not exaggerate — to various apartments, offices, and library carrels around the world. Such a disorderly exterior, such an orderly mind.

A certain amount of Arnaldo's and Edward's conversation, having to do with such (to me) arcana as Oxbridge gossip or classicists in the Soviet Union, floated amiably above my head. Usually, though, I found it most amusing. I remember one conversation about a student who Edward and Arnaldo agreed was altogether too good looking ever to become a true scholar — they were perfectly serious about this. When one of Arnaldo's best students left the University of Chicago for Princeton, both he and Edward were disappointed, and Arnaldo said, wistfully, "Ah, a Jewish boy. The Ivy League beckons, what do you expect?"

Edward had brought Arnaldo to the University of Chicago as something like a permanent visiting professor and argued for his remaining there when the administration, failing to be properly impressed with his greatness, wanted to release him at normal retirement age. Edward took personal responsibility for him. When Arnaldo's bad heart condition worsened, Edward, the Jewish grandmother in him kicking in, moved Arnaldo out of the room he occupied at the faculty club and into his own more capacious apartment. There, with an oxygen tank in his room, Arnaldo continued to see his students until he returned to England, alas, to die. Edward cooked for him and did his laundry and attended to all his needs. I recall Glen Bowersock, a dear friend of Arnaldo's, saying that he had never seen anything quite like the way Edward looked after Arnaldo — usually a lesser man might look after a greater, but here was one great man extending himself completely for another.

Had things worked out the other way around, I am fairly sure that Arnaldo would not have done the same for Edward. I say this not in the least to disparage Arnaldo but to highlight the extraordinary generosity of which Edward was capable. Through the son of a friend who had been a student at Cambridge, where Edward kept a small house on Tennis Court Road near his college, Peterhouse, I recently learned that Edward was thought a tightwad. This came from his sometimes taking leftover desserts home from college lunches and serving them for dinner at his own table. At the Greek Islands Restaurant, he used to have the waiters put the extra lemons and unused bread into a bag that he would take home. But these were habits of Edward's Depression-era mentality — he simply hated seeing food go to waste.

At the same time that he would take home bread and lemons, he would give — not lend, *give* — a graduate student ten thousand dollars to help her finish a difficult final year of her studies. He might give another young couple a five-thousand-dollar Christmas gift, merely because he wanted them to know he loved them. He was immensely generous to his own son and daughter-in-law and, had they permitted it, would have done even more for them.

Edward was even more generous with his time. He would see students through the day and night. He would take them to restaurants. He lavished great care — and vast quantities of his green ink (Mr. Alfred's [Dunhill] Ink for Writing Instruments) — on the papers they wrote for his classes. He was sometimes contemptuous of how little his colleagues seemed to do by way of imposing standards on their graduate students' dissertations. If you wrote a dissertation under Edward, you were sent to the south of England, thence to Sumatra and back, but when you were done, you really knew everything about your subject. Many a student must have left his apartment, heart weighted down with a list of another thirty tomes he would have to plow through and head spinning from having discovered that, to take the next logical step in his studies, he would have to learn Polish. But, if the student was fundamentally sound, he would know that what Edward had asked him to do was right.

Edward's effect on me was inevitably to make intellectual effort seem worthwhile. He was like a great ship captain in Conrad, not standing at the helm, but seated at his desk at all hours, working through the problems he had set himself as a young man and felt he had not exhausted. He was a man who seemed to get by with four or five hours of sleep. One might drop him off at ten at night, and he would get in another three hours at his desk: making corrections on student papers, perhaps working on the ninth draft of an essay, dictating letters, or writing lengthy testimonials for students and friends for jobs, grants, and further schooling. A testimonial from Edward could be a dangerous thing. The problem was that Edward not only had standards, which are easy enough to possess, but he applied them, which is not so easy. He might praise a student, or a former student now in his forties or fifties, for honorableness, upstandingness, and industry but not for being deeper than Goethe, more brilliant than Stendhal, or subtler than Proust, and the absence of these qualities could be dampening in the current inflationary academic testimonial market. At the same time, a recent student of his told me that Edward had written him a brilliant many-paged testimonial showing how his, the student's, own work made him a perfect fit historically for the sociology department to which he had applied. Edward knew the history of this department, I have no doubt, better than anyone currently in it.

As Henry James could never lie about art, so Edward could never lie about intellect. His high standards caused him truly to anguish over the state into which the universities, and intellectual life generally, seemed to him to have fallen. He, who perhaps knew more about the history of scholarship than anyone living, looked about him and everywhere saw compromise, dumbing down, politicization. (Anyone who thinks that the attacks on the politicization of academic life are themselves at base political ought to look into *The Torment of Secrecy*, Edward's book of 1956, written during the heart of the congressional investigation of security in the United States, to see an example of majestic disinterested political thought in action. In the pages of that book, Edward, without underplaying the genuine menace of the Soviet Union, shows why Senator McCarthy and other opportunistic congressmen were able, through menacing work of their own, to stir up the country.) The great university traditions that he so much admired — had really devoted his life to carrying on — were everywhere, in his view, being worn away, undermined, all but sabotaged.

His anguish often turned into rage. I have been personal witness to some of his spectacular tirades on the subject of the swinish behavior of academics. Edward was one of the world's fastest talkers, and I have heard tirades of his that lasted no less than an uninterrupted half hour. This made for a vast number of well-chosen words from a master of vituperation. His anger at what he saw before him gave him the reputation of a curmudgeon, when in fact he was a man driven to the deepest sadness by the spoilage of all that he most loved in the world.

Edward's position as a strong figure who disapproved of so much that was now de rigueur in academic and intellectual life tended, even within the University of Chicago, to set him on the margin of things. He continued to teach at the university, without payment of any kind, until only two months before his death at the age of eighty-four, but his counsel was only rarely sought on any matter of important university policy, which hurt him greatly, though he never made this complaint out loud, at least not to me.

While Edward Levi was president of the University of Chicago, Edward was something akin to the cardinal he dreamed Jacques Maritain had made him. He was not a gray but a purple eminence; he was a powerful and not at all behind-the-scenes influence, whose advice was sought and very often followed. In good part it was owing to the two Edwards — Levi and Shils — that the University of Chicago did not knuckle under to student protest in the middle 1960s and was never humiliated and, subsequently, diminished by it in the way that Berkeley, Columbia, Michigan, and other universities had been.

The degradation of the great academic traditions was not something with which Edward could ever come to terms. He functioned once again as a conscience in these matters, but the truth is that people don't feel the need of such a conscience, least of all those who are flourishing quite nicely without this important, invisible organ of the spirit.

Courage has its price, though Edward would have dismissed the notion that he was ever genuinely courageous. When he gave the Jefferson Lecture in 1979, he chose as his subject the regrettable incursions of the federal government into higher education. People afterward told him that it had taken courage to say what he thought. Not at all, he responded; it takes courage in the Soviet Union or in South Africa to say what one thinks, not in the United States.

The price of Edward's courage was loneliness. He was not only excluded from the inner councils at the University of Chicago, but he was invited out less and less. He maintained some friendships at the university, but increasingly his life was spent among students and a few friends not in positions of any power. His many English and European friendships bucked up his spirits. He used to say that, if his son and three or four friends didn't live in Chicago, he would have retired permanently to England.

Luckily for me, he never did. His friendship and wisdom meant a great deal to me. I used to check in with him regularly on subjects about which I was writing and found him unfailingly helpful. He once told me that, without the element of personal intellectual progress, life was pretty empty, a notion especially useful for anyone who teaches and hence is tempted to repeat himself endlessly. Another time he recited for me the four intellectual possibilities: to be unoriginal but right; to be original but wrong; to be unoriginal and wrong (the most common possibility); and, rarest of all, of course, to be original and right. He always asked me what I was reading; and I could not mistake the slight disappointment in his voice when I reported reading at length a writer who he thought not really worth the time.

If I have made Edward out to be lonely — without the large family life he would have enjoyed, with an attenuated connection to the university where he had taught for more than fifty years — I don't want to make him sound tragic. His curiosity was too wide, his mind too lively for him ever to seem a broken reed. He knew how to take pleasure from the everyday delights life provided: good food, good books, good friends. "Through all my days I have never known more than momentary boredom," he once told me. With his mind, boredom was not really a possibility.

Edward never degraded the material life. Up to the very end, he remained an enthusiastic collector of books. He would go into Williams-Sonoma to buy some kitchen *tchotchke*, knowing full well he needed it, as he said, like a *loch in kop*. He claimed that acquiring new things gave one a sense of futurity, of life continuing, no matter what one's age. His own age, once he reached his middle seventies and beyond, became a standing joke with him. "As the United States seems to have passed, as Bryce remarked, from barbarism to decadence without attaining civilization," he once told me, "so I seem to have gone from ignorance to wisdom without ever having been considered very intelligent." Once, when two former students of his from the 1930s came to visit him, men now in their seventies, he capped his report of their visit by saying to me, with his winning smile, "Nice boys."

Edward had extraordinary physical gifts. He could keep later hours, eat more and spicier food, talk longer, and get up the next day in much better fettle than I or just about anyone else I knew. His energy remained amazing until his illness. I always thought he would die in England of a heart attack. I thought I would receive a call, and a voice in a gentle English accent would tell me that Edward had died in his sleep or, better, at his desk. "I want to go with my boots on," he told me more than once. "No tubes up my nose, lashed to three IVs, strangers milling about."

What he died of was cancer: colon cancer metastasized to the liver. (He might have said, like the archbishop in Willa Cather's novel, "I shall die of having lived.") Although he was eighty-three when the cancer was discovered, he enrolled himself for the full-blast regimen of chemotherapy. After the first rounds proved ineffective, he signed up for a second, this time experimental, round. When people who knew what he was going through asked how he was, he replied, "Apart from dying of cancer, I feel just fine." He was only intermittently in great pain, but chemotherapy can be to cancer what psychoanalysis often is to neurosis: the illness, as Karl Kraus said, for which it purports to be the cure.

Edward must have lost fifty pounds, his eyes stared out of his head, he began to shuffle, he looked particularly fragile from behind. Whereas before the intrusion of cancer, Edward, for the twenty-odd years I knew him, seemed a permanent age sixty, he now looked all of his eighty-four years and more. Among the other penalties exacted by cancer — by the chemotherapy, really — was that he lost his sense of taste. He told me that he would fantasize about dishes, then order them or prepare them himself, only to find most of them tasteless. One day I brought, at his request, a jar of spinach borscht called schav, which he ate with great dollops of sour cream. "I don't know how much longer I'll be alive," he said to me, "but however long it might be, I shall never eat this horrible soup again." Our last meal together, before he took to his bed, was a cold smoked pheasant followed by a special brand of chocolate ice cream, each of us eating the latter out of separate pint-sized containers.

Edward told me that he felt he had, over the years, acquired the character to face death without terror. And so he did, little as he wished to leave life. Except for only occasional lapses into delirium, he kept his lucidity to the end. The extreme weight loss caused the very shape of his face to change. His nose, which was normally fleshy at the end, now came to seem longish and slightly aquiline, which made him look like a distinguished Roman senator. To me his face always suggested great playfulness, and I have seen him in a state of intellectual passion, after a day of solid work at his desk, when he seemed to me nothing less than radiant. But he never seemed more beautiful than at the end of his life. Until the end, he continued to see students. Old friends, my wife among them, came in a week or so before his death to bid him good-bye. As my wife said, he did all the work: telling her how much her friendship had meant to him, how he would miss her, instructing her not to grieve for him but to remember the lovely times they had had together. I had taken to kissing his forehead when I came into or departed his bedroom. He would lift my hand to his mouth and smile.

Four or so weeks before he died, I told him that he had been a very good friend, the best friend I expected ever to have. He told me that I had been a dear friend to him as well and added the qualification "even though we rarely spoke together of things of the heart." I tried not to show shock at this, and I have since pondered its meaning.

We shared a happy intellectual candor, as only two people whose general views are congruent can. From early in our friendship, we told one another the amount of fees we collected for lectures and for magazine pieces or what we paid for this or that article of clothing or meal. I felt there was nothing I could not say to him about other people, we could even analyze the personalities of persons we both admired, and, such was his tact, I never had to tell him that anything I said was *entre nous* — he could make those delicate judgments nicely enough on his own. Our loyalty to each other was complete. And yet, at the end, Edward felt that "we rarely spoke of things of the heart." What did he mean?

What he meant, I have come to believe, was that we chose not to speak to each other, except in the most fleeting way, of our doubts and disappointments and griefs. We didn't, in part because neither of us was therapeutic in our impulses — better, we both felt, to eat than to spill the beans — and in part because we each lived by a code in which a man does not whine or weep, even on the shoulder of his dearest friend.

Edward applied his own high standards to himself, and if he found so many contemporaries wanting, he knew that, as good as he was, he was not as good as he wanted to be. He left unfinished vastly ambitious manuscripts; and as excellent as his published work was, he always felt it could have been better. In his intellectual life, Edward suffered what I used to think of as encyclopedism: he wished to get all around every subject he took up. This could make him sometimes garrulous in conversation and cause him to bring in manuscripts forty or fifty pages longer than the possible outer limits of the space available. He was immensely tolerant of my editing of his manuscripts, which chiefly entailed radical cutting, and he used to joke about bringing out a book consisting entirely of things that I had cut from his essays. (I gave the book the working title *From the Abattoir Floor.*) Powerful as so much of his writing is, and permanent though I believe his contribution to the study of society has been, he would, I do not doubt, have preferred to have left behind a single masterwork. But, alas, he didn't. It was not something we talked about.

He hungered, too, for a richer family life than he had. He loved the *idea* of Christmas, for example, though he didn't do much about it; and his notions here may have derived as much from Dickens as from the sad reality of the rather hopeless binge of gift giving that this holiday has become. By the time I knew him, Edward had long been divorced, though he had had chief responsibility for raising his only child. In all the time I knew him, he never told me that he had been married twice, and I only learned this from an enemy of his who told it to me to spite him. Yet, such are the paradoxes in the human heart that, despite his love of family, Edward may have been one of nature's true bachelors, with his frequent travel to international conferences, his penchant for working at all hours, and his domestic schedule open to invasion by students, visiting scholars, and old friends.

Along with his hunger for family, Edward had a genuine regard for religion. He once described himself to a devout Catholic acquaintance as a "pious agnostic." He just couldn't make the leap into faith. I don't think this was by any means the central drama in his life. Faithfulness to his own exacting standards provided that. But he believed in religion, as he believed in family, because he thought both enhanced society by strengthening its bonds, preserving its traditions, making it deeper and richer. We spoke often of these things, Edward and I, but usually in a detached rather than a personal way.

Any but a fatuous man will be disappointed by his own life — will feel that he could have done more and better than he did. The truer test is whether a man has disappointed others. An entry from my journal of April 13, 1973, very soon after I first met Edward, reads:

Dinner last evening with Edward Shils. Always a pleasure: very good food, even better talk, and a lovely overall feeling of intellectual glow that lasts for hours afterward. What an impressive figure he is, by turns serious, severe, wildly humorous, marvelously anecdotal, and above all disinterested. While on the one hand he seems unconnable, on the other he can be — and often is — a great appreciator.

When Edward was in Chicago, we spoke over the phone every day, usually for forty minutes or longer. In twenty-two years, we never ran out of things to say. My problem now is that I still have so many things to tell him. I remember wanting to call him to laugh together about the story in the *New York Times* about Tip O'Neill's pals in North Cambridge — Skippy McCaffrey, Pinky Sullivan, and Mickey O'Neil — who met to remember their friend Tip at their favorite bar, a story Edward would have loved. I wanted to call him to tell him the joke I heard about Yeshiva University's rowing team, on which one man rows and the other twelve yell. For the remainder of my life I shall have stories that I shan't be able to tell to Edward, and this will make them less satisfying.

Edward taught me how best to peel an orange, where to buy olive oil, how to spot intellectual fraudulence, and how to laugh in dark times. Since his death, a word, a phrase, a formulation will occur to me that has his own lovely comic spin on it, and I know that it is Edward speaking through me, as he so often did in life. Edward's life was devoted to the fundamental, the primordial truths we all know and are ever in danger of forgetting. Chief among them is that only a life lived with courage, passion, and honor is worth living. This was, precisely, the life Edward lived, indomitably, right up to the very end.

JOSEPH EPSTEIN is the author of the *New York Times* bestseller *Snobbery: The American Version*, among many other acclaimed books. He was born and educated in Chicago, where for thirty years he taught English and writing at Northwestern University. From 1975 to 1997 he was the editor of *The American Scholar*. His work has appeared in *The New Yorker*, the *Atlantic Monthly*, *Harper's Magazine*, *Commentary*, and other publications.

"Joseph Epstein's gifts are true and abundant
and altogether enviable." — *Chicago Tribune*

FABULOUS SMALL JEWS. *Stories*

EPSTEIN'S MARVELOUS SHORT STORY COLLECTION features artists,
writers, a commodities trader, a concert pianist, lawyers on the make, all
at various crossroads and turning points in their lives. As always with
Epstein, the magic, the charm, and the humor are in his lavish details.

ISBN 978-0-618-44658-2

FRIENDSHIP. *An Exposé*

IN HIS WRY AND SKEPTICAL EXAMINATION, Epstein charts the unexpected and surprising forces that have squeezed and shaped modern
friendship — from technological leaps like e-mail and instant messaging
to the (very recent) assumption that your spouse will be your best friend.

ISBN 978-0-618-87215-2

IN A CARDBOARD BELT! *Essays Personal, Literary, and Savage*

EPSTEIN'S SPLENDID ESSAY COLLECTION includes personally revealing
essays about his father and about his years as a teacher, deeply considered
examinations of writers from Paul Valéry to Truman Capote, and sharp
takedowns of such cultural pooh-bahs as Harold Bloom and George
Steiner. *Houghton Mifflin hardcover (forthcoming)* ISBN 978-0-618-72193-1

NARCISSUS LEAVES THE POOL. *Essays*

IN THESE SIXTEEN SPARKLING ESSAYS, Epstein again displays his dazzling wit and charm. Among his targets this time are topics such as name-
dropping, talent versus genius, the cult of youthfulness, and the information revolution. ISBN 978-0-618-87216-9

SNOBBERY. *The American Version*

THE *NEW YORK TIMES* BESTSELLER *Snobbery* explores the shallows and
depths of status and taste. In these essays, Epstein skewers all manner
of elitism in contemporary America, offering his arch observations of the
new footholds of snobbery: food, fashion, high-achieving children, schools,
politics, and much more. ISBN 978-0-618-34073-6

Visit our Web site: www.marinerbooks.com.